T0286070

SOLITUDE

The average adult spends nearly one-third of their waking life alone. How do we overcome the stigma of solitude and find strength in going it alone? Whether we love it or try to avoid it, we can make better use of that time. The science of solitude shows that alone time can be a powerful space used to tap into countless benefits. Translating key research findings into actionable facts and advice, this book shows that alone time can boost well-being. From relaxation and recharging to problem solving and emotion regulation, solitude can benefit personal growth, contentment, creativity, and our relationships with ourselves and others. Learning what makes us better at spending time alone can help us move toward our best possible selves.

Netta Weinstein is an internationally recognized psychologist and director of the European Research Council's "Solitude: Alone but Resilient" (SOAR) project. Her research focuses on motivation and well-being. She is also Professor of Psychology at the University of Reading and an associate researcher at the Oxford Internet Institute, University of Oxford, UK.

Heather Hansen is an independent science writer and author. She joined SOAR in 2020 to lend her expertise in interviewing and communication. She has won awards from the American Society of Journalists and Authors, the Society of American Travel Writers, and the Colorado Authors League.

Thuy-vy T. Nguyen is a pioneer and expert in studying solitude in laboratory experiments and investigating the factors that lead to different concepts of solitude. She is also Associate Professor in Psychology at Durham University, a fellow at Wolfson Research Institute for Health and Well-being, and principal investigator of the Solitude Lab at Durham University, UK.

SOLITUDE

The Science and Power of Alone Time

Netta Weinstein
Heather Hansen
Thuy-vy T. Nguyen

CAMBRIDGE
UNIVERSITY PRESS

CAMBRIDGE
UNIVERSITY PRESS

Shaftesbury Road, Cambridge CB2 8EA, United Kingdom

One Liberty Plaza, 20th Floor, New York, NY 10006, USA

477 Williamstown Road, Port Melbourne, VIC 3207, Australia

314–321, 3rd Floor, Plot 3, Splendor Forum, Jasola District Centre,
New Delhi – 110025, India

103 Penang Road, #05-06/07, Visioncrest Commercial, Singapore 238467

Cambridge University Press is part of Cambridge University Press & Assessment,
a department of the University of Cambridge.

We share the University's mission to contribute to society through the pursuit of
education, learning and research at the highest international levels of excellence.

www.cambridge.org
Information on this title: www.cambridge.org/9781009256605

DOI: 10.1017/9781009256599

First published 2024

Printed in the United Kingdom by TJ Books Limited, Padstow Cornwall

A catalogue record for this publication is available from the British Library.

Library of Congress Cataloging-in-Publication Data
Names: Weinstein, Netta, author. | Hansen, Heather, author. | Nguyen, Thuy-vy T.,
1986- author.
Title: Solitude : the science and power of being alone / Netta Weinstein, Heather Hansen,
Thuy-vy T. Nguyen.
Description: Cambridge, United Kingdom ; New York, NY, USA : Cambridge University
Press, 2024. | Includes bibliographical references and index.
Identifiers: LCCN 2023025715 | ISBN 9781009256605 (hardback) | ISBN 9781009256612
(paperback) | ISBN 9781009256599 (epub)
Subjects: LCSH: Solitude.
Classification: LCC BJ1499.S65 W45 2024 | DDC 155.9/2–dc23/eng/20230719
LC record available at https://lccn.loc.gov/2023025715

ISBN 978-1-009-25660-5 Hardback

Contents

Note to the Reader

Unlike its mythologies, which you'll read about throughout this book, the science of solitude is very new, and insights are emerging every day about its values and costs. We are learning a lot about the topic by studying everyday solitude both in artificial laboratory environments and by talking with people whose stories can enlighten researchers about how time alone impacts their lives.

That said, it's tough to study solitude in real time, because by its very definition, people can't be alone and talking to researchers! And that begs certain questions – can we assess real (meaningful) solitude in a lab where participants don't create, or even know, their space? When we ask research subjects about past episodes of solitude, are they able to accurately report what that time felt like? In general, solitude has proven harder to study than other human phenomena, but it's intriguing enough to be worth the effort. With an understanding of these potential limitations, we have to make suppositions in our work about solitude as many people experience it.

Because of who we and other researchers have focused on in our inquiries, we also know more about certain groups of people. Psychologists across different fields of interest including solitude often study college students because they happen to have them around. This isn't a great solution to the problem of demographic diversity in research in general, and we have to keep in mind that a college student's relationship with time alone is unique to that time in their lives and to the socioeconomic conditions that have placed them there. Thanks to the work of other researchers who have focused instead on older adults (who have had more time to build relationships with solitude), there are also some good data on that age group. Similarly, alone time and children also has been well studied. That's an important topic that we touch upon in these pages, but because this is a book about adults, we do not give it full treatment. By contrast, there is much less research than we'd like on people inhabiting the major gap between young and old. Much of the research that we've done over the past several years, which we talk about throughout these chapters, aims to begin filling that void. In the same breath, we acknowledge that there is much more work still to be done.

Another limitation that we want to make readers aware of is that researchers have largely studied the solitude experiences of people in Western countries. When appropriate, we try to extrapolate what those data may mean from a broader cultural perspective, and we make every effort to give voice to those ideas and studies that have come from underrepresented places. In our own work, we have also tried to recruit study participants from as many relevant demographic groups as possible. Again, we recognize that even that approach will leave certain voices unheard for the time being, and we can only endeavor to be more thorough going forward.

Because the study of positive solitude is, in many ways, "straight out of the oven" (as Netta describes it), we also have to acknowledge that ideas and findings about it exist at various stages of development. Although most of the scientific knowledge we present in this book has been peer reviewed, there is also fresh information gained from new data that have not yet been published (at least at the moment of this book's publication). In those cases, we share that learning along with data and materials in an effort to be fully transparent. We have carefully analyzed those data before sharing them in this book, but we welcome readers to consider the merits of those ideas and are open to differing perspectives.

Some of our recent research includes a substantive narrative study that we draw upon heavily in these chapters. Those include lengthy conversations with dozens of people around the world from fairly diverse demographics about their experiences of solitude. Many of those participants are precisely quoted in the text to honor the depth and context of their contributions. Although their words are exact, we have endeavored to protect their privacy by changing their names – using only first names – and avoiding the use of any information that could precisely identify them. In all cases, their ages and countries of origin have been maintained.

INTRODUCTION

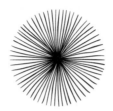

I MAGINE YOU'RE SITTING IN THE COCKPIT of a single-engine plane, cruising 2,000 feet above the surface of the Atlantic Ocean. It's pitch black outside, and you're flying blind into strong headwinds and driving rain. There's no radio on board, and you are the plane's sole occupant. You are no longer an earth dweller with feet planted on terra firma, but you don't belong to the sky either, not really – the immense roar of the engine and the pungent smell of petrol in the cabin make that clear enough.

Now, somewhere over the frigid northern waters, your engine sputters and dies, and you're momentarily hypnotized by the glowing, spinning dial of the altimeter as the plane plummets toward the sea. The profound silence of the powerless plane at first is stunning, but then you spring into action to revive the motor. At least thirty seconds have elapsed since the engine quit as the plane drops below 300 feet in altitude and continues its decline. You wonder how high the waves below may rise to meet you when, finally, the engine roars back to life and you ascend back into the clouds.

This harrowing scene is how aviatrix Beryl Markham described her historic journey as the first person to fly solo across the Atlantic from east to west (from England to Canada). That was in September 1936, nine years after Charles Lindbergh made the first solo transatlantic crossing and four years after Amelia Earhart was the first woman to do it – but they had both flown with the prevailing winds from west to east. Instead, Markham flew into the wind and, with her twenty-one-hour twenty-five-minute flight, accomplished what no one else had up to that point. (She was aiming for New York, but after her fuel vents iced over, Markham was forced nose down into a bog in Nova Scotia, breaking the windscreen with her head during the rough "landing.")

Despite falling a bit short of her original goal, Markham had solo-piloted her flashy Vega Gull with a turquoise body and silver wings straight into the history books. This is how she described sitting in that seat: "Being alone in an aeroplane for even so short a time as a night and a day, irrevocably alone, with nothing to observe but your instruments and your own hands in semi-darkness, nothing to contemplate but the size of your small courage, nothing to wonder about but the beliefs, the faces, and the hopes rooted in your mind – such an experience can be as startling as the first awareness of a stranger walking by your side at night. You are the stranger."

To solitude researchers, including the three authors of this book, Markham's powerful account speaks volumes about what it means to be alone for any of us. Solitude is, in essence, a solo flight. A lot of what can make people feel uncomfortable – or exhilarated – in that state is that it insists that we face ourselves, with all of our troubles and triumphs, emotions and expectations. For many people, there is a comforting familiarity in that, whereas for others, there can be a startling strange-ness. Sometimes we are flying blind in that space, and things can go wrong while we're in flight, but with the right awareness, preparation, and tools, as we talk about at length in this book, we can ultimately make it a successful journey. In short, regardless of whether we are skilled or a novice at spending time alone, it can be as defined or amorphous, as empty or full, as certain or uncertain, as we choose to make it.

In Markham's time, as in ours, the decision to *go toward* alone time was an uncommon one. Like many in history who recognize that humans are largely social creatures, she knew that spending time in solitude was unconventional and perhaps even undesirable for most people. "You can live a lifetime and, at the end of it, know more about other people than you know about yourself. You learn to watch other people, but you never watch yourself because you strive against loneliness," wrote Markham. "The abhorrence of loneliness is as natural as wanting to live at all." Yet Marham had ultimately spent so much time alone while flying planes and training racehorses that silence had become a habit, solitude a haven – and loneliness the stranger.

Markham was born in England in 1902 but raised in colonial Kenya, where she learned to fly planes. By the time she climbed into the cockpit for her record-breaking flight, age thirty-three years, she had already logged some quarter million pilot miles. Markham was realistic about the dangers of flying during the dawn of aviation, and of flying as a woman alone, but outweighing all of that were the freedom and transformative solitude that it allowed. She alluded to that in her thrilling memoir *West with the Night*. While cruising over the southern tip of Ireland during her historic flight, she remarked on some of the last rain-drenched lights she'd see for many hours after heading over black water: "I am above them and the plane roars in a sobbing world, but it imparts no sadness to me. I feel the security of solitude, the exhilaration of escape. So long as I can see the lights and imagine the people walking under them, I feel selfishly triumphant, as if I have eluded care and left even the small sorrow of rain in other hands."

Flying alone across the Atlantic, and in particularly foul weather, obviously took tremendous courage and confidence. Likewise, while it's seldom death-defying, solitude in any form requires all of us to muster up some moxie. That's because there's a lot, particularly in our modern world, indicating that we should *run from* time alone, that it is a problem to be solved, a waste of time, or, paradoxically, an illegitimate indulgence. According to some experts and many headlines, many of us are enduring an epidemic of loneliness (even in the days prior to the epic social strangeness inflicted by COVID-19). Some current books and media coverage are fraught with misconceptions about solitude, presuming that those who want or need it are introverted or socially inept or that one's alone space is a zone of nothingness (a zero-sum game). In popular culture, in particular, we are led to believe that solitude is something to avoid or endure; just consider the sad singletons desperate to connect with a mate, like Bridget Jones or the *Sex in the City* clan. Women in particular are saddled with the stereotype of aspiring to be social butterflies, in communication with others 24/7. (We three researchers/authors know from our own experiences that this isn't true and regularly crave and pursue time apart from our loved ones.)

Little in mainstream society today indicates that when we choose it, solitude can be wonderful, even transformative. Instead, all that talk of loneliness in modern life can make us think that solitude is a disease requiring treatment, and perhaps cured by avoiding solo moments altogether. Until recently, science has supported those assumptions because decades of prevailing research have focused on humans as "social animals" and on the fact that fulfilling relationships are integral to happiness. Being social has been highly valued by most researchers, and society has devoted its resources to understanding, developing, and embracing relationships with others. Researchers have studied relationships for so long that we now know a lot about how those interactions affect well-being. We know exactly what we mean by "close relationships" (romantic partners, parents), "conversations" (sit down and talk), and "horizontal" (friend) or "vertical" (boss) relationships.

From that work, we have also learned a lot about solitude in the extremes, for example, for prisoners and astronauts and in early childhood development (a different kind of captive and space cadet!). While there is value in studying the effects of alone time on the very young and among isolated people, including some elders, that laser focus has left a gaping hole in terms of what role solitude plays for everyone else in the middle, and in our everyday lives. In an effort to fill that gap, we draw from many of the major theories that have formed psychology as we know it to understand the role of social relationships *and* the relationship with the self. Those include developmental psychology (research on children and adolescents), humanistic psychology (writings by psychoanalysts or research related to meaning and *self-determination theory*), social psychology (research related to societal norms), and environmental psychology (research related to nature).

From that research, we know that just as we have physical needs, we also have mental ones. Just as our bodies need food and water to sustain us, to help us grow and strengthen, our minds need the experience of relatedness with others (for some people, this includes a kinship with nature) *and* autonomy within ourselves. Those gains are not muscle and bone but their mental equivalents. That relatedness need is an easy concept to understand, and it probably comes as no surprise to hear that we need to feel close and connected to others to feel content. Even in a book about solitude, we can't ignore the importance of relatedness to others, and we consider in these pages what our need to connect with others means for the time we spend alone, and vice versa.

Basic psychological research and theories tell us that, yes, other people matter hugely to contentment. "Social" is an inherently positive concept, while its flip side – unsocial or merely alone – is viewed negatively, even stigmatized. So, by comparison, scientists have spent very little time and resources on understanding the role of solitude, and the power of positive solitude in particular, in shaping our lives. These mysteries have never really been grappled with, and that was intriguing to the three of us researchers/authors. Because, in reality, the social sciences are not always about the "social" world, and in our own professional (and personal) journeys, we have been drawn to concepts like "personal growth" and "self-connection" and to how the nonsocial environment, such as we experience in the beauty and power of nature, can impact those aspects of our lives. In short, we believe that there is much more to well-being than our social relationships.

When we pushed beyond the body of existing research on being alone, which was limited for our purposes of understanding *positive* solitude, we found ourselves in a territory uncharted and explored by few others. That's why we put together the Solitude Project – both a physical and a virtual space – and have spent several years researching what time alone means to different people around the world. As a result, we had to draw a new map of what our outer and inner landscapes could look like when we make solitude a sought-after destination. That was a daunting but exciting space to be in, and what we learned from our research subjects has revolutionized the study of solitude in some ways – and made us leaders in understanding and interpreting what everyday solitude looks like for people on diverse paths and in different phases of life. Our research participants' perceptions continue to guide the direction of our work and to impact who we are and how we spend our days.

We three came to the study of solitude with very different backgrounds and expertise, which we believe combine to offer unique perspectives on solitude from the dawn of humanity to the present day. Netta is a social psychologist and university professor who has spent much of her career focused, paradoxically, on relationships and motivation. The shift to looking at individuals spending time alone was, therefore, a big one. The idea that we each have the power to think about and to regulate ourselves in solitude, and the fact that time alone can have a profound influence on who we are out in the world (including in our relationships), changed her identity as a researcher and her understanding of solitude in her own life.

Thuy-vy is a professor of psychology who has been researching solitude since she got hooked on the topic during her graduate studies years ago. Like Netta, Thuy-vy uses rigorous experimentation and scientific understanding gleaned from that process to try to improve the quality of our lives. Using that quantitative or "hard science" approach, scientists learn through statistics – objective evidence that describes and explains phenomena. But to truly understand people's lived experiences in solitude, both Thuy-vy and Netta realized that they had to push beyond the hard data to get at why solitude has become an essential yet overlooked part of daily life.

Realizing the limitations of a quantitative approach in capturing the richness of individual wisdom and experiences, they recruited Heather, a longtime journalist and science writer, to help gather and interpret those conversations with research subjects. Our shared goal was to conduct *qualitative* research with three objectives: letting people from all walks of life speak for themselves about their solitude, analyzing those contributions, and describing those findings for the benefit of a wider audience. The result of that work, in part, is this book.

Despite our different paths as researchers, our destination was the same: an understanding of what role solitude plays – and can play – in the daily lives of ordinary people like us. We three have experienced the push and pull (mostly pull!) of solitude in our own lives and know its value for each of us, individually, in helping to establish our personal identity and beliefs. (We side with Beryl Markham and countless others who have seen, and presently see, a universe all their own in solitude.) But that wasn't enough, and we needed to hear from as many others as possible, and over time, dozens of our research subjects – whose voices you'll hear throughout this book – have offered myriad insights that have changed the way we authors view time alone.

Learning about many people's ordinary experiences of solitude turned out to offer, in a way, some of the most extraordinary insights. In talking to a diverse group of people, including a nineteen-year-old Black, male medical student in South Africa and a white, female retiree in Scotland, we heard some remarkable similarities in the potential to recenter and reenergize oneself in solitude. We also heard differences about the meaning of that time in different phases of life. We began to see that solitude *happens* throughout life, whether or not one specifically seeks it, and we recognize that most of us can be better positioned to be resilient in that space and to maximize its benefits.

It may surprise some people to learn that the average adult spends nearly one-third of their waking life alone (that proportion was rising even before COVID-19 pandemic restrictions became part of daily life), and even more as we get older. Also, the number of people living on their own now is higher than at any point in history, and in general, fewer people in wealthy countries are now marrying or living in a cohabiting union, and if they do, it is later in life. Whether they landed there by chance or choice, that trend toward solo living is seen by some as a crisis of well-being and as the unraveling of our social fabric. Remember, that's because we are taught from the time we're in diapers that being alone is bad, and that message is reinforced throughout our lives. As a result, loneliness and solitude – two unrelated states and ideas – have gotten muddled together.

It's true that the experience of being alone can be painful or, at the very least, unwelcome for some people. To them, solitude is a place where dark thoughts bubble up, where we can get lost in feelings of uncertainty, inadequacy, or disconnectedness. We recognize that, at times, fending for ourselves can be intimidating. All the authors of this book have moved around the world for work and school and have endured lonely, uneasy periods. But simply spending less time alone or more time with others isn't a "cure" for loneliness. As many of us know, we can feel deeply lonely even in the company of others. In the coming chapters, we talk about what really causes loneliness and how to avoid its pitfalls in solitude.

While it wasn't our original intention, we largely researched and wrote this book at a unique time in history – a moment that reinforced many common misconceptions about time alone. The COVID-19 pandemic shut down the world to greater and lesser degrees in early 2020 and came to be defined by who we were with or without. The quantity, and not so much the quality, of our relationships and our alone time was in the spotlight, and there was a tremendous emphasis during that time on how we could stay *in touch* with one another. By contrast, there was little focus on how we could be our own touchstones, and few experts suggested that the open space of alone time represented an opportunity for well-being. Instead, the message we got was that there was danger from the virus "out there" but also "in here," in our silent, private, vacant places, where loneliness could creep in and hobble us.

While the pandemic hadn't relented completely at the time of writing, in many parts of the world, we have been returning to a more familiar, if changed, landscape. In the best-case scenario, that period of being physically cut off from much of what we knew has been a break from the treadmill of ordinary life, an opportunity even, in which to reprioritize. Do we really need to spend time on those "filler" friendships? Do our kids need to have every minute of free time scheduled? Before the pandemic, many of us were feeling like we were in constant contact with friends, family, and coworkers (and then came the Zoom calls!). We now know that there are many more quality ways we could be spending that time – listening to music, reading, learning a language, sewing, baking, and on and on.

As we expand on in the coming chapters, we don't see solitude as a threat to our need to belong; rather, we see the two as complementary parts of our lives, each offering different benefits. Unlike a solitary polar bear roaming the snowy tundra or colony-dwelling honeybees, humans are a hybrid species. We require a balance of solo and social (whether we're so-called introverts or extroverts), and we don't have to pick one over the other as we're often led to believe. The facts, insights, and stories of solitude in this book show that the "solo self" is not at odds with the outside world but is fully compatible with the "social self." The assumption is that time alone fragments society, but at its best, it can be a unifying force that positively shapes our understanding of our own minds and others' and transforms our social circles for the better. Solitude is an opportunity to occasionally shut out the noise of other people's lives and gain an understanding of our inner worlds while offering a chance to perhaps, paradoxically, improve the quality of our relationships.

Ideally, solitude is not a shift *away* from others but an intentional move *toward* our best possible selves. Only when we make the decision to focus on ourselves in a meaningful way can we dispel and transform misconceptions about solitude in our own minds. That's important because, as critical as healthy outside relationships are, our number one relationship should be with ourselves. Drilling down to the core of who we each are is critical to understanding important aspects of our being, like what our true beliefs are, where our priorities lie, and what our goals should be. As researchers, we share a passion for understanding how people relate to their core selves – the most important values, emotions, and beliefs we have – and we find solitude stories told to us by research subjects both fascinating and informative in that regard.

Those insights highlight an alternative narrative, spanning history and cultures, that enforces the concept that spending time alone matters deeply for transcending social conventions, gaining wisdom, and identifying a personally meaningful path. In this volume, in fact, we take a rare multidisciplinary look at what solitude has meant throughout human history and what it means now. With the help of historians, philosophers, writers, anthropologists, and neuroscientists, among others, we break down solitude to understand its component parts – and then we build it back up. Through that process, we begin to see that there is something sacred (not in the religious sense, unless you want it to be) in the decision to disengage from society, for however short a period.

Alone time – which, remember, you have been doing your whole life to some extent – has been misunderstood and, we believe, drastically underestimated. Research on the benefits of solitude is still in its early stages, but what we know so far from experimentation is that alone time can have many perks, from relaxation and recharging to problem solving and emotion regulation. Our research also shows that authentic solitude (when we are truly ourselves) is key to well-being because it is the zone where we best connect with our values, interests, and emotions. In that space, there can be truth, sincerity, independence, and intimacy. We can choose solitude for any number of reasons, and those can shift from one minute to the next. Regardless, we believe that time well spent in solitude is critical to embracing an insightful, meaningful, and peaceful life. Our research also points to how we can learn to be comfortable and more resilient in solitude, and we share that information as well.

One theme that has arisen time and again in our discussions of solitude is another myth we seek to debunk: when we can imagine solitude as positive, we tend to think that excelling in aloneness is a holy grail, or lost art, that can be mastered only by retreating to a secluded Tibetan monastery. But our research paints a much different portrait, one of opportunity – the advantages of solitude are readily attainable in our daily lives if we choose that path. As researchers, we have learned that there is no universal perfection in solitude, no right way to do it; there is only the individual exerting their personhood there, and that's enough. As the architects of our own solo space, we can build a shelter to house the inner resources that help us make sense of our world.

Although it doesn't require monastic devotion, pursuing solitude does require embracing its inherent paradox – that it's a space where we may be limited to our own thoughts and desires but at the same time have zero boundaries containing us. Ultimately, seeking solitude is an act of self-care that anyone can undertake, but choosing it can be a radical act for some people. In that place, we can learn to recognize that solitude is not the absence of anything, not really, but rather the presence of everything. And when we do that, we can see that what we used to think of as punishment becomes possibility.

Like pioneering aviator Beryl Markham, any of us may find ourselves in solitude and feel, at times, as if we are unaccompanied pilots bumping around in the dark, a stranger to ourselves, alone without a guide. But we can also know solitude as a solo flight where our wits and wisdom, our tools and training, can be tapped to help us along the way. Markham wrote, "Flight is but momentary escape from the eternal custody of earth." We can see solitude that same way, as a chance to disconnect from tethers, as an opportunity to lift off and be free with frivolity or intensity, and to learn, examine, play, and dream.

CHAPTER 1

Solitude Is Not Just for Hermits, Poets, and Billionaires

IN A SMALL HOUSE ON THE SHORE OF HOOD CANAL, a huge fjord carved into Washington State's densely forested coast, a man sits alone at a desk. If he looks up from his stack of books, he can see beyond brimming window boxes and across tranquil water to the snowcapped Olympic Mountains in the distance. He might even spy a great blue heron cutting through the air with slow swoops or an orca slicing powerfully through the water. But he spends most days reading voraciously, or scratching ideas on a notepad, occasionally getting up to crack open a Diet Coke.

Since the 1990s, that guy – Microsoft magnate Bill Gates – has been going on what he calls "think weeks," during which he steps away from everyone and everything in his daily life for several days to be completely alone. The über-entrepreneur, and now philanthropist, escapes to the quiet cabin to still himself and to distill his ideas – essentially, to problem solve and look ahead. In the Netflix documentary *Inside Bill's Brain*, Gates calls it "CPU time," named for the central processing unit, or the part of the computer that does what a program tells it to. "Hey, I just need to think," Gates says, explaining his need for solitude. After all, without a functioning CPU, a computer is just a useless pile of metal and wire.[1]

This serene scene begs some fundamental questions about the condition we call solitude, who has access to it, and if it is essentially a positive or negative state (or neither). The concept of solitude has existed in stories and paintings, and in practice, for centuries. Looking at that history, as we do in this chapter, tells us a lot about the preconceptions we have about solitude today. Should we conclude from Gates's example that enjoying meaningful solitude is only for billionaires or "tech-bros"? Is it only good and effective when we sequester ourselves completely in a secluded cabin, and for days or weeks at a time? (Spoiler alert: the answers are no and no.) Breaking down the myths and realities of solitude, as we do in our research and in this book, clears a way forward to better understand what solitude is and how we can all benefit from it, every day.

For better and worse, we see and relate to solitude in part due to the way our various cultures treat it. The images we see and the stories we hear, both historical and contemporary, create impressions about what it means to be alone and why we would or wouldn't want to be throughout our lives. By "culture" we mean not just the part of the world we grew up in, or the languages we speak, but also the dynamics of our families and other relationships from childhood through adulthood. We may have been raised in so-called individualist or collectivist societies that imprint on us the power of being alone, and revere or revile it, depending on those traditions. Or growing up in noisy or quiet families may have provided role models for positive alone time or led us to fear it. But we have found, in interviews with people in dozens of countries and by reflecting on our own experiences, that we can each hold unique ideas about what solitude means in our lives while collectively revealing certain universal truths about it.

This is important, because although each of us has an innate sense of what solitude is, there is surprisingly little consensus on its definition among those of us who study it. For the past forty years, psychologists have probed what it's like to be alone,[2-4] though, during that time, they have studied mainly children. The lone kid on the playground sparks concern in caregivers, and everyone wants to know if avoiding social interactions means trouble. Accepting its limitations, that research is still helpful in beginning to understand when solitude is good or bad and who tends to like or dislike it. But that approach has left a gaping hole in understanding the experience of solitude for us adults in our everyday lives.

For the past several years, in our own research, we have focused on filling that gap and on recognizing the many dimensions of solitude. With the input of thousands of people from all walks of life, we know much more about time spent in solitude, and we now lead the field in defining what it means to be in solitude and understanding the impacts of that time. What makes it necessary or enjoyable, painful or feared? What effects does solitude have on the rest of our lives and on our relationships beyond the one we have with ourselves?

As we talk about in the coming chapters, we know now that solitude is not the same as loneliness, isolation, or withdrawal, even though those states are associated with the condition of being alone. And although psychologists used to treat solitude as "being alone" in a space absent other people, we now recognize that solitude can also happen in crowded parks and cafés full of chatter. We also see now, despite what history implies, that solitude isn't reserved just for the powerful or spiritually accomplished.

So why is the lone genius on a woodsy retreat (often depicted as male, if we're being real) the way many of us think about solitude? It's a simple question with a fascinating answer played out over millennia and compacted down into the baggage we now carry when considering the who, what, where, when, and why of solitude today, in our daily lives. This book isn't meant to offer a definitive history of solitude from the dawn of humans, but even a flyover look at how it's been viewed over time helps shed light on some biases and beliefs. Looking at how solitude has been treated, and still is, can help us untangle why we approach it in the ways we do today, both as a society and as individuals. With that knowledge, we can also illuminate some of the misconceptions of solitude that impede us from enjoying it today and move ahead toward our own "you"-topias.

FIRST, A LITTLE HISTORY

One of the reasons solitude is so interesting to study is because, as we have discovered in our research, the state or condition of being alone is an element of the human experience that transcends time and place, language and religion, age and gender. That doesn't mean humans, since we first walked upright, have always experienced alone time in the same way or equally (gender and socioeconomic status have been important exceptions, as we'll cover), just that it's been a state sometimes celebrated, sometimes criticized – and most always marginalized –

throughout recorded history. Understanding that solitude has been embraced or shunned, worshipped or feared, discouraged or tolerated, through the ages hints at its power.

For millennia, solitude remained on the sidelines because, frankly, we weren't physically equipped for it. Solitude as an opportunity to experience a separate, internal space was outside the realm of the everyday lives of ancient hunter-gatherers. From this perspective, we are not "wired" to be alone (more on this in Chapter 6), and while we now top the pecking order on Earth, for most of history, we were fairly easy prey. Our ancestors, trying to avoid lions and leopards, knew that there was safety in numbers, at least for most members of a group. Before devising the technology required to flip the script on predators, we stuck together. This defensive behavior also served us well in forming societies that benefited from collective efforts like hunting and foraging.[5]

Nowadays, most of us don't need our neighbors' help to catch dinner, and our survival doesn't require putting others in peril. But this early history of primates may be responsible, in part, for why solitude is still outside of what is considered normal or expected, or practical. Even though we no longer need to be "selfish herd"[6] members like flocks of birds or schools of fish, humans still frequently adopt that mentality – and especially at times of danger, when individual reasoning is suspended in favor of pack trends (experts see this during structure fires or even when following stock market surges). "Group mind" can hijack our individuality and encourage alternative behavior we may not ordinarily exhibit. That innate desire to be part of the "in crowd," research has shown, also makes us less responsive to changes in our environment than we should be. It also makes us less likely to choose different ways of being that may ultimately benefit us – like spending time in solitude.[7]

Even as we moved off the savanna and into towns and cities, an understanding and acceptance of solitude continued to dwell on the fringes of human experience. In the best of times, solitude has come into favor as a fad, or at least a fascination, only to fall out again according to norms governed largely by academic, religious, and political leadership. (We delve into the science of that stigma in much greater depth in Chapters 2 and 6.) All the while, it has been greatly underestimated and undervalued in the mainstream.[8]

Some ideas about what solitude means in society today are driven by enduring stories and imagery from generations past that can influence, for better or worse, how we think about alone time and whether we welcome it. Those are sometimes clichés, such as the lone poet lying in a sunny meadow or a brooding philosopher sitting in an armchair by a fireplace. Other depictions of solitude have reached the masses via major religious traditions from around the world. They offer some of the earliest views of solitude, represented as a path to insight, growth, and spiritual transcendence (away from messier, "imperfect" social realms).

Ancient texts and countless images based on them (see Box 1.1) are infused with tales of prophets seeking guidance and wisdom in the "wilderness."[9] Islam teaches that the prophet Muhammed went solo to a mountain cave for one month per year. He was visited there by the angel Gabriel, who revealed to him the first verses of the Qur'an, the faith's sacred, central text.[10] Prophets in Jewish and Christian traditions, as depicted in the Bible, also tended to spend a lot of time alone. Both Moses and Elijah were advocates of solitude; Hebrew prophet Moses (traditionally credited with writing the Torah, which, in Judaism, is the law of God) "entered the cloud" of deep solitude on Mount Sinai to have God divinely reveal to him the Ten Commandments.[11] Ancient Persian prophet Zoroaster (also known as Zarathustra) seemingly outdid them all by retreating to wander the rocky, sparse Iranian mountains on and off, and alone, for a decade.[12,13]

For centuries more, those teachings continued to inspire the idea of solitude for spiritual transformation, and the hermits and monks who followed the prophets – still far from the mainstream – continued to seek sublimity.[14] This idea may seem oxymoronic on its face – that holy people shunned the presence of others for a self-serving purpose (transcendence) – but it wasn't selfish to them. Instead, solitude was required to achieve utmost focus on something beyond themselves; time alone was meant for connecting with the divine. That need was understood at the time, and their deprivation was revered (and perhaps envied) by more common folks who knew suffering to be a route to salvation and happiness. Solitude represented an experience inaccessible to most, and it created, at least for some, an unrequited, romanticized longing for it.[15]

BOX 1.1 BUDDHA BENEATH THE BODHI TREE

Perhaps the most recognizable, and maybe idealized, image of solitude is the Buddha sitting under the Bodhi tree. His eyes are closed to indicate an inward focus, his legs are crossed in a meditative pose, and on his face is a slight smile of peaceful contentment. Quite often in this ethereal imagery, the Bodhi tree, with its gnarled but leafy branches stretching outward in all directions, represents spiritual growth and development of selfhood. But how did the Buddha – the enlightened one, the knower – get there, and what lessons exist for us about the value of solitude?

The young Buddha, called Siddhartha Gotama at birth, was raised in wealth and comfort in Nepal, ignorant about the suffering of the poor. When he first ventured beyond his castle walls, Gotama believed the rest of the world shared his lucky birthright, and he was shaken when he saw, for the first time, poverty, illness, and death. To make sense of such a divergent and painful reality, Gotama sought help from the spiritual leaders around him. They suggested he fast and pray, but that didn't seem to do the trick, and after years of trying, a still-confused Gotama decided to go it alone in search of answers. It was then, in the solitude of a nearby forest, that he is believed to have found enlightenment. That formed the basis of what we now know as Buddhist doctrine, which professes that an existence based on attachment causes suffering and that pain can only be alleviated by freeing ourselves from the illusion of permanence.[16]

Through his attempt to understand the world on his own, the Buddha was able to return to society as a wise teacher with his own unique views and a new philosophy of the "good life." Today, we generally frame what the Buddha was doing in solitude as meditation or its cousin, mindfulness – both popular but not required practices for finding meaning in time alone.[17]

Beyond its designated path to spiritual enlightenment, for most of history, solitude has been reserved for devotees like monks or cloistered nuns, those willing to swap societal and family ties for isolation and the doorway, they believe, to both a higher being and a higher purpose.

Excepting those idealized forms of solitude undertaken by religious figures, solitude was viewed mostly with suspicion over the following millennia. The fear of solitude seems, paradoxically, to stem from what gives it appeal – in the absence of social influence, people have the freedom to try out self-reflection, self-sufficiency, and independent thought. That was a power entrusted only to a few, and over time, it's been seen as dangerous in the hands of the shiftless majority.[8]

During the move from the Middle Ages into modernity, many physicians believed that a person's natural balance was thrown off by certain ways of life that affected their mental health. They warned that ascetic nuns and monks were at grave risk of melancholy from extreme self-discipline. Marsilio Ficino, an immensely influential scholar, priest, and philosopher in mid- to late fifteenth-century Italy, instructed scholars to lay off overthinking in solitude. Ficino, who also dabbled in astrology and medicine, believed that too much cogitating caused people's brains to dry out, which he believed led to depression.[18] It wasn't the beginning of that line of thinking – medical folks since Galen of ancient Greece (circa the second century) conflated being solitary with melancholy, a kind of vague sadness – nor was it the end, and it continued in that vein for centuries.[19] Oxford academic and vicar Robert Burton wrote in his best-selling encyclopedia of depression *The Anatomy of Melancholy* in 1621 that solitude transforms people from "sociable creatures, [to] become beasts, monsters, inhumane, ugly to behold."[20]

Even up into the mid-nineteenth century, solitude was highlighted as deviant in many ways. In his *American Practice of Medicine* from 1846, physician Wooster Beach talked about several maladies believed to be either caused or intensified by solitude, including grief, melancholy, epilepsy, "love sickness," and hydrophobia (a key symptom of what we now know as rabies). His conclusion: "Solitude should, therefore, by all means be avoided."[21,22] Sentiments toward solitude weren't much different across the pond. In the 1850 edition of the *People's Medical Journal, and Family Physician* – at the time, a publication rivaling the prominent *Lancet* – British doctor Thomas Harrison Yeoman wrote, "The leading characteristics of melancholy are – a love of solitude, gloom, fear, suspicion and taciturnity."[23]

At best, some people seemed to have had a complicated relationship with the concept of being alone, or perhaps a dawning recognition of its possibilities. Despite the mainstream being dominated by discouraging messages about solitude, there have been moments when it has been more or less "in fashion," albeit among those privileged with downtime and/or privacy. During the Renaissance in Europe (fifteenth to seventeenth centuries), some folks began to think differently about spending time in their own company.[15,24,25] They wanted to revive the teachings of ancient Greece and Rome, and in that context, they talked a lot about the "self" and the "individual." The ancient Greeks believed, as Aristotle professed, that humans are political animals, but some also toiled over the value of the individual. Socrates was a chatty, city-loving philosopher – one famously indifferent to popular opinion – who argued for the supremacy of the individual conscience over the approval of society.[25–27] Later, the Roman Stoic known as Seneca wrote, "The primary indication, to my thinking, of a well-ordered mind is a man's ability to remain in one place and linger in his own company."[28]

Volumes of candid personal essays on the pros and cons of solitude were written during the Renaissance. Some of the most controversial were penned by reluctant politician and French philosopher Michel de Montaigne in the mid-fifteenth century. One is called "Of Solitude," in which he insisted, "We must reserve a withdrawing-room wholly our own, and entirely free, wherein to settle our true liberty, our principal retreat and solitude." He was most likely talking about noblemen like himself, and not the women or servants around him, but Montaigne's thinking nevertheless represented an evolution in the understanding that there is a wholeness in being alone (and that it doesn't cause your brain to dehydrate like a raisin). "We have a mind that can turn to itself, that can be its own company; that has wherewithal to attack and to defend, to receive and to give. Let us not then fear, in this solitude, to languish in an uncomfortable vacancy of thought," he wrote.[29]

At the same time, Montaigne lived at a moment when economic conditions across Europe were improving for many. Privacy became a real possibility and objective, first for "nobles," then for others who could afford to build either more rooms or at least more partitions in their homes. For the first time, a growing number of individuals could seek solitude, if only for a short time. In some cases, even women – particularly if they were part of genteel society – could enjoy more than just a few moments of quiet apart from familial and social responsibilities.[24] (More on this in Box 1.2.).

Despite the shift in thinking for some people around "solitariness" (the term used back then), time alone remained a divisive topic. Most people still believed the individual was defined only in relation to society and that those who found themselves outside of that paradigm should be criticized – or pitied. That thinking may have stemmed more from a fear of the unknown than from anything else, because the masses likely had little firsthand knowledge of complete solitude. During the early industrial era in the mid-eighteenth century, seeking solo time wasn't realistic because just making it through the day often relied on continuous social interactions. Even if someone did want to be alone, living in small, crowded homes or working in congested sweatshops would have made that difficult to do for any stretch of time. The working classes had little time for the Buddha's brand of self-reflective solitude – though they may have had solitude "breaks," according to David Vincent, author of *A History of Solitude*. On the flip side, and for some people, being alone may have been more a by-product of long hours of labor in the fields – more depleting than peaceful.[24]

During this time, there was also little enthusiasm among ruling elites for working individuals to find their own paths to wisdom (seen at the time as closely related to religious faith and morality). Most people were also illiterate and therefore unable to interpret spiritual teachings for themselves. Expounding on spirituality was the purview of religious leaders, who defined right and wrong, and spiritual pursuits were appropriate only in churches and social gatherings. Beyond those contexts, discovering one's own untaught truths threatened an established social order and was discouraged by religious leaders.[24]

That narrow view didn't change much during the hypersocial period of the eighteenth-century Enlightenment, when churning over progressive and liberal ideas in countless "salons" was all the rage and solitude was seen by many as a perversion. Eminent Scottish philosopher David Hume (1711–76) wrote in *A Treatise of Human Nature*, "A perfect solitude is, perhaps, the greatest punishment we can suffer. Every pleasure languishes when enjoy'd a-part from company, and every pain becomes more cruel and intolerable."[30]   But there were exceptions, such as

Daniel Defoe, author of *Robinson Crusoe* (1719), who recommended everyday solitude for anyone who had the right mind-set for it. In a follow-up to that book, in his essay "Of Solitude" (1720), he wrote that the essence of solitude did not lie in the seclusion of a monk's cell and could just as easily be found on the trading floor of what's now the London Stock Exchange. The trick, he said, is for us to become "perfectly retired from the world" and ready and willing to be content on our own.[31] For some outliers like Defoe, who suspected that society held more questions than answers, time apart from others became an appealing place for self-discovery.

BOX 1.2 WOMEN IN SOLITUDE

The experiences of women throughout history are often difficult to discover, at least from the written record (while men have penned most of history, women have lived it in ways rarely recorded) – and their relationship to solitude is no exception. But as three female researchers and three women with different but profound relationships with solitude, we are acutely aware of the need to try to represent a true diversity of experiences. The history of women and solitude up to the present day is most certainly incomplete, but several prominent voices hint at the enduring importance of time alone to many women throughout the ages – including our own.[47]

The "herstory" of solitude exists on the fringes of society over the centuries, just as it did for many men, but how and why women have achieved solitude differs in some intriguing ways. That's due, in large part, to gender stereotypes that exist in some form to this day, such as that women are "talkers" who want, or even need, to communicate to satisfy emotional needs. We are also perennially seen as "caretakers" who are thus expected to be available to others constantly and to relegate our own needs to partners and children at home, and at the office too (women are still overrepresented in occupations focused on social contribution and interpersonal communication).[48]

Historically, the picture was grimmer in terms of women's secondary status in society. Women were believed to be the weaker sex, and men thought a woman left to her own devices would not have the mental strength to resist the devil. The definitive handbook on witchcraft,

Malleus Maleficarum (or *Hammer of Witches*), from 1486, which prompted two centuries of European "witch hunting" hysteria, gives us a peek at why. "When a woman thinks alone, she thinks evil," it says. This meant that women who wanted to be on their own had to ride a swinging pendulum to the other extreme by declaring religious devotion.[49]

So-called desert mothers are not nearly as well known as their male counterparts, but nevertheless, there were female Christian ascetics in the Middle East, North Africa, Europe, and the British Isles in the fourth and fifth centuries. Those *ammas*, as they were often called, joined monastic communities, but many also lived on their own as hermits. Choosing such an extreme religious vocation was a script flip on expected social values and expectations and, arguably, a mental and physical "way out" of living under patriarchal oppression. (In particular, the vow of chastity that ammas took was a solid workaround for women seeking physical independence.)[50]

Solitude, however, wasn't just a means of escape but a meaningful space in which women could think and profess as spiritual teachers. Syncletica of Alexandria, living in fourth- and fifth-century Roman Egypt, was one such woman.[51] She was reportedly rich, beautiful, and educated but gave away her wealth and moved to the desert to live a holy, hermetic life. Even though she was certainly a fan of quiet contemplation, many people took pilgrimages to hear what she had to say. One of Amma Syncletica's bits of wisdom rejects the idea that one must be a recluse to access solitude and its benefits, while also warning of the potential for rumination there. "It is possible to be a solitary in one's mind while living in a crowd; and it is possible for one who is a solitary to live in the crowd of his own thoughts," she said.[52]

The eremitic tradition petered out somewhat in the ninth and tenth centuries but surged again when, in the latter half of the Middle Ages (roughly 1100 to 1500 CE), women in Britain and Europe were again seeking solitude, in a different but no less extreme way.[24] That was the age of the "anchoress," during which time hundreds of laywomen chose to live alone (as long as they could financially support the endeavor), walled up in twelve-foot-square cells with no means of physical escape, to devote themselves to prayer and contemplation.[53]

The word *anchoress* derives from the Greek *anachero*, meaning "to withdraw." That life of relative isolation – they also counseled visitors from within their "anchorhold" – was believed to elevate them to a higher level of existence. They were a kind of supernun, though they didn't take any vows, in that they had the power to seek salvation for others; some even believed the anchoress could usher the dead past purgatory. Beyond her obvious physical constraints, the anchoress fulfilled a powerful spiritual purpose far beyond other Christians – and most women – of her day.[48]

Many anchorite guidebooks written over centuries praised total solitude and made frequent reference to the preceding desert hermits as role models. One thirteenth-century guide, *Ancrene Wisse*, reminded the anchoress that the consolation for her sacrifice was the service it provided others. "The anchoress is called an 'anchor,' and anchored under the church like an anchor under the side of a ship to hold the ship, so that waves and storms do not capsize it," it said. This unique role represents a rare moment in history when the spiritual authority of women was recognized, even sought. (There were also male "anchorites," but they were always outnumbered by women seeking the role.)[54]

Unlike an amma, the anchoress was on her own in the middle of town. Her cell was generally attached to a church and had three windows – one that overlooked the church interior, one that faced a parlor where a servant swapped food for waste, and another that opened to the outside. (There were no doors – an effort to "protect" her physical body from temptation and sin.) She was advised to keep her hair short and her clothes simple, as did the desert mothers and fathers. But holding an important position in the center of the community set the anchoress apart from what we know of hermits. While they shared the choice to live apart from society in extreme ways, the anchoress moved – at least intellectually – between society and solitude with remarkable intention.[53]

In that way, anchoresses represent an interesting anomaly in the history of solitude for women, and they illustrate the extremes to which women were willing to go to be left alone to think. At the same time, the reality of women being voluntarily locked in cells as their only acceptable way to achieve significant periods of solitude (and to escape the uneven landscape of legal and social rights afforded only to men) is a grim one, at least to us in the modern day. Still, unlike most of their female contemporaries, anchoresses had a degree of autonomy over their physical bodies – they weren't expected to marry or to bear children, for example – and they were encouraged to read and write. Julian of Norwich, also known as Mother Juliana, is arguably history's most famous anchoress. She spent decades in her chosen confinement and, during that time, wrote her *Revelations of Divine Love*, which describes being on (what she thought was) her deathbed at age thirty – while not yet an anchoress – and experiencing a series of celestial revelations. The book, written in the mid- to late 1300s, is the first work in the English language that scholars are certain was authored by a woman.[55]

Women have taken greater risks in seeking solitude throughout history (and some argue we still do, be it physical and/or psychological) and by living in unconventional ways. A good example of this are the *beguines*, who came on the scene around 1200 in northern Europe and later spread south. The beguines were laywomen unaffiliated with any religious order who had nevertheless devoted their lives to poverty and service (in vocations like teaching or nursing).[56–58] Some lived solo, while others chose a more communal setting, but regardless, they were often investigated, suppressed, and even persecuted by those suspicious of women living without direct male oversight. If a woman and her body weren't governed by someone other than herself, if she wasn't under constant surveillance, then she seemed useless and potentially dangerous to men. (Despite attempts to shut down the beguines, they persisted in some form until the late twentieth century.) One exception to this harsh reality was Mugai Nyodai (1223–98), born into a noble samurai family in - modern-day Japan. After being widowed and raising her daughter, she chose to study with monastery abbots and eventually take her own monastic vows. After years of meditation, she attained enlightenment, becoming the first female Zen master, and (after being denied leadership of her teacher's monastery) founded the first Buddhist convent in Japan.[59]

Historian Naomi Pullin at the University of Warwick has studied how experiences of solitude and society have differed for women and men, historically. She has written that, in seventeenth- and eighteenth-century Britain, following others' guidance and example was customary, and departing from the norm could be a profound act. Bearing the weight of relentless domestic responsibilities, women's time was rarely their own, but occasionally, they carved out a way to be with their own minds. Pullin tells the story of Lady Elizabeth Anne Dormer, a gentlewoman from Oxfordshire who (unhappily) married Robert Dormer in 1668 and wrote revealing letters to her sister about her relationship – with solitude. "She extolled the emotional and domestic benefits of her private closet, 'a safe shelter,' where she could read and write in privacy. She contrasted this with the chaotic and over-bearing domestic situation 'out of it,' where she could find 'little quiet,'" wrote Pullin.[60]

Skip ahead to the mid-eighteenth century, and some remarkable women were also expressing their thoughts on solitude. Anne-Thérèse de Marguenat de Courcelles (a.k.a. the Marchioness de Lambert) hosted intellectual salons in her Paris home from 1710, where hot topics of the day were debated. She wrote about the importance of women carving out periods of internal shelter for independent thought. (Lambert could appreciate the paradox of espousing the Enlightenment-era philosophy of individual sovereignty in a parlor crammed with people.) In one of her most famous works, "Advice of a Mother to Her Daughter" (1729), she talks about solitude as a virtue to be cultivated. "Secure then a retreat in your own mental acquirements, whither you may at any time return and be yourself," she wrote. "You should therefore from time to time retire from the world to be alone."[61] Lambert and similar writers around that time accepted that women were confined to a particular sphere (mainly the home) but argued that there were some choices still inherent within, or despite, that domestic confinement. Independent thought in solitude was one of them.

Later female writers had a more complicated relationship with solitude and saw it as a place of reflection and growth, but a precarious one – like wild-spirited, London-born, pioneer feminist and writer Mary Wollstonecraft, who wrote about solitude as both a gateway to heaven and a woeful retreat to take when she was rejected by lovers or strangers alike. "Solitude and reflection are necessary to give to wishes the force of passions," she wrote in *A Vindication of the Rights of Woman* (1792). Wollstonecraft died at age thirty-eight, eleven days after giving birth to her second daughter and just six months after marrying William Godwin. Both were societal misfits; Wollstonecraft had affairs and advocated for women's rights, and Godwin was a known anarchist. Their daughter, Mary Shelley, went on to write *Frankenstein* – the story of a creature feared and spurned for being "different" and doomed to the loneliest solitude.[8,62,63]

Nineteenth-century women talked about and used solitude in a way we might today better recognize as feminist. Kate Chopin's fictional Marianne in the "Maid of Saint Philippe" (1892) is a strong, self-sufficient seventeen-year-old French American (and skilled hunter) living in present-day Louisiana on the cusp of a British takeover of her village. As an only child and newly orphaned, Marianne rejects multiple suitors, pursuing solitude instead and the independence she feels when she's on her own. Chopin writes of Marianne, "At once she felt that she was alone, with no will to obey in the world but her own. Then her heart was as strong as oak and her nerves were like iron."[64]

In that same year, Elizabeth Cady Stanton (1815–1902), by then a famous suffragette agitating to gain the women's vote, addressed the US Congress on the "Solitude of Self." "In discussing the rights of woman, we are to consider, first, what belongs to her as an individual, in a world of her own, the arbiter of her own destiny, an imaginary Robinson Crusoe with her woman Friday on a solitary island. Her rights under such circumstances are to use all her faculties for her own safety and happiness," she said.[65] Essentially, Stanton was arguing that what women did in solitude – indulge the sovereignty of their human souls – proved that they are equal to men. "To guide our own craft, we must be captain, pilot, engineer; with chart and compass to stand at the wheel; to match the wind and waves and know when to take in the sail, and to read the signs in the firmament over all. It matters not whether the solitary voyager is man or woman," she said.[65]

Twentieth-century women picked up that baton, arguing further that women needed their own spaces to feed their intellectual hunger. "A Room of One's Own," a now-classic feminist text based on two lectures given by Virginia Woolf to undergraduates at Cambridge University in 1928, was just one of Woolf's works alluding to the power of solitude.[66] That "room" was literal and figurative, and Woolf argued that it was one of the many advantages men had over women at the time. Having the place and the time to enjoy solitude – whether to work or just to think – was key, especially for writing. Woolf sometimes experienced loneliness in solitude and depicted her characters in both positive and negative relationships with it, but she also capitalized on those moments, which seemed to fertilize her thinking. She wrote in "The Waves" (1931), "How much better to sit by myself like the solitary sea-bird that opens its wings on the stake. Let me sit here for ever with bare things, this coffee cup, this knife, this fork, things in themselves, myself being myself."[67]

That concept was well understood by the prolific Belgian American poet, novelist, and diarist May Sarton. In her 1973 book *Journal of a Solitude*, she wrote that time alone was her "real life." In solitude (both literal, on the windswept coast of New England, and figurative, as a lesbian female artist born in 1912), she wrote, "I hope to break through into the rough, rock depths, to the matrix itself."[68] Sarton went in search of solitude in her mid-forties, when she felt societal demands were tamping down her inner fire. Her youth had been filled with many friends, lovers, coworkers, and correspondents, but she felt she had to reach inside for something more. In her work, Sarton explored universal themes, such as the quests for inner peace, self-knowledge, and individual satisfaction. In her collection of poems called *Inner Landscape*, Sarton wrote in "Canticle 6," "Alone one is never lonely; the spirit adventures, waking / In a quiet garden, in a cool house, abiding single there."[69]

Women are no longer seen as the devil's playmate if they steal away by themselves, but there still seems to be special scorn reserved for women wanting to fly solo today. Choosing solitude is often associated with the negative stereotypes of being difficult, selfish, pitiful, or sad. Oftentimes, those negative stigmas can be internalized, leading single women to form a negative impression of their own lifestyles.[70] For example, in an in-depth interview study of thirty-two Norwegian women age thirty-five to fifty-five years, researcher Bente Heimtun explored how it felt to travel alone. She asked her subjects to reflect on their best and most difficult moments, and they reported feeling inhibited and suppressed by the "tourist gaze" when on vacation or eating out alone. Her participants felt lonely and self-conscious when they couldn't hide from perceived social judgment. "It's not nice to sit in the middle of things and be stared at, then you really are alone, no matter how many books you've got with you," elaborated one interviewee.[71] (Sociologists have argued that conquering dining alone, in particular, is important for women's ability to claim their public space, shake off the fear of negative evaluations by others, and embrace their own solitude.)

Choosing to spend time in solitude continues to be viewed as a somewhat radical act, and some women are still compelled to make some extreme moves to stake a claim to alone time. Today, we have the "hermettes," a term coined by Risa Mickenberg, head of a quasi-clandestine society of women and a New Yorker demanding for women the respect normally reserved only for male hermits.[72] In a rare radio interview on the subject in 2022, she said, "I'm feminizing it because I feel like female aloneness is such a taboo." Instead, Mickenberg (now retired from a career in advertising) and others are bucking the stigma of being seen as hags or old maids, stereotypes that persist for women who have chosen to spend their lives solo and are hoping to shape a new feminine ideal. "I've seen now, there are so many women who really love being alone. And instead of it being a shameful or embarrassing thing, or kind of a secret, I think it should be the thing that we really all want to do," she said.[73]

At the same time in Continental Europe, the Romantic era was getting ready to launch, bringing with it more mainstream recognition of a potential upside to solitude. Johann Georg Zimmermann, a renowned German physician, wrote a four-volume tome, *Solitude* (1784–85), about how time alone offered moments for self-regulation and self-reflection and, for those reasons, provided a space to actively cure what ailed one's soul.[32] Zimmermann was critical of the picture of the pious, navel-gazing hermit completely removed from others as the only or true form of solitude and instead embraced the idea that solitude could be a collection of moments that complemented social life.

Zimmermann discussed solitude with nuance – he understood that there were risks as well as rewards – and he emphasized the importance of having the right mind-set, the right amount, and even the best context for time alone. Still, his writing caused discord at the time, according to David Vincent. Some people read *On Solitude* as a blanket "positive stamp" on solitude and reacted with hostility, as if Zimmermann's work was threatening the established social order. "There was all the difference between the withdrawal to the closet or the countryside for the purpose of self-collection, and the retreat to the same spaces because of emotional defeat or misguided passion," wrote Vincent.[24]

On the heels of Zimmermann's unusual take on solitude came Romanticism, an intellectual and artistic movement characterized by its rejection of Enlightenment ideas and its embrace of emotion, transcendence, and the individual. The Romantics of the late 1700s and early 1800s and their American counterparts, the Transcendentalists, couldn't have been more different than the Enlightenment folks. During that time, poet William Wordsworth walked in the Lake District as "lonely as a cloud"[33] and in the "bliss of solitude," and Ralph Waldo Emerson strolled in the hemlock, red oak, and white pine woods of Concord, Massachusetts, engaged in thinking about self-acquaintance, independence, and self-reliance.[34] Both groups held a certain suspicion about society and the masses and didn't desire the constant company of others, preferring instead a solo space to figure out who they were, often using the natural world as a guide. (Much more on the science behind the impact of nature on humans in Chapter 7.)

Solitude also found its place at the time in the carefully designed "self-reflection" gardens of Great Britain. In the mid-eighteenth century, it became fashionable to stroll around one's property seeking spirituality and wisdom. Again, solitude was only for wealthy families who found themselves with more time for "thinking."[35] During this time, some rich families even employed "garden hermits" to occupy remote spots on their properties (some landowners also used the huts or grottos themselves from time to time for meditation and self-reflection). The hired hermits – picture a living, breathing lawn gnome – lived in artificial caves or hermitages and were visited for an occasional reminder of what spiritual transcendence through solitude could look like. Some were asked to dispense advice to visitors; others were told to stay quiet, not to bathe or cut their hair or nails, and to don robes like Druids (members of the learned class of ancient Celts).[35]

The hermits may seem to us now like a bizarre carnival act (and a somewhat inhumane one at that), but the introspection they were meant to encourage – however cultivated – was prized by elites at the time, and the hermits were meant to be revered. The popularity of gardens and grottos and the spectacle of "pet" hermits illustrate people's complicated relationship with solitude: those with more leisure time increasingly tried to reconnect with wisdom in a way previously only accessible to spiritual figures. But, still, solitude was a curiosity, a fringe element.[24,35] Many people seemed tantalized by it, understanding that there was something there worth exploring, but they failed to connect with the concept that it was fully open to them, whenever and wherever they chose.

SOLITUDE WITH A LOWERCASE *s*

So far, we've looked at the history of solitude with a capital *S*, which seemed largely reserved for prophets, priests, poets, and the like, or at least, they are the ones privileged with enduring stories. But solitude with a lowercase *s*, the kind experienced every day by most folks, is tougher to pinpoint. It's difficult to know what the experiences of most people were, say, roaming the landscape in prehistoric times or dodging the plague in the fourteenth century, but it's likely most ordinary folks were too busy trying to stay alive to think much about the meaning of solitude in their daily lives. That doesn't mean they didn't desire more time on their own, and at least from a modern perspective, it's hard to imagine they didn't long for alone time when living and working (and infrequently bathing) in cramped quarters. They may also have had a kind of alone time – in the company of others – that we researchers find particularly interesting: while kneading bread in the kitchen, washing clothes in the river, or sowing crops in the fields, side by side in easy silence, many people may have been experiencing a variety of positive solitude without even knowing it.

We know a little more about the experience of "empty" time as civilization progressed and the somewhat universal perception of being stuck doing something more recently described as "dull" or "monotonous." Social historians tell us that, up to the mid-nineteenth century, people accepted "downtime" as part of the human condition. They didn't necessarily love it or embrace it, or hate it for that matter. It was just part of living.[36] But some portion of society was beginning to recognize that a period of time could be differentiated as hollow or meaningless, and the word "boredom" first appeared in print in the 1820s.[37] In the following decades, writers portrayed tons of bored dilettantes and debutantes, some of whom even took pride in a social standing that allowed them to do nothing in particular – and to be cranky about it.[38]

In the 1930s and 1940s, the American artist Edward Hopper became famous for painting solitary figures in everyday scenes. In contrast to the hypersocial Roaring Twenties, his images of people looking intently out a window, sitting casually on a bed, or sidled up to a counter in a diner (not physically alone but certainly caught up in their own thoughts) became synonymous with the loneliness of modern life. Hopper was celebrated for capturing poignant moments experienced by people hovering on the edge of whatever American dream was supposed to be within their reach. Outside observers saw sadness and defeat in his subjects because that's what most people believed was supposed to happen when one was alone. But that's not what Hopper was getting at; instead, he was depicting people who were largely content in their own space, engrossed in a task or a thought.[39]

Then as now, misinterpretations of Hopper's work continue to illustrate the false correlation between *alone* and *lonely* that still dominates overall perceptions of solitude. A good example of this occurred recently when Hopper's work dominated social media as the COVID-19 pandemic forced most of the world to isolate to varying degrees. "We are all Edward Hopper paintings now," one writer quipped in a tweet gone viral.[40] But decrying the state of being alone doesn't seem to be what Hopper, a taciturn, self-contained man himself, had in mind at all. "The loneliness thing is overdone," he once said. It is just as easy to see him as a chronicler of solitude – with a lowercase *s*, the more accessible kind we all experience.

In our research, our subjects have given us countless snapshots of moments in their daily lives spent in quiet contemplation while cutting the grass or hanging the laundry – which align well with Hopper's images. The voyeuristic feeling we may get when looking at one of his paintings – like one that peeks into a single woman's bedroom – is natural, not because we're peeping on her physical state but rather because she is experiencing the intimacy of solitude, in heart and mind. It's a pseudo-sacred space where her singular self – in what Hopper called an "elation of sunlight" – is purposefully set apart and distinct from others.

Despite our take on Hopper's work depicting empowered solo spaces, much of early 1900s society held tight to the idea that solitude meant sadness. The perception of "alone" as something largely undesirable evolved in earnest when the word *loner* was first used in 1940 in a pejorative way. *Solitude* fell by the wayside as the term *loneliness* took center stage. In the mid-twentieth century, American industry regarded being bored or lonely as shameful or treacherous, as something bad for our health because, well, it helped companies sell more cheerfully sociable stuff like telephones and movie tickets – and it still does.[41] At the same time, in the aftermath of World War II, social psychologists were looking at the ill effects on the human psyche of constantly marinating in other people's thoughts, needs, and desires (more on this, in depth, in Chapter 6).

In the 1950s, particularly in America, millions fled cities for the barbecues, block parties, and coffee klatches of the hypersocialized suburbs, which were considered a salve for boredom and loneliness. The 1960s were marked by a backlash "hippie" exodus from the suburbs (which paradoxically also extolled communal thinking and activism), and "loneliness" was pathologized in the mainstream media.[42] The

January 1960 issue of *Maclean's* magazine looked at that "commonest and least examined social problem of our times." The article led with the line "Loneliness, according to the psychiatrists, is born with each and every one of us at the moment when we are thrust into the cold world from the warm comfort of the womb. It threatens man from the cradle to the grave." As if that weren't alarming enough, the article continued, "It seems that man is born with a need for contact and tenderness. If he is removed from his fellow men, his mind may become confused and deranged."[43]

Twenty years later, calling out this prolonged hysteria, Alfred Kazin wrote in the *New York Times*, "Apparently, to be alone for a minute in this country is to seem 'lonely' – at least to others." In fact, Kazin was writing about a Hopper retrospective that regurgitated many of the same tired impressions of the artist as a purveyor of lonely hearts. "What obviously obsessed him was not 'loneliness' but the taut surface of some deeply engrained solitude," wrote Kazin.[39]

So far, these glances at how alone time has been experienced by people throughout history have shown us that society, by and large, has always been a mix of people who thought being on one's own was either a tragedy, critically important to spiritual development, or simply out of reach. And, while it may have been entirely commonplace to spend time alone, or to want to, at many points throughout history, we see solitude relegated to the extremes. That's because of the enduring sense we have that only special people could, or should, choose to be alone, and for very specific reasons.

Consequently, many of us still have a sense of solitude as something peripheral to our daily lives and as exceptional and/or extreme – both in good and bad ways. It's still synonymous with privilege – with tech elites like Bill Gates, with the time and money to purposely seek out wisdom in the style of spiritual leaders – or seen as the domain of cranky wilderness militants like Edward Abbey in *Desert Solitaire* (1968)[44] or troubled people ejecting themselves from society to fight demons and find themselves, such as Chris McCandless in *Into the Wild* (1996)[45] or Cheryl Strayed in *Wild* (2012).[46]

Looking at solitude and how it's been treated throughout human history is enlightening and a little frustrating, but, we believe, it can also be freeing. As researchers, we, too, can feel the inertia that has positioned solitude as negative over time, but we're also focused on contrasting that entrenched social dogma with new understanding. Enduring mystique and misconceptions around solitude energize us to show what solitude *really* looks like today. Our work draws the solitude experience in from the margins of history and, with the help of our many research participants, unmasks it and puts it smack in the middle of our busy, evolving, and promising lives.

CHAPTER 2

Everyday Solitude for Everyday People

ONE OF THE AUTHORS OF THIS BOOK, Heather, spent eight years in Catholic school, and even back then, before she became a journalist, she asked a lot of questions. The two conditions – inquisitiveness and parochial school – were largely incompatible. Being curious made her somehow "difficult," and sincere inquiries like "Why can't the pope be a girl?" often led exasperated nuns to eject her from the classroom into the cold, hollow hallways. All by herself there, she felt alienated and misunderstood. Occasionally, she'd even miss a sugary treat someone had brought in, which was a special kind of torture. (Don't be too sad, though, she evened the playing field years later when teaching religion to schoolchildren and devoting hours to "silly" questions.) More recently, Heather has found profound relief and immense perspective in alone time in most settings.

All three of us have also felt how difficult and isolating solitude can be when moving to a new country. When Thuy-vy was fifteen, she left behind a busy household in Vietnam and moved to Dayton, Ohio, to study. In a population that was less than 1 percent Asian, she stuck out while struggling to communicate in English, which compounded her feelings of alienation. In that circumstance, solitude was more of an escape than a pleasure. But now, Thuy-vy gets up early in the morning to spend time alone in peace. Netta felt similarly at age twenty-eight, leaving America for a job at a German university. On her first night in a small apartment (which still had no appliances), she wondered why on earth she had decided to move across the world from her home, culture, and partner. Netta filled the profound emptiness of the new place by watching videos

34

online, nonstop. Later, her relationship with solitude changed entirely with her first-born child; now solitude was a dear, long-lost friend. At that time, a quiet shower or a brief walk became necessary for her to recenter and restore balance.

These are all examples of our own multifaceted relationships with solitude. For us three, like for most people, time alone has played a sometimes major, sometimes minor (and sometimes positive, sometimes negative) role, depending on our needs, desires, and personal life circumstances. We three span decades in age and can reflect meaningfully on the role solitude can play from early adulthood to middle age, both while single and partnered, with children or without. We have navigated several languages and cultures and were raised within different family structures, under different economic conditions. Still, we share one thing: we deeply value solitude as a common condition in our daily lives. By reflecting on our own experiences, and in recording those of our research subjects, we now recognize that we can access solitude in many places, under diverse conditions, and use it in myriad ways to achieve a range of goals (more on this in Chapters 3 and 4).

For us, solitude is about much more than simply being alone. Its meaning and qualities differ substantially, depending on who's doing the defining, but for most of us in the modern world, it doesn't generally take the extreme forms we've seen in the past. We have found that almost all moments of solitude today reside in the middle ground, in the huge space between zero and total solitude, which we researchers think of as garden-variety solitude happening every day to regular people. This is the important but neglected space we have been exploring in our work.

What exactly we mean when we say the word *solitude* is still up for debate in the research world. That's a problem for scientists who study the topic because sharing and comparing research findings requires agreeing on a common language. Imagine two physicians who take a patient's temperature but don't agree on what number constitutes a fever. Based on their two different assessments of the same number, one doctor will treat the patient as sick and one will not. If the patient is burning up and goes untreated, they could die. In this instance, as in most, physicians and researchers must use specific words and definitions to communicate clearly about shared problems and to identify solutions. The stakes may not be quite as high when we talk about solitude, but there is ground to be won and lost, depending on how we're programmed. One person may be able to go days without any time to themselves without hating life, whereas another may become crabby and unproductive (ahem, Heather) if not left alone for at least some portion of each day.

Defining solitude using the experiences of ordinary people – and not just the musings of the poets and prophets we met in Chapter 1 – became one of our most important objectives. To create a definition of solitude that we and other researchers could share, we had to pin down its basic components, at least, to build a better picture of the nature and conditions of solitude as many people experience it. When and how does it happen? Where does it happen, and why? When is it good or bad, or neither? We hoped that answering these questions, among others, could help us describe solitude in an accurate and inclusive way that allows researchers to evaluate its potential benefits and costs. With the generous input of many people around the world, we could do that, and much more. We were able to begin to distill the essence of solitude and what lies at its heart for many people. Some data we gathered didn't represent entirely new ideas to us, or to other researchers of solitude, but a lot of data truly surprised and inspired us.

During one phase of our research, we began each interview with the question "What comes to mind when you hear the word *solitude*?" We asked that basic question because we knew that solitude often has a negative connotation; even the dictionary definition conflates it with being "alone," "lonely," or "uninhabited," which are three completely different states objectively unrelated to each other or to solitude. We wondered if that undertone affected our participants' experiences with it. We didn't realize just how illuminating that simple inquiry would be until the answers started rolling in.

Initially, some people we asked gave a definition of solitude that differs from how they experience it in their own lives.[1] Some of the sixty participants with whom we did in-depth interviews during our "narrative study" mentioned monks in hushed monasteries and some of the other stereotypical images we've already talked about. Others thought immediately of isolation, remoteness, and loneliness. But when we encouraged them to define alone time in *their* lives, most descriptions were much different and overwhelmingly positive. It seems that solitude is still often mistaken as having an uppercase *S*, even by people who see themselves as wanting or needing solo time.

We learned from the people we interviewed that solitude is in the eye of the beholder. It is as simple or complex, as freeing or confining, as our own perceptions and circumstances. We want to shine a light on their stories because they help us pull solitude in from the margins and clarify the fact that lowercase *s* solitude can be meaningful on a regular basis for all kinds of people. We hope that understanding that alone time takes many forms will open up a world of possibilities for those who don't yet see how they can make a place for positive solitude amid busy, happily social lives.

We sought to be global in our understanding of solitude, which ultimately comes from thousands of research subjects from around the world – from the United States and Europe and from nations including (but not limited to) Bangladesh, India, Iran, Mexico, Egypt, Vietnam, Hong Kong, China, Malaysia, the Philippines, and central and sub-Saharan Africa. We spoke to struggling single moms, "starving" students, comfortable retirees, prolific artists, and budding Wall Street tycoons. We got dozens of colorful and inspirational takes on solitude in response to our questions. And that was wonderful, but it also posed a problem.

As we mentioned in the Introduction, Netta and Thuy-vy came to the study of solitude as *quantitative* researchers, meaning they were focused on what statistics can tell them about the aspects of human behavior we are studying. This means they design studies in which they can measure human experience in terms of numbers. That helps them test theories, which, if accurate, result in consistent patterns. It's the way of doing science they're most comfortable with because they were taught early on in their careers that conclusions they draw from those types of data are generally reliable and trustworthy. Numbers *can* tell us some things about solitude, of course, and help us group subjects together in some ways, but Thuy-vy and Netta quickly realized that those data are far from the full story. If they wanted to capture the nuances of everyday solitude, they knew they'd have to get off the beaten path. So, we three researchers then waded into the waters of *qualitative* research, which aims to capture how people behave and experience the world in a more subjective way. Doing this means accepting that each person experiences reality in their own way – an exciting and sometimes mind-bending proposition for scientists.

We were fascinated to hear about the experiences of our research subjects but, frankly, somewhat taken aback at first by the individuality and richness of the replies. For example, one person told us he can tap into solitude on a busy crosstown bus in Reykjavik. Another sets an early-morning alarm in Oxfordshire to get a few minutes to herself before her home stirs to life. One participant needs a silent hour on the beach in Waikiki to reap the benefits of alone time, whereas another can dip into its positive effects during a ten-minute lunchtime walk in Central Park. How could we hope to generalize such diverse findings to explain solitude in a way that would benefit a larger population?

In short, we had to earn some new researcher chops. Qualitative research and analysis is a dynamic way to do science, and it requires adhering to a different rule book than when dealing solely with numbers. When analyzing the lengthy conversations we had with our subjects, we had to recognize recurring themes, categorize them based on that learning, and build our own models to explain the phenomena being described to us.[2] By talking about participants' attitudes and activities in solitude, and what is desirable for them about that state, we were able to reflect on how those experiences shape their personal definitions of solitude and how they characterize what goes on there.

Some of what we found supported some basic assumptions about alone time, but we were caught off-guard by other findings. We discovered that not only does everyone have their own definitions of solitude but we each also have our own set of conditions and expectations that make alone time a positive experience. That said, when recording stories of people in positive solitude, we identified several overall themes regarding how people achieve that state in their daily lives. To begin with, those themes address if a person needs to be physically alone for solitude to be gained and whether they need to be mentally or psychologically apart from others. Many people said, perhaps predictably, that physical separation was important, but interestingly, there was no consensus around needing it to achieve positive solitude. There was, however, strong agreement that solitude requires a mental independence from others. As a result, we came up with a conceptual model that recognizes both physical and mental separation as legitimate forms of solitude.

Our study subjects shared their experiences so richly and openly, helping mold our definition of solitude as "a state in which the self is intentionally placed at the center of one's attention and, if not physically alone, then mentally distanced from others." This definition is intentionally open-ended, allowing for a range of experiences, but is also very direct in its requirements. In our conversations, we also saw four distinct "forms" of solitude take shape: complete, private, companionate, and public. Each category offers a fascinating window into how we each move between and within our solo and social worlds.

COMPLETE SOLITUDE; OR, BUDDHA-STYLE SOLITUDE

As researchers, we struggled to name this "whole enchilada" type of solitude, which is characterized by being physically *and* psychologically separate from others and devoid of outside stimuli. *Pure, total,* and *perfect* are some of the terms other researchers have used to describe this alone state in which one is willing and able to focus entirely on oneself with zero distractions, other than one's thoughts.[3] This type of solitude has a deep, uninterrupted, focused quality. It may be the most obvious description of solitude that springs to mind, and understandably so, owing to the legacy of seeing solitude as practiced in very physically and mentally restrictive ways (as discussed in Chapter 1). This Buddha-style solitude didn't resonate widely with our research subjects, and it doesn't agree with our own experiences of solitude, so we don't include an extended discussion of it here. Instead, we focus on the other three types of solitude most often experienced.

Still, it's helpful to consider briefly what that drastic version of alone time means today, because it is still sometimes lionized in the mainstream. The media loves "modern-day hermit" stories,[4,5] which all seem to consider similar questions: what do they *do* with all that time alone, and why do they do it? The implication is that solitude itself is extreme, and that creates confusion. We may think, wow, I couldn't live in the woods for thirty years and not talk to anyone, so I must not like – or be able to endure – "real" solitude. Or people may think that if that's what solitude amounts to, they'll take a hard pass.

"Pure" solitude is also used as a benchmark by certain researchers who try to simulate those "clean" conditions within a lab to assess whether it's substantially different from other ways aloneness is experienced.[6] Many researchers cling to this description of solitude simply because it's practical and straightforward. If we consider that solitude could include any social elements or distractions (like playing a video game while on your own), that begs the question from other researchers if we're really studying solitude at all. Complete solitude is an understandable go-to for researchers, and we three authors can accept it as an absolute state achieved and/or required by some people, but we have found that such a narrow concept precludes us from talking about other ways of being alone that may be rewarding and satisfying.

In our recent process of gathering people's stories of solitude, we did hear about the need to be psychologically *and* physically separate from others (what we call "private" solitude below), but only, on occasion, did we hear about the need for the extreme conditions that define complete solitude. Some of our participants talked about requiring that kind of "nothingness" at times, with total silence and complete isolation from others, to achieve positive aloneness. Most often, however, solitude seems to happen along a continuum, meaning that all kinds of experiences, under many conditions, "count" as solitude.

By interviewing regular people who spoke meaningfully about their daily solitary experiences, we gained insights into more normative views of solitude as neither a struggle nor a triumph over extremes. As a result, we don't subscribe to the complete "solitude is the only 'real' solitude" model. As we have heard from many people, and experienced ourselves, other forms of solitude are real and achievable without taking draconian measures.

PRIVATE SOLITUDE; OR, DOWN-TO-EARTH SOLITUDE

This commonplace brand of solitude is the kind described by most people in our research. There's a lot of variation within this more middle-of-the-road state of aloneness, but the hallmark of "private" soli- tude is, as the name suggests, the state of being physically separate from others. For many people we spoke to in our research, regardless of the reason they choose to spend time on their own, positive solitude can be achieved only when they are alone in their own physical space. Think of private solitude as a more down-to-earth version of complete solitude. It is a space in which we can do anything we like – read quietly, blast music, stream Netflix, and for as short or as long as we like – as long as we do it solo. Run-of-the-mill solitude doesn't require waxing philosophical about the meaning of life. It doesn't insist we think about or do much of anything, really, if we don't want to.

Some people told us that they couldn't fully retreat or relax, that they couldn't get into the depth of mind they like or be wholly themselves, with others around. One participant described a need to "secure the physical environment," somewhere they wouldn't be disturbed, to be able to tap into "[their] own sphere in [their] own head." For some, even the idea that an outsider may interrupt their private solitude – family members returning from a trip or the postal carrier ringing the doorbell – derails some positive moments of solitude.

Among our study participants who described themselves as empath- etic, or as caretakers, the desire for solitude, and, specifically, the need for private solitude, seemed more prevalent. They described carrying others' emotional baggage and needing to balance the weight of others' feelings and needs (and opinions and noises) by carving out a time and place where they could be free. One of our study participants, Ella, age forty-nine, told us, "I think empathy, in general, is one of the reasons that I need solitude. . . . What I crave partly from solitude is some respite from people's needs and their problems, because I think I kind of take them on in some way. I think it's only when I'm on my own that I can ditch [others' feelings]."

Similarly, Rebecca, age forty-eight, from Iceland, talked about the need to escape the role of mother, wife, sister, and manager, even for a brief time, to focus on herself. "I'm empathetic, in fact, I think that's one reason I need some time alone. ... [Solitude] is more about those moments where I can let go even if it's for a moment and not have the constant thinking about work or family, or somebody else's needs," she said. Sam, age thirty-nine, from the United States, described a relation-ship in which he and his partner are acutely aware of needing time away from everyone – including each other. "I think we really pick up on the emotions of the other person. And so, if the other person is in a bad mood or stressed out, we're a bit too empathic, we can really feel it," he said. Sam also emphasized the intentionality with which they step away from each other and toward alone time and how that's achieved without taking offense.

Among our subjects, the desire for physical aloneness was especially appealing to those who were caregivers, either as a result of life circum-stances or because their work, as therapists, nurses, and stay-at-home-parents, keeps them tapped into others for prolonged periods of time. Scott, age sixty, from England, was a longtime caregiver to a spouse with multiple sclerosis. "Most of the time, you have to consider other people, whether they be partners, whether they be somebody in the street. ... But if you're just sort of sitting and contemplating ... then that's just you, and so you don't need to consider anyone else," he said. Terry, a sixty-eight-year-old former vicar in a small English village, described a life in which – even after retirement – "normally, there's somebody else wanting some-thing from me." But in retirement, she has chosen to intentionally lean away from caregiving and toward self-care. Terry described carving out one day per week spent in her home without contact with anyone else, doing whatever she wanted. "I was coming to terms with all sorts of things at the same time, and I wanted to reflect," she said.

We also heard about private solitude being important for people who want to use that time to be uninhibited in their actions – to sing loudly or dance wildly without the fear of disturbing others. Elliott, age twenty-eight, told us he needs a private space where he can be open, free, and wholly himself. "I'd go and practice guitar or put on headphones and sing and awkwardly dance around in my room, that's not something that I want to do when everyone else is watching," he said. Private solitude is necessary for people like Elliott because it's impossible for them to disconnect from the presence of others, even strangers, because they believe they are being noticed or judged. Social psychologists call this the "spotlight effect," or the sense some people have that there's a beaming bulb shining down on them, illuminating all their flaws. This self-conscious way of moving through the world, which can range from mild to severe, can make it difficult to feel alone, even when surrounded by strangers.

This is a fairly common phenomenon, but the truth is that, while people may be noticing you on some level, likely nobody is scrutinizing that obvious-to-you baby barf stain on your pants. Two fascinating studies highlight this point – one published in 2000 by Thomas Gilovich at Cornell University with colleagues at Northwestern University and Williams College[7] shows that most of us overestimate the extent to which others notice what we do or how we look. In one part of that (somewhat hilarious) study done at Cornell, a recruited "target" student was asked to wear a shirt with an image of Barry Manilow on it. (Despite having sold nearly one billion records as a solo artist, Manilow was unpopular among college students at the time, and those asked to wear the shirt among their peers recorded feeling "embarrassed" to do so.) The target had to walk into a room where "observers" were already sitting and take a seat. Later, researchers asked the target and observers who noticed what. Confirming the spotlight effect, the targets overestimated – by double – the number of people whom they thought would notice their mortifying attire. In the following four parts of the experiment, the researchers tested the spotlight effect on targets with "cooler" shirts, including some subjects who did and said things they perceived were hard to ignore. No matter the context, the observers consistently failed to award the target with the attention they expected. The researchers concluded that "people tend to believe that they stand out in the eyes of others, both positively and negatively, more than they actually do."

A second set of studies done at Yale University by Erica Boothby and colleagues, published in 2016,[8] replicated the Cornell findings, but with an interesting twist. The spotlight effect seemed to be in play when, again, researchers asked a target to wear a specific shirt, this time depicting notorious Colombian drug lord Pablo Escobar. Those wearing the shirt again overestimated the impact it would have on others. But the study also revealed another phenomenon that researchers called the "invisibility cloak illusion," under which people actually *underestimate* how much others are paying attention to them. It sounds contradictory, but the two states exist at the same time – we assume others' attention is on the same thing we're focused on (an offensive shirt, a bad haircut), but that's rarely true. We are both more *and* less anonymous to others than most of us generally perceive, but importantly, others likely are not focused on our perceived flaws.

Why do some people feel this way, and is there any way to get over it, to access types of solitude that don't require physical separation from others? Like many ways we feel when alone or in the presence of others, the spotlight effect likely has evolutionary origins. In a 2013 study, researchers in Britain and Australia showed images of faces to their subjects and asked them to report whether the images' eyes were looking at the subject or off to the side. They determined that "humans have a prior expectation that other people's gaze is directed toward them."[9] This preconception dominates perception particularly when the faces are difficult to see, meaning that subjects assumed they were being looked at if they couldn't be quite sure. In terms of evolution, at a time we were preyed upon by large carnivores, we assumed that a predator was looking at us even if it wasn't, because that was the safer bet. While not applicable to most of our daily lives now, that wiring can be tough to ignore – but not impossible to overcome.

The findings of these studies could help some of us – who feel like we're not truly alone unless we're physically alone – to think differently about how and when we can access solitude. There are ways to combat the spotlight effect and blunt self-consciousness (that's a whole other book),[10] but it may free some people to know that they are likely more alone in the presence of others than they think. This may help people living in busy households, crowded cities, or both to put positive solitude within reach even if they find it impossible to break away from others. And even if one cannot overcome the spotlight effect, understanding one's need for private solitude is also important. Knowing that we may require physical aloneness to benefit from solitude can prompt us to carve out that individual space, if only for a short time.

COMPANIONATE SOLITUDE; OR, PARTNERS-IN-SOLITUDE

The two types of solitude we've talked about so far – complete and private – rely on being physically apart from others. The second two –

companionate and public – perhaps surprisingly do not. By "companionate," we mean partners and spouses, of course, but also any other person with whom we have a familiar or close connection. We heard positive solitude stories from our research subjects who achieved that state with family members and friends. In that company, many of our participants felt they had the freedom to turn inward and connect with themselves. Essentially, they have an ability to be psychologically separate from others even when sharing the same airspace.

This opened our minds as researchers to the idea that companionate solitude is just as legitimate a form of solitude as any other. In some cases, the presence of people even enriched rather than detracted from solitude. Those occasions have often lived long in the memories of some of our participants. "My father was very into fishing – and we would often go with him. Just sitting at the riverbank dangling my feet in the river Thames, just next to my father in perfect peace and quietness. That's a very, very vivid memory . . . just sitting next to my father perfectly quiet, not because I had to but [because] I enjoyed it," said Scott, age sixty, from England.

"Partners-in-solitude" also describes enjoying peaceful activities in nature, at home, and even while traveling. We heard from Kaitlin, age forty-eight, about the meaningful solitude she has achieved while seeing new things, like a sculpture in a museum, with a friend. "I was traveling just with one other person and there were plenty of times where we would go see something and we were together, but we were quiet and separate in some way and we were . . . basically having different experiences. . . . So there was a sense of obtaining that solitude but I wouldn't have said I was alone." Experiences of companionate solitude are akin, in a way, to monks in a monastery "sharing" solitude and vows of silence.[11] Austro-German poet Rainer Maria Rilke (1875–1926) considered his wife the "guardian of his solitude."[12] In a letter to a friend, he wrote, "I hold this to be the highest task for a bond between two people: that each protects the solitude of the other."[13] Whether a monk or a museum buddy, the key is a tacit agreement to give one another the psychological space to achieve solitude while in each other's company.

In our research, companionate solitude was achieved by people with children at home (generally teens or older), but it was most often described by those in long-term relationships. Colleen, age sixty-nine, from England, told us that she's very rarely alone at home but that she's often "totally relaxed . . . in a little bubble in myself." She can even be in the same room where her husband is watching television yet feel completely apart. "I'm not actually *with* him because I'm immersed in my book," she said. Sometimes finding solitude in the company of another was a learning process. Claire, an American widow in her eighties, came to understand the value of solitude over her long marriage. Whether in a small Manhattan apartment, or later in a larger home, she and her husband found ways to retreat into their own psychological spaces when necessary.

Although half Claire's age, thirty-nine-year-old Sandra shared something similar. She told us that she and her husband can be in their flat together but also be content to give each other the mental space to be entirely separate in their thoughts and actions. That was something entirely new to Sandra. "[Solitude] is not something I really experienced before, and it's kind of something that I didn't really understand very well when he would explain it to me," she said. "That's actually a gift he's given me, learning how to get in touch with my own needs and my own solitude and appreciation for time alone."

Companionate solitude became evident, and perhaps more prevalent, during pandemic lockdowns with work- and school-from-home setups, when sharing physical space with loved ones over longer periods of time than usual was a common condition. For some of our participants, moments of solitude were formed when each person was free to have their own experience and perspective despite sharing the same general area. At times, these were even described as the most memorable experiences of solitude during that time. Rebecca, age forty-nine, a mom of teenage girls, told us about working side by side with them on art projects. They all sat at the same table but didn't talk or interact in any significant way. All three were inhabiting their own worlds, in a way, while being aware and comforted by the presence of the others. "I was with my two daughters, and that for me was very special because we were somewhat in solitude but with each other, rather than ... in three different places around the house. ... We wanted to create together," she said.

PUBLIC SOLITUDE; OR, ALONE IN A CROWD

Our participants talked about another form of solitude that involves psychological but not physical separation: being alone in public, in the presence of others. This is very different from companionate solitude because the only person you know there, or care to acknowledge, is you. (On this point, solitude historian David Vincent talks about an in-between kind of aloneness experienced when another person is not a "partner" in solitude but not a "stranger" either.[14] In the past – and perhaps still in some places – subordinates may be treated as invisible by their "employers," who may access solitude by dehumanizing those workers.)

Public solitude is sought in a less secure environment than the companionate kind. Those around you don't necessarily know you want to be on your own, and intrusions can happen at any time, directly or indirectly engaging you and bursting your solitude bubble. On the other side of the coin, public solitude could be easier to access in some ways because there is less investment to be made in those around you. "If you're walking along with a partner you have to talk, or you don't have to, but you tend to talk, if you're walking by yourself you're just enjoying the view," one of our research subjects, Peter, explained to us.

Our subjects offered a lot of other interesting examples of when they are out in the world and in solitude. Silent retreats were a popular example of one activity in which people were surrounded by strangers but felt secure about delving deeply into their own psychological spaces. But a silent retreat wasn't required for most people. Again, Peter: "Sometimes, it's nice just to sit, like, if you're on holiday, just to sit and watch the world go by. That's solitude, as well, because you're just sitting there, maybe on the seafront or something, and you're people watching, but you're actually sitting there quite quiet and relaxed."

Being able to access solitude in public may be particularly beneficial for city dwellers. Two of our participants – though separated in age by more than twenty-five years – described having lived in north London at some point in their lives and having taken advantage of some public swimming holes in a park there. Grace, age sixty-five, described the experience of swimming in the "silkiness of an open pond," where she does a slow breaststroke, enjoying the "deliciousness" of the activity and feeling alone even among others. Alex, who is originally from a much warmer climate than the United Kingdom, nevertheless enjoys outdoor swimming in winter, calling it an "exhilarating" experience (we'll take his word for that!). During that time, he focuses intensely on his own connection to the environment. "You just feel, you don't need to talk there, you just become part of nature," he said. (More on solitude in the natural world in Chapter 7.)

Whether in solitude or not, people are often wrong when predicting what they'll enjoy or hate. Imagine you and a friend have tickets to the opera and he cancels at the last minute. You hesitate, imagining an empty seat next to you, and consider not going. But you were looking forward to the performance, so you go anyway and end up having a great time. You missed your friend, but you didn't miss the way he normally whispers commentary in your ear during a show. So why did you assume you'd have a bad time going solo? Some research findings demonstrate that social norms play a part in shaping our perceptions of what is acceptable to do alone in public spaces.

The pursuit of solitude in spaces traditionally designed for communal activities, like parks and restaurants, might come with unique challenges. The fear of being judged or watched, of boredom and loneliness, distracts many people in those settings and stands in the way of positive solitude. One consumer survey including individuals in the United States, India, and China showed that people often anticipate less enjoyment and fear others' judgment more when asked about engaging in "fun" activities alone in public, such as going to a restaurant or movie theater.[15] Those participants expressed concern that others would think they were alone because they had few friends with whom to enjoy those activities. By contrast, if the primary goal of the activity is utilitarian, like shopping for groceries or walking in a public park (presumably for exercise), fear and hesitation were diminished because those were perceived as more "acceptable" solo activities.[15]

Eating, which we argue is both fun and utilitarian, presents a particularly complex picture of public solitude. The social history of eating with others is so ingrained in our collective psyche because, since the time humans first cooked with fire, we've been gathering.[16] Consider festivals like Chuseok in Korea, Iri-ji in West Africa, Thanksgiving in America, and it's clear that food brings people together.[17] Alternatively, supping solo can seem like an aberration. One recent experiment shows us why this is the case. Researchers[18] asked 248 US adults who had dined in a restaurant in the past six months to imagine eating a meal in the presence of other customers and subject to one of the following conditions: (1) with other customers dining alone or (2) with others in groups, and when the restaurant was (3) full or (4) empty. Participants were asked how lonely they'd be given the various scenarios and if they would anticipate others looking down on them. Those who imagined themselves eating alone surrounded by other customers in groups anticipated more loneliness and negative evaluation from others, especially in a busy restaurant, and said they would be less likely to eat alone under those circumstances.

To mitigate those negative feelings, even people who love traveling alone sometimes attempt to deflect potential negative judgment from others by using "props" (books, smartphones) to show they are engaged during meals and not "missing" a companion.[19] Those subtle cues might be strategically used to communicate the purpose of their aloneness while other people are around. (Those props are also sometimes used to communicate that they want to be left alone.) Eating alone still gets such a bad rap that scientists from Australia are designing a robotic table mate, Fobo, that behaves like a fellow human.[20] (No word on whether it's programmed to burp and then, of course, excuse itself.)

Whereas some people are turning to mechanical meal mates, there are many people rejecting the perception that "fun" things shouldn't be done alone. The growing "table for one" phenomenon is a great way of tapping into what is wonderful about public solitude.[21] Say someone leads a hypersocial life, always dwelling and working in the presence of others with few solo moments possible. Maybe breaking away for lunch and dining alone offers them an opportunity to have an enriching experience on their own. "I'll go into a café or whatever, order food or order a drink, whatever it may be. And it's not that it's not possible to have conversations with people, I choose not to. I just enjoy the experience of being there," said Cliff, who is in his sixties and lives in the United Kingdom.

And consider the case of Finnish "foodies" who extol solo dining as a way to fully experience food and the atmosphere in which it's served.

The authors of a 2022 paper on "recreational eating out" in Finland talked about the growing cultural phenomenon of solo dining spawned by a desire to better appreciate the aesthetic qualities of food and drink, akin to how one would experience objects in a museum (ah, if only one could crack open one of Andy Warhol's Campbell's soup cans).[22] Whereas some people enjoy discussing works of art, or how their steak tastes, others find that doing so detracts from their experience, whereas being on their own actually enhances it. The phenomenon is not just a Western one. A study of nearly 500 Chinese diners in Macao showed the appeal of dining alone was commonplace in China and questioned the assumption that dining should be group based.[23] Similar positive emotions were associated with solo dining in Japan, where singletons did not anticipate negative evaluation from others.[24] The exception in the research literature is Taiwan, where solo diners saw the activity as a lonely one.[24]

Other positive solo diners have expressed righteousness in the face of judgment. In a study of Instagram posts, researchers extracted posts hashtagged #tableforone and looked for recurring themes.[25] What they found was a sense of empowerment expressed by those who enjoyed eating alone and a recognition that it's valuable to them because of the pleasure of being with oneself. Like the Finnish foodies, they found that going solo gave them the space to savor the tastes and experiences of high-quality restaurants. The posts expressed "the importance of valuing alone time," said the researchers, and the idea that eating alone is a form of self-care, legitimate in its own right. Some of the social media posters also rebelled against the stigma of eating alone and against the assumption that they *had* to do it with someone else if they wanted to enjoy the experience.

As compelling as we three researchers find our subjects' descriptions of public and companionate solitude, others who study time alone disagree that those are legitimate. They contend that any time spent in the presence of others, even if they aren't interacting with us, makes us vulnerable to social influence, to subtle nudges to behave in certain ways. For example, while sitting in a restaurant, we may notice how others are ordering and eating, and this might influence us to do the same. These researchers also suggest, as earlier, that we may feel outsiders' affirmations or judgments, and our feeling and thinking at that moment may be colored by that stigma. They contend that this "noise" adversely impacts the quality of solitude, if they consider it that at all.[26]

But many people, including some of our participants, can deflect negative attention, or they are simply not susceptible to it. Among our research participants are several people who seem to be able to secure a space around themselves, at least mentally, in which they are insulated from what's going on externally. "I can just lock into what I'm doing, and I'm alone in my head anyway without it being an issue if there's things that are happening on the periphery. And I can sort of dip in and out if asked a question or something like that, but often, I'm just absorbed," one person told us. (Heather's mom was like that; she could do cross-word puzzles despite a fire alarm shrieking overhead.)

By examining the rich, lived experiences of our research subjects, we have been able to offer an alternative narrative to the narrow idea that solitude is only for certain kinds of people in particular places and in defined ways. For this reason, we're able to legitimize forms of alone time dismissed by other researchers. With that new knowledge in hand, we can turn our attention to *why* solitude can be such an abundant space and to its many possible benefits.

CHAPTER 3

What Makes Solitude Great?

WHEN THUY-VY WAS IN EIGHTH GRADE, she moved with her family from the countryside of Vietnam into the city. She was allowed out on her own for the first time there, and she seized every opportunity. She'd hop on her rusty but trusty bike, paper map in hand, and explore new routes. Up to that point, the "unfamiliar" had been scary, but she went out alone anyway, eager to discover and to navigate her expanding world. During those outings, Thuy-vy learned that the world was not such a scary place without her parents around and that her fear of something was generally greater than the thing itself. She was cautious in unknown spots, of course, but was also observing, adapting, and looking out for herself. On those solo adventures, Thuy-vy found her way around the city and, in a way, her own mind.

Netta has had some similar experiences in solitude. When she graduated high school, she traveled for the first time without her family. She walked through the English countryside and into a space where she was making her own decisions for the first time. She got lost a lot and "misplaced" her passport and money but still relished the independence and seemingly infinite possibilities for exploration. Now, years later, and with two school-aged children, solitude has taken a different shape. When she does get time to herself these days, Netta feels a sense of relief in that space. While there, she can breathe more deeply not having to think about what to say or how to react to someone else. In solitude, Netta can do whatever she wants, and she can do it as well or as badly, as slowly or as quickly, as she wants to.

Similarly, Heather uses solitude as a place for discovery and, most recently, for healing. Not long ago, she took her own travels around the

United Kingdom after the death of her mother. In the hollow of grief, she dreaded being alone with her own thoughts but also knew she needed to be out on her own and walking. During those months, Heather took refuge in a quiet rhythm – lacing up her boots, pulling on her backpack, and setting her own pace. Within that solitary ritual, she began to hear her own heartbeat again. In solitude, Heather drew a map to an in-between place where she was not whole again and would never be the same, but she had begun to incorporate the traumatic loss of her mother into a different version of herself.

Our reflections on these overall positive solo experiences also illustrate that solitude isn't always amazing for the three of us, or for anyone. It can sometimes be a difficult spot plagued by doubts and rumination (maybe in the same ten-minute period). But, most often, solitude starts out neutral like a lump of sculptors' clay that we can shape into whatever we want. Our experiences, and those of our research participants, have shown us that many positive outcomes are possible when choosing to carve out some time alone (much more on that in Chapter 4).

Why is solitude so potentially powerful for all kinds of people? That's a question that has driven a large part of our research, and we continue to build on what we have learned. What we've seen so far points to the fact that solitude creates an environment in which two important things can happen: each of us can captain our own ship, and while in that role, we can connect to our true selves. Think of it as the ultimate place to *do what you want* (autonomy) and *be who you are* (authenticity).

DOING WHAT YOU WANT

What helps people flourish in the way we've described in the three foregoing stories is related to a framework psychologists call "self-determination theory."[1,2] The idea behind that is, just as humans have physical needs like eating and drinking, we have mental needs. Those three core necessities are relatedness (connection to others), competence (feeling we're capable), and autonomy (having the sense that it's us, not others, driving our own meaningful actions). If those needs are met, we feel a sense of well-being, we grow and mature in healthy ways, and we take on life's tasks with energy, even passion. If those needs are not met, mental health tends to suffer, and motivation lags.[1,2]

Autonomy is a key quality of positive motivation, performance, fulfillment, and well-being. Being "autonomous" means feeling choiceful and free from outside demands. We all want to think our own thoughts and chart our own destinies, and if we're denied that, we're more likely to grumble (there's a reason revolutions have been fought over the desire to self-govern!). Solitude naturally gives us opportunities to be independent agents, fully in touch with what we really think, value, and need while behaving in ways that are consistent with that knowledge (more on this in Box 3.1).[3]

We witnessed a powerful indication of the link between solitude and autonomy at the beginning of the COVID-19 pandemic. In general, some people had a lot of time alone, while others were running on fumes. That translated into too much or too little solitude, depending on what each of us had considered "normal" or "ideal" before the pandemic. Of course, a lot of people were unhappy because they couldn't move around in the usual way. Many of us also missed face-to-face contact with family, friends, coworkers, even the barista at our neighborhood coffee shop.[4]

Others' experiences were marked by extreme togetherness (parents of small children, *we see you*), and their autonomy and happiness took a hit. For example, Netta walked every day in the fields by her home to reflect and recenter. She benefited so much from those walks because, as we mentioned earlier, it's her go-to place for feeling autonomy. Likewise, in the beginning of lockdowns, Heather struggled to manage being at home with her partner all day, every day. She was used to being entirely on her own most days, and then suddenly, she was attempting to work side by side with someone while the endless drone of Zoom meetings echoed through the house.

Among those who experienced extreme aloneness were many who struggled in that space of isolation. The lockdowns imposed by many governments during the early stages of the global health crisis had many researchers and medical professionals wondering about the short- and long-term psychological effects of confinement and a lack of social contact.[5]

BOX 3.1 SOLITUDE(S) AT THE POLES

In 1992, Norwegians Liv Arnesen and Julie Maske made the first unsupported crossing by women of the Greenland Ice Cap. Two years later, at age forty-one, Arnesen made headlines again as the first woman to ski solo and unsupported to the South Pole. For fifty days, she glided and grunted 1,200 kilometers (745 miles) across the "huge, featureless white spaces" of Antarctica, as she put it in her book *Skiing into the Bright Open*.[7] The mental and physical strength required for such a grueling expedition under any conditions is clear (subzero temperatures, near-constant wind, heavy sledges, and treacherous crevasses). To do it alone requires rising to another level – yet Arnesen took comfort in that. "I remembered all those who, before my departure, thought that being on my own would be the worst part of an expedition such as mine. On the contrary, even though I'm no lone wolf, it was being alone for so long that I most looked forward to," she wrote. "Solitude is just as necessary as food and sleep; only in that way can you find calm and make contact with yourself."[7]

In preparation for her own polar feats, Arnesen read numerous accounts of explorers who'd come before her (all men, up to that point) and about the required planning that could mean life or death in the field. In her memoir, Arnesen wrote that, to her, "it meant being alone and independent with everything that you need: tent, food, sleeping bag, cookstove, and fuel. It meant being able to manage with simple means. Much later, I was able to give this a name: a sense of freedom."[8] Arnesen had such intense quiet on her own that when she reached the Amundsen-Scott South Pole Station on Christmas Eve 1994, she was somewhat overwhelmed by the reception. She told a magazine at the time, "I was more tired after three or four days at the South Pole than after skiing alone for 50 [days]."[9]

In 2001, Arnesen and American explorer Ann Bancroft became the first women to cross Antarctica – a ninety-four-day, 2,725-kilometer (1,700-mile) journey of companionate solitude. In Bancroft, Arnesen had found an expedition partner who shared her desire for peaceful coexistence in the wild. "I didn't want to spend a hundred days on the ice with someone who needed to talk, talk, talk all the time. For me, part of the appeal of the remote wilderness is the solitude, the ability to be with one's own thoughts," Arnesen wrote in *No Horizon Is So Far*, an account of their historic feat, coauthored with Bancroft. (One of this book's authors [Heather] had the privilege of meeting Arnesen in Oslo years ago. She was humble and grounded – and inspiring! – talking about the sense of doing what she wanted, and being who she is, on her historic polar explorations.)[10]

At the same time, others unexpectedly flourished even when forced to reduce physical interactions with others. Thuy-vy, for example, had lived alone for several years in graduate school and seldom went out socially. While she wasn't used to the disruption in routine brought on by the pandemic, like not going in person to her university to teach and attend meetings, the additional solitude had few adverse effects. She shared that sense with many research participants we spoke with during that time who felt like the rest of the world was just now getting a concrete lesson in how many people lived before the pandemic struck.

In the first few months of the pandemic, we ran a study capturing the experiences of 2,035 individuals (age thirteen to sixteen, thirty-five to fifty-five, and fifty-nine to eighty-five years).[6] We found that autonomy as a benefit of solitude was a common theme across age groups (though it was less frequent in adolescents, who also expressed the least self-determined motivation for solitude). Themes related to autonomy included a sense of self-reliance, freedom from outside pressure, and increased self-connection. Those who described autonomy as a benefit of solitude also reported a more peaceful mood during that time and more self-determined motivation for solitude, creating a kind of feedback loop of choosing solitude and then benefiting from it. Some of the comments we heard from participants included ways in which autonomy makes solitude good: "I can rely on my parents, but I would prefer to do things myself and my own way" (male, age thirteen) and "[I can] be more independent and think for myself" (male, age fifteen). One female, age thirty, talked about learning "how to love and be comfortable with my own company. It has made me more confident about myself."

Some other telling comments in our milestone study about solitude and autonomy spanning different age brackets included the following:

I learnt to listen to my own desires, needs and wishes. I tried to enjoy the moments and the activities I really like. (male, age thirty-six)

[I have] freedom to relax and be myself whilst alone. To do things that I want to do without distraction or interruption. (male, age forty-one)

I found the times on my own to be good as I was able to devote time to doing the things I enjoy. (female, age sixty-three)

I have been able to feel quite relaxed, feeling I had nobody to answer to but myself. (male, age seventy-seven)

In other aspects of our recent research, we also heard that spending time in solitude is an important act of self-care because it involves prioritizing oneself and fulfilling the need for autonomy. Solitude is a space in which we can shift ourselves to the front burner and do what we want in a way that suits us. "In my head, solitude is *me* time," said sixty-seven-year-old Jean from Wales. "I think it's important to have that time on your own to think things through and to do things that are just for you."

Choosing some of that free/me time doesn't require much effort for some people, whereas for others, turning inward can require a bit of push and pull with those around them. A family, friend, or community culture of "togetherness" with various expectations and responsibilities can limit the availability and acceptance of an individual's alone time. In that environment, seeking solitude can sometimes amount to a personal act of defiance. One forty-seven-year-old mother of two teenage boys from Germany described it as "putting my foot down and saying I need to go do something for me, all by myself."

BEING WHO YOU ARE

Autonomy in solitude has a twin power: authenticity. If autonomy is being free *to do* what you want, authenticity is being free *to be* who you are. "Know thyself" is one of the three so-called Delphic maxims, or moral rules, carved on the entrance of the Temple of Apollo at Delphi, Greece (according to second-century writer and geographer Pausanias). At least since then, acquiring self-knowledge has been an engaging pursuit for thousands of years.[11] Ancient teachings in Buddhism and Christianity also talk about the importance of wise reflection to spiritual evolution.[12,13] Knowing ourselves is another way of saying that we're being authentic in our thoughts and actions. We will get to how and why solitude encourages authenticity (but doesn't guarantee it); first, though, it's essential to understand what it means to be authentic, why that's a good thing, and what happens if we're not being true to ourselves.

Lots of moral, ethical, and practical questions arise when trying to define what being authentic means, and scholars have written volumes about leading genuine lives with confidence and conviction.[14–17] In short, authenticity is awareness of our thoughts and feelings, receptivity to our real (often gut) reactions to new experiences and information, and behavior consistent with that awareness. It simply means being real or true to ourselves – and owning whatever that is[18] – but, in practice, that can be a complex undertaking. Being true to ourselves is tough because it makes us vulnerable and open to scrutiny and rejection.[19] Who among us hasn't tweaked a photo of ourselves before posting on Instagram for that reason (what will people think if they see my wrinkles, pimples, etc.)? And many of us hide real opinions from friends, family, and coworkers for the same reason.

Being genuine can also make us feel separate from the pack and thus exposed[20] (remember in Chapter 1 how we talked about the evolutionary imperatives of not being out on the savanna alone). But it can also foster a sense of real versus fake, full versus empty.[21] Authenticity is one of those holy grail–like attributes, like independence and individuality, that many people aspire to but find difficult to attain. We tend to applaud people who "keep it real" – like celebrities who post unretouched photos of themselves on social media – yet we still may tweak photos of ourselves. That's because, although following our own path can be immensely rewarding, it can also be risky.

We humans seem to have a hot/cold relationship with authenticity – we may dislike it from others, at least in certain settings, but deeply value it for ourselves across the board. An analysis of 136 studies on "fitting in" rather than "stepping out" in the workplace revealed that authentic folks get worse performance reviews than their less-genuine (or more "self-monitoring") peers and are also much less likely to get promoted into leadership positions.[22] But researchers have also found that, in general, we are happier when we are true to who we are. Multiple studies have shown that authenticity results in lower stress, anxiety, and depression and higher self-esteem and life satisfaction.[23,24] Think about the moments in life when you were most genuine. Those may be, in fact, the most meaningful times you can recall, instances when you felt fully connected to yourself and/or to others. At times like those, it seems like everything in the universe is in alignment and contentment is within reach.[25] Take it from Mahatma Gandhi (1869–1948), who said, "The inner must be in harmony with the outer. We ought to be able to think and feel as we act."[26]

Authenticity – though it may be expressed differently – is important not only in Western cultures (as studied in the United Kingdom and United States) but also in Eastern cultures (as studied in China, India, and Singapore). This is somewhat surprising because researchers tend to think of Western cultures as "me" oriented, prioritizing traits like individuality and knowing and connecting to the self. On the flip side, Eastern cultures are "we" focused and centered on being part of a collective, connecting to others, and conforming to social norms. Or so go the stereotypes. If we bow to those oversimplifications, we may expect that authenticity, a strongly me-related concept, doesn't play a role in Eastern cultures. But researchers from the United Kingdom and Germany putting that assumption to the test did a cross-cultural investigation of whether the experience of authenticity is a by-product of Western ideals, such as freedom and independence. Their findings suggest it is not and that striving for authenticity is natural to being human.[27]

By contrast, when we are inauthentic, we say and do things to please or accommodate others.[28] Consider how most of us deal with sadness while out in the world. If someone at the post office asks us how we are, we quickly respond "fine," even if we want to cry, because we assume strangers don't want to see or hear our true emotions. We often endure these difficult moments by creating highly inauthentic social interactions because even those of us who are typically more authentic may feel we do not have the space to be ourselves. There are also times when many of us hide our emotions amid worry they won't be validated or reciprocated. In those situations, inauthenticity might feel better than social rejection, but it still doesn't leave us feeling particularly good about ourselves or our experiences. The bottom line is that feeling judged, socially incompetent, or isolated and conforming to social expectations create the most inauthentic experiences. Studies show that being *inauthentic* can lead to stress and burnout and even to feelings of impurity and immorality – heavy stuff.[29,30]

GETTING REAL IN SOLITUDE

In the still-new study of authenticity, scientists and psychologists have wondered mainly about what *social* authenticity does for us – when we are around and sharing our true selves with others. Little attention has been paid to authenticity in solitude, but there have been a handful of compelling findings to date. One early study on the subject showed that, despite what may seem like a strange concept, it is possible to feel fake in solitude. Even when we're on our own, it may be difficult to assess from moment to moment if we are being true to ourselves or if pressure to fit in and conform with societal norms is preventing us from being real. If someone is being inauthentic in solitude, they may feel bored, restless, and lonely.[31] Those feelings indicate a lack of connection to anything (themselves or others), at least in their minds, and a sense of alienation. Inauthenticity in solitude seems to have the same downsides as when we're with others – stress, anxiety, and depression.[32] These findings lend credence to the powerful idea that, even when we're alone, it's important that we are linked in some way to our authentic selves to access the benefits of solitude.

Because there's clearly an important connection between solitude and authenticity, we wanted to know more. In a series of studies we conducted, participants were asked to recall authentic and inauthentic moments (in both social and solitude settings). We were interested in the question, does spending time alone give us space to be real? In four separate studies, using both online surveys and in-lab interviews, we got feedback from 700 university students and adults (age eighteen to sixty-three years) in Great Britain and North America. After explaining what it means to be authentic or inauthentic, we asked them to think about those types of experiences in their own lives and how those made them feel. Some were asked to report on experiences they had on the day they were questioned, while others could reflect on the past several months.[33]

We first looked at social authenticity and saw that – no surprise – spending time with "close" others, such as a good friend, offers one way to feel authentic. Our participants were equally able to remember feeling pressured and ingenuine in separate social encounters when others' expectations were a major factor. They reported feeling scrutinized and judged, sentiments measured by rating the statement "I felt concerned about what other people thought of me." During these experiences, participants also said they felt lower self-esteem and more feelings of anxiety and sadness. Ultimately, well-being suffered from those feelings of being pressured and ingenuine. We then turned to solo moments when study participants were, or were not, their "real" selves. When they were asked to think back to an "inauthentic" time alone, they often reported moments when social evaluation and pressure had intruded on their solitude.

Ultimately, we found that authentic social interactions and authentic solitude share some common, positive ground. That included allowing participants to act or be true to themselves; experience a sense of confidence, achievement, or pride; be comfortable, relaxed, and experience inner peace; accept themselves for who they are; and engage in hobbies or activities they are passionate about. We also learned that there are some perks unique to authenticity felt in solitude. Participants described those as the opportunity to choose activities aligned with their own interests and having the space for self-reflection, where they could attend to their own thoughts and feelings. By contrast, inauthentic solitude did not allow participants to gain an understanding of themselves. These findings add to the existing literature on authenticity in a couple ways. We learned that solitude gives us as many, if not more, opportunities to be authentic than when we're with others. And, equally as important, we heard from research subjects that they experienced inauthenticity more frequently when they were with others versus on their own.[32]

Our narrative studies based on sixty lengthy interviews with people in many parts of the world confirmed many of those factors linking solitude and authenticity. One of our participants, twenty-seven-year-old Baris from Turkey, said solitude is a crucial time for self-reflection that can help him evaluate where he is in the present and where he should go in the future. "It shows me the place that I am in now, that I can see myself," and it helps him answer the question, "Should I stay here or [should I] go there?" he said. And Lucas, age twenty-one, from Portugal, confirmed the concept that being authentic in solitude boosts well-being. "I love myself when I'm being myself, and one important thing in our lives is loving ourselves. We need to accept ourselves and that alone time for me is for accepting myself. Being who I am, with all my flaws and all my doubt, and all my over thinking, and all my curiosity. I need to accept all of that," he said.[34]

Why is solitude such a good space in which to access authenticity? We can only speculate, based on what we've heard from our research subjects, but it seems there are a few main reasons. First, solitude allows many people to let go of others' scrutiny and the vulnerability that comes with those feelings. Instead, it can be a space that lacks self-consciousness and encourages self-inquiry. Solitude is a "letting go," or at least it can be. (Remember, alone time can be tough for anyone sometimes and for some people all the time. We can respect that reality while also learning in Chapter 9 how to be more resilient in solitude.) Worrying about what other people think only really fades away for many people when they connect with their true selves – our deeper thoughts, feelings, and values – in solitude.

Solitude also offers a powerful opportunity to be self-governing. Studies have shown that when we focus inward, we feel better able to be ourselves. In one online study of 619 adults mostly in their twenties and thirties, those who invested in self-reflection were more likely to feel authentic or true to themselves. They showed this by agreeing to statements like "I love exploring my 'inner self'" and "My attitudes and feelings about things fascinate me." The researchers, from the southern United States, suggested that people who are generally more in touch with themselves experience "meaning" more readily and feel more satisfied with their lives overall.[35]

We saw evidence of that in our narrative studies as well. For some people, being true to who they are comes more naturally when they're alone under various conditions (maybe public solitude or companionate solitude, as we discussed in Chapter 2), whereas for others, being secure in solitude is essential to the process of coming into their authentic being. For one of our research subjects, a fifty-three-year-old woman, authenticity in solitude is achievable only when she's completely alone with few prospects for interruption. "I feel, even if they didn't disrupt me, there's the potential for disruption, and then I feel self-conscious about what I'm doing in solitude. I feel observed and I feel I can't be myself. I feel then you have to still perform in some way, that even if they don't come into the room, I couldn't sit there and write or I couldn't get on with what I might want to do by myself," she said. But when people do relax into solitude, it seems a great place to access their true nature. Jack, age twenty-two, from Malaysia, said, "These moments of solitude [are] more of an opportunity for me to explore my interests, and explore my hobbies, and I think that was one way that I could remain true to myself. . . . It really helped solidify me as a person."

We heard many times from that same batch of research participants that time alone can lead to a greater awareness of "self" and toward truer versions of themselves. One participant expressed it eloquently: "I feel like it's full of authenticity, it's full of honesty, it's full of awareness, mindfulness in a way. Like when I'm alone, it gives me time and space, an undisturbed phase, to have a conversation with myself, and gives me space to recognize what I'm feeling." Fifty-six-year-old Phil from the United States told us, "Throughout the day, I recognize, I'll be more aware of why I feel what I feel, how I feel, and [solitude] gives me a space of reflection and looking inward." And Samantha, age forty-two, from Switzerland, said, "It feels like you're kind of unsheathing the type of energy that's normally contained and wrapped up in all this other stuff. You're kind of peeling away the layers and getting at something that's really true." Elliott, age twenty-eight, of Germany, said that solitude allows him to set aside others' opinions and focus on his needs, perspectives, and goals. During alone time, he said, "it feels like I remember how *I* feel."

In solitude, a kind of how-to guide to our own operation can be written as we tap into our own thoughts and fundamental nature. That can help us better understand our strengths, weaknesses, values, emotions, and motivations. Helena, a thirty-nine-year-old single woman from California, told us, "For me solitude is learning yourself, learning who you are, and learning what you're capable of." And Rebecca, age forty-eight, from Iceland, described it this way: "I think you miss out on an opportunity to just get to know yourself if you're constantly distracted by everything else." It also gives people a chance to discover and reinforce ideas that are core to who they are – even if these ideas conflict with those of their family and community. As a young person growing up in Bangladesh, thirty-year-old Kaamil would "retreat to solitude" to reconcile societal expectations (of marrying young and having children) with what she felt in her heart – the desire to study abroad and see the world. "What helped during that time is I know my ideas are different, my thoughts are different, and I have to develop a sort of fortress between myself and the rest of society," she said. As a result of her connecting with her true self in solitude, Kaamil left home to attend university in another country and is studying happily in several more nations while completing an advanced degree in business.

Achieving authenticity in solitude, much like maintaining autonomy in that space, doesn't have a finish line. They are both ongoing processes requiring intention, however bold or modest, each time we have a moment or two to ourselves. In those instances, solitude shifts from that formless blob of sculptor's clay we mentioned earlier into a zone of potential perks. We turn next to those many benefits.

CHAPTER 4

Mapping the Benefits of Solitude

WHEN THUY-VY WAS IN GRADUATE school and first started researching the state of being alone, she wanted to focus on experiences that contribute to human flourishing. But when she perused the psychological literature on solitude, Thuy-vy found that it was mostly negative (and focused on adolescents). It's no surprise, really, that researchers have only begun to explore the potential benefits of solitude in the past twenty years or so, because, as we talked about in Chapter 1, seeing solitude as a positive phenomenon has been a fringe concept throughout human history. Sometimes solitude was actively discouraged by authorities, or passively looked upon with suspicion, or just simply logistically impossible for many people.

Those challenges all still exist in some form today, and researchers and laypeople alike have had difficulty breaking out of that mind-set. Still, Thuy-vy persisted, knowing personally that solitude was connected to well-being in some way and wanting to understand how and why in order to benefit others. Meanwhile, Netta approached her scientific inquiries into solitude from a different angle. She is a relationship researcher turned solitude lover who became intrigued about how one state may affect the other (they are more closely tied than one may think, as we'll talk about in Chapter 5). The challenge she encountered was that, unlike the richly researched field of relationships, the role of solitude in well-being was still a mystery.

Both Netta and Thuy-vy quickly found that studying solitude and homing in on its possible benefits is particularly challenging in a few ways. As we mentioned in Chapter 2, they learned that knowledge is born of data in the form of numbers. In that quantitative world, they learned how to observe behavior to test if one part of the human experience was similar enough, or different enough, from another part of the human experience to indicate commonalities or anomalies. Those statistics help us build scales with which we can say something new and interesting about the human condition. That process is, ultimately, how researchers generalize their findings to a larger population beyond their own subjects. But with a research topic as new as solitude, and one so laden with false assumptions, there were fundamental and yet still unanswered questions that required a broader, more inclusive – but no less rigorous – approach.

At first, abandoning pure statistics was daunting because we researchers have always heard whispers, and sometimes shouts, that qualitative research – which gives weight to information that cannot be easily quantified – is "storytelling," not science. But there are clear limitations to the pure numbers approach when looking at solitude. That's because we all attempt to make sense of the world in our own ways, and we each have individual concepts and experiences of solitude that are not well elicited in traditional quantitative analyses. That's when Heather came into the picture. As a science journalist, she likes objective evidence gained through experimentation and statistics as much as Netta and Thuy-vy. But only in conducting lengthy interviews with research subjects could we begin to dig into why solitude is positive for so many people and what its main benefits appear to be.

During our research, we heard about so many different upsides of solitude that we began sorting and categorizing them. At first, we struggled with how to represent the possible perks of alone time – initially, we thought of a layer cake (because, frankly, cake is never far from our minds). We also considered scaffolding that rises level by level from some of the simpler perks of solitude to some of the more complex. In those analogies, the basic benefits of solitude as we see them, like rest and relaxation, were topped by "higher-level" rewards like creativity and so-called peak experiences. But the "layer" concept didn't quite fit, because experiencing one attribute of solitude doesn't necessarily rely on having achieved another. For example, the pianist Ludwig van Beethoven banging out one of his stark, forceful compositions may have been seizing immense creativity in solitude, but he wasn't exactly relaxed while doing it.

Instead, imagine entering solitude, as either a familiar or foreign landscape, getting the lay of the land, then choosing a direction in which to go. With that approach to organizing our research subjects' many diverse experiences, four categories of benefits emerged like cardinal directions on a map – north, south, east, and west. The idea is that, in solitude, we draw our own map and orient our individual compass as we venture down our chosen path. The direction one goes, toward a new or familiar destination, may vary depending on the day or moment, stage of life, or the necessity or desire to achieve a certain goal.

All directions on the solitude compass originate from the essential meta-features of autonomy and authenticity that we wrote about in Chapter 3. Given that initial bearing, there's no right or wrong way to go (really, perfectionists, there isn't). When developing the concept of the solitude compass, we used a somewhat UK- and US-oriented way of navigating, and we recognize that someone in Mexico, for example, will not think of the "south" in the same way as someone living farther north, but nonetheless, the overall themes should be universally accessible.

Bearing that in mind, the solitude compass is marked quite unscientifically by *north*, the stereotypical direction of realness (such as "true north"), which represents using solo time to self-reflect, examine authentic feelings and beliefs, and consider true priorities and values; *south*, which refers to rest or relaxation (think hanging out on the coast of the Mediterranean or on the lazy shores of the US Gulf Coast) and is also a place to "refuel" or "recharge," as our subjects described it; *east*, which is the direction of enrichment (and, not coincidentally, the rising sun) – periods of solitude can be intensely productive and creative for many people; and *west*, which represents prosperity and peak experiences, where we have the potential to achieve a sense of joyfulness and connectedness, even transcendence. (The reason west seemed like the natural direction for these potential perks is because, owing to the direction of Earth's eastern rotation, prevailing winds blow from the west in many parts of the world. We imagine that having the wind at our backs can drive us toward exploration and new experiences.) Note that although there are four directions equally weighted with benefits in our minds, not all have achieved equal attention in the research world up to this point, and that is reflected in our descriptions here.

Also, these basic categories are a framework and not meant to indicate that we're limited in any way in solitude. Each category has fathoms of possibilities to be discovered by us as individuals. For example, *north* is described, generally, as a space in which to connect with ourselves and to reflect. That reflection can, and does, take many forms. We heard from study participants heading *north* in solitude that it is a space for solving problems, making decisions, prioritizing, getting perspective, and gaining confidence and greater life resilience. Similarly, orienting *south* meant, in general, taking a route of rest and relaxation. In many of the interviews we did, people described some moments of solitude exactly this way, while others used words including *restorative, nourishing, recharging, balance, calibration, breathing space, calm, grounded, content*, and *purifying*. Similarly, creativity (*east*) and peak experiences (*west*) can take, as we'll see, many intriguing forms.

NORTH: TOWARD SELF-REFLECTION

On most days, navigational compasses don't accurately indicate the precise direction of the North Pole. Instead, they point the way toward magnetic north – the direction in which a compass needle shifts as it aligns with Earth's magnetic field. Magnetic north is ever changing, whereas true north is a fixed location indicating the exact location of the pole. When unsure about their compass bearings, navigators long ago defaulted to using stars and charts to avoid getting lost. As long as they could see Polaris, the North Star, they'd keep heading the right way. Most of us aren't navigating the high seas like explorers on an expedition, but the stakes are just as high for being able to discern our true north – our authentic self – from a false one. That can impact life decisions, big and small, and affect our steering one way or another. And solitude, as a stellar setting for finding autonomy and authenticity (as we talked about in Chapter 3), can be an invaluable space in which to do that. We can think of it as a place and time to get back to basics, to listen closely to our inner voice, to see our north star clearly.

In our research, we have heard a lot about solitude being used to "take stock" because, we suspect, time alone gives us a chance – without input from others – to make sense of the variety of experiences we have on any given day.[1,2] Such self-reflection can influence what goals we set, allow us to recalibrate, and sustain movement toward those objectives. Time on her own gives Elizabeth, a working mother of two, time to "truly think and clear my head" by disengaging with outside thoughts of work and family. It also gives her the energy to sort out what's most important to her. "I think being in solitude is the only way you can get to know what really matters about life for you. In solitude, I gradually came to a kind of self-awareness of what my priorities are in life, and so I have a strong sense of what I want in life and what matters to me . . . rather than getting overly influenced by other people's views," she said. That thought resonated with Elliott, from Germany, who uses solitude to evaluate "short-term goals and medium-term goals and [for] kind of recentering myself and being aware of my own timeline in life, where I am." Solitude is a key space for him to disconnect from others and connect with himself because otherwise, said Elliott, "it's really easy for me to kind of just latch onto outside stuff, other people's stuff."

We have seen some evidence of the importance of solitary self-reflection in other research as well. In one study of the upsides of solitary, long-distance walking, subjects experienced both short- and long-term benefits.[3] The walkers' fleeting positive outcomes included feeling energetic and enthusiastic once they left the trail and returned to their daily lives. The long-term benefits, however, were linked to the self-reflection they experienced while going solo on the trail because it allowed the walkers to disengage from normal life and gain a different perspective. The subjects said that having a space just for them facilitated thinking deliberately about their goals and priorities, finding personal meaning and growth, and expanding their capacity to move forward with that knowledge – even after their walks were finished.

That potential for self-reflection was acute for some during the pandemic that began in 2020, when many people had time in isolation. The lucky ones not dealing with illness or death, or serious financial instability, had more time to reflect on their lives and evaluate their purpose, beliefs, and values. For many, clarity emerged, and relationships, careers, and lives began to shift intentionally and meaningfully.[3] During that time, normally itinerant writer Pico Iyer, who wrote *The Joy of Quiet,* commented, "We're remembering what we choose versus what's handed down to us, it's a hiatus, and ... I think almost everybody who's part of this conversation will say that she has a clearer sense of what she cares about now than she had last month. Suddenly, she can sift what is trivial from what is essential. In many ways, that's such a blessing."[4]

Some of our research participants also said that engaging self-reflection and self-connection in solitude had a restorative or healing power. A twenty-four-year-old from Portugal who had recently broken up with her partner commented, "Although I was alone, I started to heal a lot faster than going out or constantly asking for my friends' company, because I had time to think about all of it and most importantly, to heal and to start taking care of myself. It was in solitude that I found myself again and now, being alone isn't something that bothers me, in fact, I need a lot of time alone to heal, to recharge and to connect with myself again."

Solitude offered a number of our participants (and one of this book's authors) the space to begin to make sense of the death of a loved one and the quiet in which to examine who we become in the wake of immense loss. Grief sometimes creates what researchers call a "crisis of meaning," and introspection and self-reflection can help in the process of reconstructing significance.[5] Samantha in Switzerland couldn't find her place among other people while her father was suffering with cancer and in the aftermath of his death. She was putting up a front to avoid burdening others with the weight of her sadness. "I felt like such a mess, I just felt like I was coming apart. I felt it was such a strain to have to hold it together for people. And it was exhausting and I was actually resentful about it, that I could only grieve in ways that were acceptable for other people," she said. So Samantha stepped away for two weeks on her own in the Alps walking, cooking, chopping wood, and sobbing. In that space, she said, "I really felt like I could be free to grieve without disturbing anyone."

SOUTH: TOWARD REST, RELAXATION, AND RENEWAL

Solitude is an important opportunity to disengage entirely from tensions and problems demanding our attention. That's powerful, because disentangling ourselves from the busy, noisy outside world tends to short-circuit impulsivity, while offering balance.[5] Think of time alone as an opportunity to do routine maintenance on ourselves just like we do on our cars. It's a chance to cool our engines, rotate our tires, and tweak our alignment. From there we can get back on the road, so to speak, better equipped for the journey ahead. "I feel some of the things that may have made me start to feel anxious or worried or stressed in life, I can deal with better if I've had some time by myself because then I can be more rational about it," said Anna from England. "I can go back to being who I am and feel calm with the world after I've had time by myself."

That's true of another one of our Solitude Project participants. Mary spent most of her seventy-one years living near Cardiff, Wales, and now lives near her daughter and grandchildren in England. Mary was widowed decades ago and has lived alone since her daughter left for university soon thereafter. "The peacefulness of proper solitude" is something she seeks. "It's a very important part of my life to maintain equilibrium," she said. "If I've been worried about something or upset over something and I can't stop thinking about it, sometimes I will just get in my car and drive out into the countryside and park up somewhere and go for a little walk, or just sit and contemplate the scenery," said Mary. There's one specific spot where she goes to find that headspace – on the western coast of Wales, where she scattered her husband's ashes many years ago. "There's something about being on the cliffs there, overlooking the sea. You're very alone, actually ... but it's not a bad thing," she said. That spot of swaying grass and seaside immensity is one of the only places that feels big enough to encompass her memories and emotions.

We can glean some interesting input about what rest and relaxation mean to people around the world, and how we achieve it, from one large-scale international poll. In late 2015, the British Broadcasting Corporation (BBC) Radio Science division, in conjunction with University College London, launched the Rest Test.[6] They recruited more than 18,000 people from 134 countries to weigh in on "conscious rest" (meaning activities other than sleep) in their lives. It was the largest study of its kind to ask what rest means to different individuals and how it is meaningfully engaged.

Keep in mind, it wasn't a study about solitude, but it happened upon the idea that time alone equates with rest for a lot of people. Participants answered the poll by ranking "spending time on my own" much higher than "spending time with friends and family." Eating, drinking socially, and even sex also ranked much lower as ways to achieve rest. When participants were asked to define rest for themselves, some chose words including *personal, quiet, still, healing,* and *deliberate.* The responses were eye-opening, and the study authors wondered, "When we say we need more rest, is it more that we yearn for time away from other people?"[6]

Achieving rest is best while on our own is not a new idea and has been expressed by some notable people over the past several centuries. From 1781 to 1782, Wolfgang Amadeus Mozart composed the piece "An die Einsamkeit" with the lyrics "O solitude! how gently you soothe me, when my strength falls so quickly! With warm longing I seek you: so seeks a wanderer, exhausted, the shadows."[7] Mozart died a decade later, and just five months after his son Franz had been born, but the boy seemed to inherit both some of his father's musical prowess and his relationship with solitude. The younger Mozart also composed and, in 1810, wrote his own "Die Einsamkeit." Despite ongoing global conflict at the time and his own complicated home life, the "other" Mozart penned a cheerful song accompanied by the words "My wish and my joy are you, solitude, and domestic peace and country calm."[8,9]

Whether or not they were composing a symphony, many of the people we interviewed about their experiences in solitude also described it as a calming place for relaxation and renewal. The feeling seemed to transcend age, gender, and country of origin. Kam, age thirty-seven, from Malaysia, told us, "For me it's kind of peace, kind of a lull, quietness." We heard about solitude being a common but also important tool used to destress and recover. Alex, age thirty-eight, from Armenia, said, "I think there's a sort of peacefulness about it, a space to explore, or the space to just be. I think that's special." And fifty-nine-year-old Joni, from Ireland, empha-sized needing solitude to step away from external forces and focus on her own needs. "Sometimes I feel like I'm in a wee bubble, not interacting with the outside world, and that's okay. Sometimes it's just a way of relaxing or resting, healing, just something you've got to do occasionally."

What's happening during that time we're alone, and why is it so refreshing for some people? Solitude is a great opportunity for rest because it shuts out others' immediate influences and expectations. It's not that we escape others' influences entirely; rather, they are simply not physically present to elicit responses from us. Among our research subjects, Samantha said, "I think it's the best way to have conversations with yourself – free of other distractions and other judgments." More than that, time alone also appears to profoundly impact our emotions. Much research has been done on the lack of certain positive emotions (like excitement and enthusiasm) experienced in solitude.[10] That makes sense, in a way, because spending time with other people can involve stimulating exchanges of information, stories, or laughter. But what about our other feelings?

It turns out that solitude has the power to disarm our negative emotions. This revelation took a while to understand, because early studies on mood and emotion that seemed definitive at the time were, in reality, woefully incomplete. That work began in the 1980s with a series of studies by developmental psychologist Reed Larson, who tracked people's moods throughout the day. He observed that time spent alone was linked to less positive mood compared to time spent in the company of others.[11] At that time, psychologists tended to oversimplify emotional states, boiling them down to polar extremes like "excited" on one end and "lonely" on the other.[12] But as anyone who experiences a far broader range of emotions knows, there's more to it than that.

Larson's studies lumped together the otherwise rich range of positive and negative states we can experience on any given day, or even in a single moment, and gave the black-and-white impression that solitude blunts positive emotions. We now know, however, that there are important shades of gray. For example, solitude may not be a common time for experiencing excitement, but it's a great place, as we've discussed, to feel calm and relaxed. Since those initial emotion studies were done, new models of emotions have allowed researchers to capture four different types of mood states: (1) high-activation positive emotions (such as excited, energized); (2) high-activation negative emotions (anxious, angry); (3) low-activation positive emotions (calm, relaxed); and (4) low-activation negative emotions (sad, lonely).[13]

In our own research, we've heard a lot about the immense range of emotion that solitude can encompass. It's helpful to talk about that because it offers a snapshot of the diversity of experiences possible and, in a way, acceptable in time alone. Our participants' experiences ran the gamut, and among them were people who described having high-activation positive emotions (those who described being energized by their time alone) and some who talked about feeling low-activation negative emotions (those who said solitude can occasionally feel lonely).

But most people described being somewhere in between, most of the time. A clear illustration of this point came from Ahmad, age thirty-seven, from Iran, who talked about walking by himself versus walking with his partner and how both events are positive, but in completely different ways. Strolling with his spouse elicited high-activation positive emotions, whereas, when walking alone, he felt more low-activation positive emotions. "When I'm walking with my wife, I'm more aware of her. I'm more aware of our togetherness and it's also quite pleasant in a different way. . . . There's a more obvious celebration. When I'm alone . . . it's not always celebratory, but more like an exploration," he said.

Thuy-vy ran a series of experiments several years ago (while completing her PhD with advisers Richard Ryan and Edward Deci) that shine a light on how solitude affects emotional states.[14] That work showed for the first time that solitude helps to modulate not only high-activation positive emotions but high-activation *negative* emotions as well – an insight that is often overlooked in research on the effects of time alone. Study participants experienced what the researchers later dubbed the "deactivation effect." Time alone seemed to "turn off" many negative emotions and act as an antidote to anxiety and worry. The researchers found that this was true when participants sat alone doing nothing as well as when they spent time alone reading or browsing social media.

In our later research, we also heard about how emotions can shift during solitude and, more specifically, how we can calibrate them in that space. Again, Ahmad: "I remember when I was younger, in my late teens and even early twenties, I was a little bit helpless sometimes because it was the first time that I would find myself in a position alone, not knowing how to regulate my emotions. . . . [Now] when I feel negatively, I know it's not the first time. I know I've been here before and I know it will not last. I know I can just wait for it to pass sometimes, or I can write . . . or I can listen to music." Many people who shy away from alone time because they fear a bubbling up of negative emotions may find some solace in knowing that emotion regulation in that space is possible, even invaluable, for many people. "My ability to relate to myself, talk with myself, to organize myself, regulate myself, my feelings, my routines, my attention. It's critical," said Ahmad.

According to a recent study with a huge number of individuals from researchers at Carleton University and the National Research Council–Canada, solitude creates a kind of mental freedom that can be, simply, enjoyable. In that study, researchers used a fairly new method called "data scraping" that involved extracting posts from a database run by the social media company Twitter.[15] The researchers pulled nineteen million "tweets" that talked about "solitude," "loneliness," and simply being "alone." They also looked for the presence of certain words that indicated whether users of the service were doing well. They found that when people posted about solitude versus loneliness, they tended to use words reflecting low-activation positive emotion, describing experiences that were more "pleasant, restorative, and intrinsically motivated," according to the researchers. Solitude also co-occurred with words having to do with contentment, whereas loneliness was more related to feeling scared or depressed. When people tweeted about solitude, they expressed that they were feeling on top of the world and experiencing peace, joy, and restoration.

EAST: TOWARD ENRICHMENT AND CREATIVITY

Recent neuroscience research gives us an idea of why solitude can be so conducive to creativity. When lacking attention-grabbing stimuli and external demands, it seems we can better tap into inspiration and creativity (see Box 4.1). That is, rather than reacting to the outside social world, we have the freedom to explore an inside world rich in imagination and opportunities. Neurologists have identified three main neural networks along which creative thoughts travel.[16] They are known somewhat wonkily as the salience, default, and executive attention networks, circuits that often work in opposition but work together to spark creativity. Salience is like a traffic cop regulating attention between inner and outer worlds and is critical to problem solving. The executive attention pathways are used for focus and targeted attention. They are both important players in connecting different brain regions involved with being expressive and innovative, but the default network – also called the *imagination* network – is the genesis of creative cognition, the place where daydreaming and brainstorming happen. (It's also how we explore what others may be thinking and how we play out past experiences or cogitate on future ones.)

BOX 4.1 ARTISTRY AND ALONE TIME

Many creative titans over time – from writers John Steinbeck[20] and Ernest Hemingway[21] to writer-director Ingmar Bergman[22] and Apple cofounder Steve Wozniak[23] – have craved the void into which inspiration often flowed for them. Amid a furious schedule of composing, conducting, teaching, and performing, Wolfgang Amadeus Mozart would roam the normally heaving streets of eighteenth-century Vienna after hours in search of revelations. "When I am, as it were, completely myself, entirely alone, and of good cheer – say, traveling in a carriage or walking after a good meal or during the night when I cannot sleep – it is on such occasions that my ideas flow best and most abundantly," he wrote in a letter to a friend in 1783.[24]

French writer and aviator Antoine de Saint-Exupéry (*The Little Prince*, 1943) used to frustrate the heck out of his colleagues with his love of alone time. He'd be flying a solo mission and often reading a book at the same time, and if he was absorbed and close to finishing a story, he'd sometimes circle the airport for an hour before landing. Saint-Exupéry would also bring a notebook into the plane's cockpit with him and jot down his own story ideas. That habit proved useful after a crash landing in the Sahara due to mechanical trouble. After several days of deprivation in the Libyan desert, while suffering from dehydration and hallucinations, he imagined-to-life the little prince, who asked the author-illustrator-pilot to draw him a sheep. (Saint-Exupéry was later rescued by a water-bearing Bedouin.)[25]

Iconic American artist Georgia O'Keeffe (1887–1986) marked her creative territory with bold, spirited paintings of the high desert of northern New Mexico and its austere and delicate features, including sculpted badlands, cow skulls, and provocative flowers. She often wandered solo in the sparsely populated American West, finding an abundance of color, shape, and light amid stark landscapes and depicting essential abstract forms of nature over a seventy-year career.[26] From 1929, and onward for decades, O'Keeffe would walk and work alone for days, toting her art supplies, camping under star-crammed skies, and dipping into creeks (not to mention killing rattlesnakes, whose tails she kept in a tin box). "The reddish sand hills with the dark mesas behind them. It seemed as though no matter how far you walked you could never get into those dark hills, although I walked great distances. I've always liked to walk. I think I've taken a bath in every brook from Abiquiu to Española," she said in an interview in the *New Yorker* in 1974.[27] At the same time, O'Keeffe was no recluse and maintained her place in a tight-knit community of artists, yet it was alone in the still, quiet desert where O'Keeffe's sense of awe and powers of observation were most keen.

Many other visual artists have also used the blank slate of solitude to fill their canvases. Agnes Martin (1912–2004), who made her own indelible mark on modernist art of the twentieth century, once said in an interview, "The best things happen to you when you're alone. You know, all the revelations."[28] Like O'Keeffe, Martin lived in northern New Mexico, though Martin had a more hermetic lifestyle than O'Keeffe. Martin also evoked nature in her work, but with spare (almost arid) grid compositions that she used to convey transcendence.[29] A contemporary of Martin and O'Keeffe, Pablo Picasso (1881–1973), also felt creativity flowed best in solitude, and he seemed to resent when outside demands pressed in on his chosen alone time. He reportedly once said, "Nothing can be done without solitude. I have created a solitude for myself that no one suspects. But nowadays the clock makes solitude difficult. Have you ever seen a saint with a watch?"[30]

The imagination network is typically activated when our mental focus is directed inwardly,[17] the kind of thinking solitude encourages. How it works is this: imagine you are pop diva Taylor Swift sitting down to write a new song. First the imagination network kicks in, and it sets off emotional activation and sensory processing (or integration), which is the time when the brain takes in, organizes, and replies to sensory input in its environment, including our own bodies. Then the executive attention and salience networks come online to lock into your memory the lyrics and melody.

In Swift's film *Folklore: The Long Pond Studio Sessions*, she talked about the importance of solitude to creating her latest album, a process she began when we were all encouraged to stay home in early 2020. "I think the pandemic and lockdown and all that runs through this album like a thread, because it's an album that allows you to feel your feelings and it's a product of isolation," she said.[18] This understanding links artists from one century to the next. While he was no Taylor Swift (for better or worse), Dublin-born author Samuel Beckett (1906–89) also attributed his creativity to his time alone. The writer embraced solitude to tell stories of humanity that lay beyond the existing social order. He wrote, "I don't find solitude agonizing, on the contrary. Holes in paper open and take me fathoms from anywhere."[19]

When trying to define what gets the creative juices flowing, British psychologist (and cofounder of the London School of Economics) Graham Wallas wrote *The Art of Thought* in 1926.[31] He outlined a four-phase process of preparation/saturation, incubation, illumination, and verification. Based on his analysis, it was that second phase – incubation – that seemed most important. Creating the space and time to let notions, theories, problems, or puzzles marinate and come to fruition was critical. Albert Einstein would likely have agreed. He loved ocean voyages, epic walks, and sailing solo (even though he couldn't swim!) because of the problem-solving abilities that such zones encouraged. "I am a horse for a single harness, not cut out for tandem or teamwork. I have never belonged whole-heartedly to country or state, to my circle of friends, or even to my own family," Einstein wrote. "What is truly valuable in our bustle of life is not the nation, I should say, but the creative and impressionable individuality, the personality – he who produces the noble and sublime while the common herd remains dull in thought and insensible in feeling."[32]

These anecdotes are certainly persuasive, but until recently, the link between solitude and creativity has been mainly conjecture. The fact that Einstein and O'Keeffe were so productive in their alone time might only have indicated that geniuses prefer solitude, or that solitude prefers geniuses – but not necessarily the rest of us. But recent research has been drilling down into why solitude and creativity may be close bedfellows, and some intriguing findings come from researchers studying motivation for withdrawal. The researchers wondered, when we skip social gatherings, are we doing it because we're shy, avoidant, or unsociable (characterized in the study by the phrase "I don't have a strong preference for being alone or with others")? Among the 295 American university students surveyed, the so-called unsociable folks were more likely to say they were engaged creatively in their time alone. The researchers touted their findings as the "first evidence of a potential benefit (creativity) associated with unsociability." They noted, "Anxiety-free time spent in solitude may allow for, and foster, creative thinking and work."[33]

What we heard from our study participants aligns closely with the famous folks mentioned here, and creative pursuits were undertaken in solitude by people across lines of age, gender, and race. "Creativity just flows, and it just gives you all these intricate threads and things that you can weave together and make this beautiful tapestry of, you know, your perception and view of life and living," Kaamil from Bangladesh told us. Topping the list of imaginative activities in solitude for our study subjects were reading and writing, but also drawing, quilting, singing, sculpting, playing instruments, writing music, and even cooking.

Wen, age thirty-seven, a visual artist and stay-at-home mom from Singapore, explained her time in solitude as "being able to have the space for my sense of wonder" to emerge. Using solitude to feed hobby-based creativity was just as compelling for many people. "It's more the freedom to just experiment and explore and go places in your mind and your heart. And art is more the vehicle for that," Monica, age forty-nine, from the United Kingdom, told us. Rebecca, a working mom from Iceland, covets her limited free time when her imagination can roam freely. "To have actual true time to myself is very rare which is very hard for me because I really love having it to myself. It's when I'm creative. It's when I can really get into things, dive deeper into issues … and sometimes I come up with an idea for a poem or something because my mind isn't filled with everything else," she said. Gerry, age sixty-five, from Wales, told us, "To have the possibility of writing in a creative and playful and focused fashion is a real pleasure. And I actually feel physical pleasure in my body as I do that."

Several studies looked at whether people experienced an increase in creative thinking, in their work and home spheres, during the COVID-19 pandemic. One French study of more than 1,200 people recruited through social networks showed that individuals who were not particularly innovative prior to lockdowns (which gave a lot of people more solitude than usual) used the time as an opportunity to be more creative in their everyday lives.[34] Another study looked specifically at creativity in two dozen managers in India who had to work from home during that time. They found that when working in solitude, individuals had more opportunities to work uninterrupted on self-selected tasks, which increased creative thinking and outcomes.[35] A clear scientific link between solitude and creativity is still being established, but from what we have learned recently, we can consider that the relationship is likely more than anecdotal. Knowing that solitude can offer space to be more creative could open up new, and potentially endless, opportunities in alone time.

WEST: TOWARD PEAK EXPERIENCES AND THE GOOD LIFE

In Chapter 3, we mentioned that when Netta graduated high school, she traveled solo in the British countryside. That time was immensely positive because of the autonomy she achieved there and because her walks opened a kind of portal to feelings of freedom and transcendence. "It was great for a whole number of reasons but one thing I noticed was these 'peak experiences' that seemed to come out of nowhere when I went out hiking and arrived somewhere beautiful, but only when I was alone," she said.

This peak experience phenomenon arises from time to time in our study of solitude. Those are moments of feeling joyful and connected to the world and, in a way, transcendent (see Box 4.2). According to Gayle Privette, an expert in the field, peak experiences involve feelings of wonder and awe.[36] They are often characterized by the depth of feeling

BOX 4.2 TRADING CROWDS AND CONFUSION FOR SOLITUDE AND SANCTUARY

Admiral Richard Byrd, an American polar explorer and the first person to overwinter in the interior of Antarctica, lived a range of extreme peak experiences. In 1934, he spent four and a half months solo at the bottom of the world to study the weather (because weather systems in polar areas have a profound effect on global climate and ocean systems).[44] A *New York Times* article at the time called it a "meteorological vigil" during which Byrd wanted to record the area's first seasonal scientific data.[45]

It was Byrd's second expedition to Antarctica, but he ventured out much farther than before and wintered solo in a cabin buried in snow at the Bolling Advance Weather Base. In his outpost on the Ross Ice Barrier, more than 100 miles and countless crevasses from his expedition mates, Byrd had a wind-up record player for classical music listening, a stack of books to wade through, and a daily diary to keep along with his weather charts. Byrd was, in many ways, looking forward to his chosen physical and social deprivation. Personally and professionally, he had been content, but, as he wrote in a gripping memoir, *Alone*, "Nevertheless, a crowding confusion had pushed in." By that point, he'd been on fourteen years of grueling expeditions – along with the constant planning, fundraising, and pushing toward deadlines and final frontiers, often in close quarters with dozens of other men.[44]

Byrd's celebrated adventures were headline news, and he lectured often about them, yet he described himself as a guy with a "need for occasional sanctuary."[44] About his historic solo expedition, he said, "I really wanted to go for the experience's sake. So, the motive was in part personal. Aside from the meteorological and auroral work, I had no important purposes. There was nothing of that sort. Nothing whatever, except one man's desire to know that kind of experience to the full, to be by himself for a while and to taste peace and quiet and solitude long enough to find out how good they really are.

"It was all that simple. And it is something, I believe, that people beset by the complexities of modern life will understand instinctively.

We are caught up in the winds that blow every which way. And in the hullabaloo the thinking man is driven to ponder where he is being blown and to long desperately for some quiet place where he can reason undisturbed and take inventory."[44]

Byrd did indeed experience many peak moments. "Here were the imponderable processes and forces of the cosmos, harmonious and soundless," he wrote. "Harmony, that was it! That was what came out of the silence – a gentle rhythm, the strain of a perfect chord, the music of the spheres, perhaps. It was enough to catch that rhythm, momentarily to be myself a part of it. In that instant I could feel no doubt of man's oneness with the universe."[46]

But being on his own for months would far exceed his "occasional sanctuary" requirement and, indeed, would turn out to challenge Byrd, body and spirit. The explorer knew he would face life-threatening cold (hurricane-force winds and temperatures dropping to around minus eighty degrees Fahrenheit), impenetrable darkness, and ceaseless psychological isolation, but he had other "bitter moments" as well.[47] A painful shoulder injury greatly hindered his daily operations, and carbon monoxide fumes from a leaky cook stove poisoned and nearly killed him. He waffled between despair and hope, eventually emaciated and covered in frostbite.

Ultimately, Byrd had to be rescued weeks early (a harrowing undertaking in those conditions), and for a long time, he felt a "sense of shame over my flimsiness."[48] It's hard to imagine anyone could describe such a mission as flimsy, or that he'd have anything positive to say about the ordeal in the end, yet he did. Byrd wrote, "I did take away something that I had not fully possessed before: appreciation of the sheer beauty and miracle of being alive, and a humble set of values. ... I live more simply now, and with more peace."[48]

or perception achieved there, and though the moment may be fleeting, the recollection of it is often long-lasting (even twenty years later, Netta's memories of that time remain vivid). Peak experiences are an understudied phenomenon in psychology – we don't really know why they happen – but they seem to occur more in people who are in one particular phase of their psychological growth. The psychologist Abraham Maslow in the 1940s described this state as "self-actualization," which is a clunky way of saying that they feel as if they are fulfilling their life's potential.[37]

Self-actualization tops the *hierarchy of needs*, a theory of psychological health described by Maslow, in which he argued that to reach that highest level of development, humans' basic needs must first be met. In short, those are food, sleep, air, safety, and love and belonging. Self-actualization is among the higher-order needs related to esteem, and Maslow argued that once one's basic physiological needs have been satisfied, the need to reach a greater level of self-fulfillment emerges – something akin to becoming the best we believe we can be.[38] Among our subjects, Ahmad described it this way: "In solitude, we move towards better versions of ourselves."

According to Maslow, one of the major facets of a person who reaches self-actualization, or has the desire to, is *comfort with solitude*.[39] This doesn't exclude people having meaningful relationships and inter-actions with others; in fact, integrating those is also important. Other characteristics of someone striving for a "higher self" include some we've touched on already – authenticity and creativity (balance and purpose also factor in, which we talk about in Chapter 6). The self-actualized person is living in line with their true nature and capabilities to reach new horizons and possibilities.[38] While this may sound like a selfish pursuit, Maslow saw the self-actualized person as also having goals and ambitions to help others and improve the world. Research supporting that concept shows that people who care more about others in need (and less about fame and wealth) achieve more peak experiences.

Some high-profile examples of self-actualized people could include humanitarian Mother Teresa[39] and anti-apartheid leader Nelson Mandela,[40] but being an icon is hardly required to reach that pinnacle. We'd argue, in fact, that the psychological zenith of peak experiences is potentially within most everyone's reach regardless of life circumstances. This assertion isn't naive of the fact that more than 8 percent of the world's population, or roughly 675 million people, live in extreme pov-erty (defined by the World Bank as living below the international poverty line of $2.15 per day).[41] But we also don't pretend to be able to speak for everyone, and we hesitate to assume low levels of self-actualization in economically disadvantaged parts of the world. Certainly income is an important metric of well-being, but plenty of people who live in relative luxury, or otherwise want for nothing material, will never be self-actualized.

While peak experiences are more common in self-actualized people, that's not a requirement, and Maslow believed anyone could have them. Peak experiences may be closer than we think – taking in a stunning sunset, a moving piece of music, or a puppy romping around a room. *How* we see may, in fact, be more important than where we look. In one study, most of the 246 undergraduate students surveyed, age eighteen to sixty-four, at a large Denver-area college reported having had peak experiences. Though nearly 80 percent admitted experiencing the phenomenon, very few had spoken to others about it. They felt those were intimate events that they did not want to, or could not easily, describe.[42]

Another study by researchers in Australia, Thailand, and the United States asked for thoughts on peak experiences from thirty-nine participants (age seventeen to seventy years) reflecting on wilderness outings. Subjects noted common restorative elements of their outings, specifically solitude and the lack of human-made intrusions and distractions, in helping them to think and reflect. In many cases, that setting also laid the groundwork for peak experiences.[43] One subject talked about finding clarity in that time and feeling connected to the energy of the mountains: "It was really powerful, for the first time in my life I could truly understand what had been happening in my life. I think it was the solitude that enabled this. I had been on my own for four days and it gave me time to properly think on my recent difficulties, in this case divorce. And then, in that one moment, I saw in nature the struggle to survive and how difficult it was. It was a validation of my own difficulties and in that came a sense of joy for the first time in a very long time."

Peak experiences marked by wonder, harmony, even ecstasy, are something we've heard about from many of our research participants as well – that they have felt a kind of transcendence, or oneness with the universe, during some periods of solitude. Alone time may facilitate these kinds of events because, in that pared-down environment, many of us slow down and pay attention differently. Some of the people we interviewed described some moments of solitude as being "present in a sensory way" and having a heightened awareness of their surroundings. They often used words like *focused, grounded,* and *alive* to characterize those solitude events.

Many people access peak experiences in nature (the relevance of which we'll talk about at length in Chapter 7), and for some people that seems to imbue their solitude with a substance and quality specific to them. "I might go for a walk, and in which case, I'm somebody who notices things when they walk, flowers and birds and blossoms, and I actively note it. So, I think I do particular things to let me feel solitude," Anna from England told us. After retiring from a hectic teaching career, Sheila, age sixty, also from England, took up walking around her neighborhood for hours each day. It was her time to get out of the house and to be alone. "I've walked to places I didn't even know existed and I've lived here for twenty years," she said. Despite having some difficulty walking, Sheila took to the streets because, she said, "I wanted to do something which allowed me the space but also to connect" to her "new" environment. The passing miles are cathartic and cleansing, she said, and "I think it makes me into a better person." Often Sheila will pause to sniff a neighbor's flowers. "I mean some people must think I'm crackers when they see me but I'll stop and I smell the roses," she said.

But being outdoors, or even looking outside, isn't required to access peak experiences, and some of our study participants have had them where they least expected. Samantha from Switzerland spends one hour several mornings per week working out in her garage – in what she calls a "small realm of concrete and steel where I get to focus on me and my needs and my efforts without interruption, without any constraints at all." On some days lifting weights is just a workout, but on others, she said, "I just really feel like I'm connecting with something within myself and that's usually on a rainy day when nobody's around and it's cold and it's miserable, and I really feel like I have to draw from within to kind of shape that empty space. And I think that can be pretty exceptional." She describes that peak experience as unplugging from the "pulse of everything around you" and tapping into her "actual inner pulse." "And you can finally reach it, for a short time anyway," she said. "There's some days where it's almost magical, I feel like I'm somewhere else. I almost feel like I'm on some special little planet, like the Little Prince or something."

For Samantha, and so many others, solitude offers a time to step away and return to our own little planets, like the title character from Saint-Exupéry's novella. At the end of the book, having explored the universe, the prince returns to his home turf, where he is the only resident, recognizing that the essence of life lies not "out there" but instead within himself. "It is only with the heart that one can see rightly; what is essential is invisible to the eye," Saint-Exupéry wrote.[49]

Having journeyed in this chapter to the four points of solitude, it's clear there is a treasure trove of possibilities awaiting one there. Accessing those, however, requires opening a lock, for which we each have our own individual key. That key is choice, and as we'll see in Chapter 5, it's a component essential to reaching all that solitude has to offer.

CHAPTER 5

What's Choice Got to Do with It?

WHEN JENNIFER PHARR DAVIS WAS TWENTY-ONE YEARS OLD, fresh out of university, she decided to take a walk – a long walk – on the Appalachian National Scenic Trail (AT).[1] The AT spans 2,190 miles of the eastern United States, from Georgia to Maine, along the rugged spine of the ancient Appalachian Mountains.[2] It is one of the longest, and toughest, continuous footpaths in the world, and its physical and mental challenges are legendary. In addition to the extreme distance, which takes most hikers several months to cover, the trail's elevation gain equals climbing Mount Everest sixteen times. The main course includes treacherous stream crossings, ice storms, and hungry bears, as well as blisters, shin splints, and hypothermia – all with a side dish of fear, doubt, and loneliness.[3]

Initially, Davis had hoped a family member or friend would join her for the trek, but none could commit to the time and physical demands of the journey. So, she decided – much to her mother's consternation – to go it alone. Choosing to walk for months on end by herself, and making peace with that decision, was one of the first hurdles she had to clear, even before taking her first steps. "One thing I realized on the trail is there's this cultural stigma or shame around solitude," she said. Before hitting the AT, even dining solo in her school's cafeteria felt awkward. "Eating by myself was something that was uncomfortable or socially unacceptable," said Davis.

Other potential drawbacks of being on her own were loneliness and a lack of stimulation. "I was really scared going into it that I was going to be bored and lonely. I thought that was going to be one of the biggest obstacles," she said. Davis weathered many of those challenges and more;

on one section of trail, she came across someone who had committed suicide. At particularly tough moments like that, she longed for comfort from another person at first, but, she said, "There are also really positive parts about being alone through those experiences. And I never felt lonely, that was a surprise."

Once Davis had committed to "thru-hiking" the AT, or backpacking its length continuously, the question most people asked was, Why? They wondered, Did Davis think it was going to be easy? Was she running away from something in the "real" world? No and no. Davis walked to fully embrace her new, postcollegiate independence and to learn more about herself. "There was this inner desire to be out there on my own, sort of in terms of personal discovery, to see what I was capable of, and just to have more flexibility traveling solo versus with a partner," she said.

Davis experienced moments of joy with the beauty, freedom, and simplicity of trail life, but she knew that walking all day every day would be a chore, a challenge, and the type of education earned the hard way. So, why would anyone *choose* to suffer like that? "Certainly, every day you're sort of choosing the challenge. But it's clear pretty quickly, I think, on an endeavor such as the Appalachian Trail that you're growing and learning and changing along the way, and it's a difficult process, but very positive," she said.

PEOPLE, NOT PUPPETS; OR, THE IMPORTANCE OF CHOICE

Imagine for a moment that Davis had been *forced* to leave her warm home and loving family to trek the AT. In that circumstance, many of the challenges would have been the same, but her autonomy – the freedom to do what she wants – would have been absent. As we know from Chapter 3, the inability to conduct our own individual orchestras adversely impacts our inner symphony, our sense of well-being. When we can make autonomous decisions, we are generally happier and/or less depressed. Choosing to do anything, even something potentially unpleasant, is more important than not being able to steer our own destiny.[4] Clearly, having a sense of meaningful choice is key to life satisfaction. But why?

Choice is a complicated issue. Some findings suggest that culture, gender, education, and socioeconomic status factor into the desire for, and expectation of, choice.[5–10] How we make decisions is a fundamental question in social science, and others have devoted whole books to the fascinating topic. Allowing for that complexity, we know that humans, in general, like having some decision-making capability, or at least the perception of it. If we're at a restaurant and the server hands us a salad when we ordered a cheeseburger, we're unhappy. Even if he tells us the salad is better for our cholesterol level and we're stuck with it, we may feel disempowered, even outraged, and storm out of the restaurant. American fiction writer and author of *A Wrinkle in Time* Madeleine L'Engle (1918–2007) explained it this way: "Because to take away a man's freedom of choice, even his freedom to make the wrong choice, is to manipulate him as though he were a puppet and not a person."[11]

In solitude, as with any human experience, choice is an important driver. In the stories we have shared so far, of hermits and hikers and others who go off-grid and alone for long stretches, all shared the conscious decision to step away from society. Those individuals endure extreme conditions deprived of food, comfort, and physical companionship because choice is a powerful source of motivation. Consider the life of Igjugårjuk, an Inuit shaman who communicated with spirits – through solitude and suffering – to find solutions to quandaries brought to him by his community.[12] We know something of his life in northern Canada from Danish Greenlandic anthropologist and polar explorer Knud Rasmussen. From 1921 to 1924, Rasmussen (who was part Inuit and spoke their native language) traveled 20,000 miles across the top of North America documenting Arctic geography and people.[13]

During the journey, Rasmussen stayed with Igjugårjuk and learned how he had become a shaman, which involved spending thirty days alone and fasting in a small snow hut during a harsh Arctic winter. In "Observations on the Intellectual Culture of the Caribou Eskimos," Rasmussen documented Igjugårjuk's shamanic process of "almost sublime simplicity." Any time he had to confront a problem, heal a sick person, or weigh in on a hunting route, for example, Igjugårjuk would spend days looking for answers, he said, "out of the secrets of solitude." "These days of 'seeking for knowledge' are very tiring, for one must walk all the time, no matter what the weather is like and only rest in short snatches. I am usually quite done up, tired, not only in body but also in head, when I have found what I sought," said Igjugårjuk. "True wisdom is only to be found far away from people, out in the great solitude. ... Solitude and suffering open the human mind, and therefore a shaman must seek his wisdom there." Igjugårjuk did what few of us would, and although we wouldn't necessarily endorse his particular method for just anyone, we can respect that he chose that path to achieve a particular purpose in solitude.[14]

Many writers and philosophers through time, and today, also seem to have been partial to solitude as a path to knowledge. We've offered some extreme examples of them already in Chapter 1. There was also semi-reclusive American writer Henry David Thoreau, who lived alone at Walden Pond for two years, two months, and two days. (During that time, Thoreau wasn't a hermit, but he did choose a place removed from mainstream society, where his movements and thinking could be mostly solitary.[15]) Unlike Thoreau, Igjugårjuk, or Jennifer Pharr Davis, none of us need to walk thousands of miles or sequester ourselves in a snow hut or pondside cabin to prove our choice for solitude is sincere. But it does need to be an intentional act.

Take David Vincent, who said that becoming a solitude historian meant choosing a lifestyle of alone time among books and archived documents from which he could earn and communicate that knowledge. He lives in a fifteenth-century English farmhouse, surrounded by green fields dotted with sheep. For him, being "at home," even in that remote location, means family time. But every day he takes the gravel path leading from his house to his office "hut" (a converted pigsty, in fact), where he thinks, reads, and writes. If he were cast out of his home instead and forced to spend his days in the hut, it would cease to be a place where he can reset and focus his energy. Instead, he chooses to take that short but important journey to a peaceful space where he can follow his curiosity – alone.

"THE LAST OF HUMAN FREEDOMS"

There could be no starker comparison to the choiceful solitude we've talked about so far than to consider the experiences of prisoners in solitary confinement. Being "in solitary" – defined by the practice of physically and socially isolating a prisoner – typically means locking them in a small cell alone for twenty-two to twenty-three hours per day. Any time that prisoners have outside of that particular cage is generally used for showering or "recreating" in a somewhat larger cell. While in solitary confinement, most "perks" other prisoners may have (like getting letters or having visitors or counseling) are also stripped away.[16]

Today, the number of people kept in solitary confinement is notoriously hard to pinpoint. That's because they are not accurately recorded or many prison authorities are not forthcoming with those details.[17] The 2021 *Time-in-Cell* report by the Correctional Leaders Association and the Arthur Liman Center for Public Interest Law at Yale Law School contains the most comprehensive national data recorded on the number of prisoners in solitary confinement in America today. It estimates that, as of summer 2021, there were from 41,000 to 48,000 prisoners in isolation for an average of twenty-two hours per day for fifteen days or more.[18] And on the global level, according to a 2016 United Nations report,[19] hundreds of thousands of prisoners around the world are kept in solitary confinement, and that number is on the rise.

Solitary confinement is now understood to be the most extreme form of forced solitude and has had devastating effects on the physical and mental health of generations of prisoners.[20] It can cause adverse psychological effects (particularly for people already struggling with mental illness) within days of a prisoner's confinement and can be long lasting – even after they are released from prison.[19] Studies have found that being kept separate with few or no daily interactions with other people can lead to "anxiety, depression, impulse control disorder, social withdrawal, lethargy, apathy, self-harming, and suicidal behavior."[16]

Researchers have been recording the psychological, psychiatric, and neurological effects of isolation for decades.[21] Some of the earliest analysis was in the 1960s, when researchers looked at what impacts being a prisoner of war (POW) had on twenty Canadian servicemen. They studied the POWs in contrast to their biological brothers who had also served but had not been held captive. Even twenty years after they had been released, the effects were prominent in the POWs, and the enduring psychological and psychiatric differences in the brothers were profound. The POWs had anxiety, depression, and memory impairment at rates four to five times higher than their siblings. All the study participants did electroencephalograms, or EEGs, a test that measures electrical activity in the brain. Those showed that, because of what they had endured, the POWs had suffered long-term changes to their brains. Those were reflected in adverse impacts to their coordination, balance, speech, reflexes, and physical sensations.[22]

Subsequent studies have reinforced those findings, showing that brain abnormalities were the same in prisoners who either had suffered head trauma (serious enough to knock them out) *or* had been in solitary confinement.[23] Some of the most recent neurological research, studying the effects of isolation on mice, shows that their neurons had shrunk in the sensory and motor parts of their brains. The effect was 20 percent shrinkage after one month of solitary confinement, which increased to 25 percent after three months.[24]

Solitary confinement is now considered torture by the United Nations, which, in 2015, adopted a resolution on the treatment of prisoners (the so-called Nelson Mandela Rules).[25] The guidelines restrict the use of solitary as a measure of last resort and dictate the humane conditions that must be upheld when it is used. Nevertheless, the practice still endures in extreme forms. That desire of some humans to strip others of freedom and dignity has created a lot of difficult feelings around the idea of solitude, particularly in the Western world. How did we arrive at using forced solitude as punishment, and what can it teach us about solitude for the rest of us?

Ironically, the practice of putting prisoners in solitary confinement grew out of the prison *reform* movement of the late eighteenth century.[26] British prison reformer John Howard advocated a three-pronged strategy of religious study, hard labor, and solitary confinement.[27] Benjamin Rush (1746–1813), a social reformer, physician, and US "founding father," picked up on those ideas. He wrote, "Solitude and darkness are known to have a powerful influence on the mind. When the avenue of external sense is shut, and every accession of ideas from without precluded – the soul becomes an object to herself, her agitations subside: and her faculties tend to the natural equipoise."[28]

In short, Rush and other activists like him believed that being solitary, with zero outside input, would reform criminal minds, promote penitence, and restore a kind of spiritual equilibrium. They were right, in a way, about the power of limiting outside stimuli, but they hadn't considered that, in the extreme, the practice could be very harmful. Nevertheless, in 1790, the first "penitentiary" block with individual cells was built at a Pennsylvania prison with the intent of rescuing inmates from crowded, disease-ridden, riotous conditions prevalent elsewhere. It was also meant to help them seek forgiveness and salvation – all day, every day, in total isolation.[29] The new practice was a "social innovation" meant to be a humane opportunity, not a punishment, but it didn't turn out that way.

The first institution built entirely to keep inmates "in solitary" was the Eastern State Penitentiary, which opened its doors (and enclosed its residents) in 1829, in what is now North Philadelphia.[30] Its small, concrete, one-man cells were strung along corridors radiating out like wheel spokes from a central surveillance axle. Prisoners were confined to their tiny cells, where they either wove fabric or made shoes or furniture, and their only human contact for the length of their sentence was with corrections officers. Author Charles Dickens visited Eastern State in 1842 and wrote about its "solitary horrors" in his travelogue "American Notes for General Circulation." He said, "Standing at the central point, and looking down these dreary passages, the dull repose and quiet that prevails, is awful. ... He is a man buried alive; to be dug out in the slow round of years; and in the meantime, dead to everything but torturing anxieties and horrible despair."[31]

The inmates at Eastern State had virtually no human contact, and it was clear to the *Bleak House* author that the deprivation was taking a psychological toll. "I am only the more convinced that there is a depth of terrible endurance in it which none but the sufferers themselves can fathom, and which no man has a right to inflict upon his fellow-creature. I hold this slow and daily tampering with the mysteries of the brain, to be immeasurably worse than any torture of the body," he said.[31] Despite the observations of Dickens and others who believed the practice was inhumane, Eastern State became the model for several hundred prisons around the world (including in Britain).

Annual reports of the prisoners' activities presented a picture of a perfect system where offenders "enjoyed" daily labor and occasional religious teachings.[32] But, for many, Eastern State was not the envisioned sanctuary but rather a "living death," as some prisoners referred to it, and accounts emerged of harsh retribution imposed on inmates who attempted to make contact with others. Punishments like iron gagging, darkening of the "God's eye" skylight in their cell, and removal of daily tasks and reading materials were regularly used as disciplinary methods to enforce complete confinement. Those methods succeeded mainly in promoting and escalating bad behavior.[33]

Given the spikes in misconduct and clear suffering of inmates, over time, extreme isolation seemed like a failed experiment at Eastern State. But the practice of solitary confinement caught on anyway and was commonplace until 1890, when the US Supreme Court heard a case involving a convicted murderer kept in solitary on "death row" in Colorado.[34] The High Court ruled in favor of the inmate, who had argued that being kept in extreme solitude prior to execution was unconstitutional (citing the Eighth Amendment, which protects against "cruel and unusual punishments"). "It seems to us that ... the solitary confinement to which the prisoner was subjected ... was an additional punishment of the most important and painful character, and is, therefore, forbidden," according to the Court.[34]

After that, the use of solitary confinement wasn't as widespread as it had been, but it was – and still is – used as a punitive device in some places. As a punishment within a punishment, it is intended to break the spirits of those perceived as noncompliant. In his book *Long Walk to Freedom*, former political prisoner and South African president Nelson Mandela described many horrors of modern confinement.[35] Beginning in 1964, Mandela spent eighteen years on Robben Island, a maximum security prison six miles from Cape Town across shark-infested waters. Beatings, torture, and hard labor were commonplace, as was solitary confinement – the punishment prisoners dreaded above all others. "I found solitary confinement the most forbidding aspect of prison life. There is no end and no beginning; there is only one's mind, which can begin to play tricks. Was that a dream or did it really happen? One begins to question everything," Mandela wrote.[35]

During the Islamic Revolution in the 1980s, political protester Shokoufeh Sakhi was imprisoned for eight years. She spent nearly two years of that time in extreme solitude, including nearly nine months in a grave-like chamber known as a Haj Davood coffin. In an interview about that time with researchers at Queen Mary University of London, Sakhi recalled how paradoxically *social* the punishment felt. Malicious guards used solitary confinement to reinforce the power dynamic and to crush the will of inmates. "So the authority, the guards, they become the only people and they want to really reduce your relationship to the world to *that* kind of relationship: you and your torturer," she told the researchers.[36]

Yet Sakhi, now an independent scholar and researcher of imprisonment and the self,[37] could understand that the physical solitude itself wasn't the main problem but rather the psychological dynamics between captor and captive. She said she actively tried to balance that dynamic by focusing on the relationships that continued to thrive inside her own consciousness. "They try to take our world away," she said. "Solitary confinement – sensory deprivation – is an attempt to remove a person from their existence, from the world. But we have a past, we have an imagination for the future, we have a world. That world is within us."[36]

During her imprisonment, Sakhi worked to maintain that pocket of freedom in her own mind. Viktor Frankl (1905–97), an Austrian psychologist, Holocaust survivor, and author of *Man's Search for Meaning* (1946), wrote eloquently about that from his own experiences. "Everything can be taken from a man but one thing: the last of human freedoms – to choose one's attitude in any given set of circumstances, to choose one's own way," said Frankl. This is a powerful idea that can benefit all of us, as we'll see, no matter what type of solitude we are experiencing.[38]

There is obviously a large gulf between what we've talked about regarding solitary confinement and the experience of everyday solitude for the rest of us. Beyond the dark reality of the most extreme forms of solitude, and the adverse effects they have on prisoners, is not punishment but opportunity. The difference comes down to choice – deciding when and how to be alone – which is key to success in solitude. Luckily, most of us have a lot of freedom in our daily lives to do that, but recently, some people also got a glimpse of that other, dimmer place and had to figure out how to navigate it.

LOCKED DOWN AND ALONE

The most significant period of social isolation many of us have ever experienced occurred when the COVID-19 pandemic hit in early 2020. Depending on our circumstances, our "social distancing" confinement was more or less complete. We may have been living with others but been denied time with outside family and friends or living by ourselves with no physical contact with other people – sometimes for weeks or months at a time. Our routines were upended, and all but essential workers were told to stay home through waves of lockdowns.[39]

Even early in the restrictions, mental health experts were sounding the alarm that the physical threat of the virus could be matched by the mental menace of loneliness with all of its negative emotions and impacts. The talk of being lonesome was not new – a so-called epidemic of loneliness already had been making headlines in the years prior to the pandemic – but the lockdowns fueled a heightened urgency to study its effects. Researchers and policy makers alike were concerned that social isolation could make us lonelier than ever before, and in larger numbers than ever experienced, and that we would continue to be scarred by our time alone potentially for years to come.[40]

Given the grave realities of solitary confinement we've already talked about, it was reasonable to think that forced isolation imposed by lockdowns could have a deleterious impact. But research done on the effect of lockdowns showed a different reality, at least for most people. A University College London study compared predictors of loneliness from more than 30,000 people prepandemic to more than 60,000 participants during the pandemic. They found that the "risk factors for loneliness were nearly identical before and during the pandemic." That is, certain groups had a higher risk of being lonely, including young adults (age eighteen to thirty years), women, people with little education or low income, people living alone and in cities, and those with preexisting mental and physical health challenges. Surprisingly, a group often highlighted as "at risk" for loneliness, adults age sixty years and older, were less likely to be lonely before and during the pandemic than people half their age or younger.[41] Other studies from early in the pandemic reported similar findings, and in subsequent research, the data remained consistent.[42,43]

Although there was a slight rise in the rates of loneliness during the pandemic compared to the "before" times, that uptick was nowhere near the level of widespread distress many experts had predicted.[44–46] Nor was it necessarily reflected in people living or sheltering (isolating intentionally to protect their health) alone.[47] A few studies have begun to look at why the twin epidemic of loneliness did not come to pass. First and foremost, if you were not a person prone to loneliness before the pandemic, you likely weren't during it either. Those with established, frequent, and quality social support in the time leading up to the restrictions carried that as a kind of shield against loneliness.[48] Generally, the amount of social support people have from family, friends, and colleagues correlates with a lack of psychological distress and an improved quality of life.[49–53] Importantly, that backing does not need to be face-to-face. During the pandemic, those who maintained their social base with the help of technology, for example, enjoyed the same psychological benefits as meeting in person.[54–56] High levels of social support facilitate what's called "psychological flexibility," another important predictor of loneliness – or the lack of it – during the pandemic. Some research backed the idea that psychological flexibility may affect the type of coping strategies that individuals use during adverse events like isolation, and how effective they are.[57]

Given the dire predictions, it was surprising (even for us solitude researchers) that countless people during the pandemic recognized for the first time, or reignited, a desire for solitude. Being able to be alone, and happily so, was worn as a badge of honor, and everything from tweets to T-shirts appeared with sayings like "I was social distancing before it was cool."[58] In August 2020, a new word appeared on the Urban Dictionary website of slang: *isolophilia* (and its related *isolophile*), defined as "having a strong affection and preference for solitude."[59]

The mainstream media, in general, amplified narratives of hyper-lonely singletons, but many people pushed back against that characterization. In one May 2020 article, the *New York Times* published experiences of some living-alone adults during the pandemic.[60] While there were plenty who expressed that they were struggling with a lack of physical contact, others did not. Phyllis Coletta, age sixty-three, a schoolteacher from Seattle, said, "I think the assumption of this *New York Times* effort to reach out to people who live alone is kind of like underlying pity, or pathos, like 'you poor people stuck all by yourselves.' Listen, don't cry for me . . . cause this is friggin' fabulous," she said. "Living alone is amazing."

PREFERENCE FOR SOLITUDE

What is the nature of people who can and even *want* to be in solitude in the way Coletta described? What does it mean to have a "preference for solitude"? There are well-worn assumptions, for sure, such as that introverts like to be left to their own devices. And even some early solitude studies fed into "loner" stereotypes by concluding that people who prefer solitude are lonelier and more prone to psychological problems.[61] That assessment may sound contrary to what we said earlier about the power of choice in positive solitude – and it is in some fundamental ways – and that's because of what many researchers used to believe (and still do in some cases) about people who desire time alone.[62]

The study of who leans into solitude and why has always been a complicated one for researchers and laypeople alike because a lot of people believe that choosing one thing (like alone time) means rejecting another (time with other people). For them, having a "preference for solitude" – that's the term researchers used – was synonymous with people who liked being by themselves more than they liked being with others.[63] Because humans are defined as social creatures, preferring to be alone implied that there must be something wrong with those people. As we gather more information and evidence alongside other solitude researchers, however, we can see that solitude and our relationships with it are more nuanced. But this long-held assumption is so entrenched that it cannot easily be switched off. Reframing a "preference for solitude" as something positive and productive is a bit like turning around an aircraft carrier. Slowing the forward momentum of what's already in motion takes a while, and only once that's done can we reverse course. Understanding what has come before in the research on preference for solitude can help in that effort.

Researchers decades ago painted only part of the picture, and predilections toward solitude have never been properly measured. The first studies looking at why some people prefer solitude took place in the 1990s, when University of Santa Clara social psychologist Jerry Burger created the Preference for Solitude Scale (psychologists have a scale for everything!).[64] That series of experiments had some interesting, and uncontroversial, findings – such as those who prefer solitude liked to read for pleasure and were less bored than others when they were alone – but the scale itself was flawed. The study specifically pitted social against solo time by asking participants to choose between statements including "I enjoy being around other people" versus "I enjoy being by myself" and "I try to structure my day so that I always have some time to myself" versus "I try to structure my day so that I always am doing something with someone."

Using this approach, participants had to "choose" which they like better: people or no people. An expressed preference for solitude was equated with disliking time with other people (those researchers also concluded that those participants were lonelier and more neurotic). On the opposite side of the coin, lacking a preference for solitude meant that those folks preferred to be with others and hated being alone, yet another characterization lacking the necessary nuance. There was no room in the scale to accurately represent the person who loves solitude but also deeply values time with friends and family – or the one who chooses company most of the time but very much needs some periods of time alone.

Ultimately, Burger's model emphasized "social avoidance," and that created a false dichotomy, making preference for solitude seem like a black-and-white issue. That set the stage for how alone time lovers would be evaluated for decades. That work shows us that when researchers don't measure the nuance of choice, they find time and again that choosing solitude is a sign that someone has psychological problems. But as we've seen in our research, there's much more dimension to choosing alone time. It has little to do with getting away from someone or something, as prior research suggests, and more about moving toward ourselves and something valuable, interesting, or otherwise appealing in solitude.

That said, simply choosing solitude doesn't necessarily mean you'll benefit from it or be content in that space. We can prefer solitude for a number of reasons, both productive and not, and understanding those circumstances – sorting out *why* we're choosing it – can be key to it being a positive experience in our daily lives. Knowing more about the phenomena of choice and motivation, in general, can help us arrive at a more accurate and complete description of the "right" reasons for having a preference for solitude.[65,66]

THE DRIVE TO THRIVE IN SOLITUDE

"Why did the chicken cross the road?" goes a popular riddle that seems to have been around forever. "To get to the other side" is the common reply. In this simplistic scenario, the chicken's motivation is clear-cut, giving the impression that making choices and decisions is an easy process. We humans can make hundreds or even thousands of choices per day almost on autopilot. Cereal or scone? Walk or take the bus? Binge-watch a fifth episode of *Game of Thrones* or clean the house (that's an easy one!)? While it's important for our mental health to be able to make all of those decisions for ourselves, which choices we make is not as important, or frankly as interesting (at least for us researchers), as what is *motivating* us to pick one thing over another.[67] For example, imagine you're offered an ice cream but you opt for an apple instead. Maybe you picked the fruit out of a desire to be healthy, in which case the apple probably tastes not like ice cream but pretty good. But maybe you don't like the way your trousers fit, and you'd feel guilty indulging in the ice cream; in that circumstance, the apple likely isn't very satisfying. In this scenario, choosing the apple for the "right" reason is key to enjoying the experience of eating it.

In truth, there are a lot of forces motivating humans to behave in one way or another. Those drivers could be biological, social, cognitive, or psychological. We authors are most interested, of course, in the psychological reasons nudging us one way or another. For example, we can be driven to get out of bed each morning by the desire for an external reward (a paycheck) or be motivated by something we find inherently rewarding (a meaningful job).[68] Which is more impactful to our well-being? The paycheck is likely necessary and useful, but being motivated instead by what we feel is meaningful will likely sustain us more in the long term and help us feel fulfilled.

Whether or not we are making decisions in this "self-determined" way also influences the quality of our lives. As in the preceding example, the drive compelling us to choose an apple over ice cream (or anything, really) is characterized as self-determined if that choice is consistent with the principles of the person doing the choosing. According to self-determination theory, based on the work of psychologists Edward Deci and Richard Ryan, most of our high-quality experiences (and overall life satisfaction) stem from doing things that we truly care about or from acting in ways that support our personal values and beliefs. To do something in a self-determined way means to do it in pursuit of growth, knowledge, or fulfillment. If our motivation is self-determined, we have the sense that we have some control over our choices and can influence our destinies. By engaging in self-determined behaviors, our need for autonomy (the importance of which we covered in Chapter 3) is also satisfied.[67]

In relation to solitude, the critical distinction around self-determined motivation has only recently been measured. In one study, researchers in Ohio and California directed participants (nearly 1,000 high school and university students) to think about the statement "When I spend time alone, I do so because . . ." For the researchers to pinpoint motivation for solitude, participants reviewed a long list of reasons – both self-determined and not – and rated how relevant each reason was to a preference for alone time. In the study, autonomous reasons for choosing solitude included, for example, "It sparks my creativity," "I enjoy the quiet," and "I can engage in activities that really interest me." On the flip side, some nonautonomous reasons included "I feel anxious when I'm with others" and "I don't feel liked when I'm with others." The researchers found that motivation is critical to determining if solitude is a positive experience with beneficial outcomes. They could also see that autonomous motivation is related to a focus on personal growth and self-acceptance, while nonautonomous reasons for seeking alone time were linked to more loneliness and depression.[69]

We heard a lot about choice, motivation, and preference for positive solitude from our own study participants as well. Mainly, they choose it because of what they're gaining in that space and the positive impact that time has on their lives in general. As we saw in Chapter 4, beneficial experiences in solitude run the gamut: spending time alone to relax, be creative, learn new skills, be authentic, set priorities, gain a new perspective, or simply think. At times, solitude offers some combination of those attributes. "Solitude is a deliberate choice, it's when I decide to do introspection, reflection, self-awareness, self-love, self-care, all of those things come into that space where I am trying to realize the truth about something, or I'm trying to understand why," said Kaamil from Bangladesh.

We also saw in our research that preference for solitude can be motivated by both nature and nurture. Like Kaamil, spending time alone became a habit for many when they were young, or it was a behavior modeled for them when they were children by the adults in their orbit, or perhaps it's simply "in their nature." Whatever moved our study participants to seek solitude, we as researchers could see the importance of recognizing a broad spectrum of motivations, and we felt the urgency in recasting the term "preference for solitude" as a positive, proactive, and mentally healthy pursuit rather than a negative one focused on avoiding others.

That thinking was solidified when meeting people with rich social lives who, nevertheless, prefer solitude and seek it out in any number of ways – renting a cabin, going for a long drive, or sitting on a park bench – by themselves. In that vein, we heard from Cliff, a widower in his sixties who takes occasional solo road trips to his childhood village in England or sometimes sits alone in a café near his home reading the news. "It's not that I don't enjoy doing those things with someone else, I do, but that has a different quality to being able to do these things as an individual on my own, at times," he said. Although Cliff is now dating someone new, he still enjoys the freedom of getting away by himself. "I don't want to spend my entire life on my own, these are just sort of periods of time, sometimes they can be quite brief, but they are all important to my sense of comfort and well-being," he said.

In our research, we also heard people describe themselves as being "born to solitude" (and by some who are not necessarily introverted). Participants called solitude "a defining part of me," "the air I breathe,"

"the water I swim in." Helena from California told us, "It's become clear to me that it's something that I need, that it's not something that's wrong with me. That it's just the way I've been built, the way I always have been if I think back to myself playing as a child. This has always been a big part of my life and the need is not going to go away." Still others feel they are motivated to spend time alone because they learned to follow the lead of the adults in their lives. "I don't know if it's more innate for myself or rather it's something that I had modeled for me or I had learned it at such a very early age that it just becomes kind of like ingrained in your sense that this is something I've seen people do and I know how to do this too," said Cate, age thirty-nine, from France.

Others we spoke with became accustomed to time alone in childhood and have continued the practice throughout their lives. "I'm happy with my own company, I'm sort of comfortable with being alone and sort of not needing to be the center of attention," said Scott, age sixty, from England. "When I was a child, I used to be playing in the garden, or I was out on my bike, just sort of pottering about, generally on my own. And then when we moved to a larger village, and there were a few children around then, I did make friends and have playmates and what have you, but again I was just still quite as happy, and sometimes happier, to be doing my own thing," he said.

We also spoke with plenty of folks who described themselves as "sociable" introverts who love spending time with family and friends but who nevertheless have a strong preference for solitude. Alex from Armenia explained it succinctly: "I'm quite independent. I'm a very social person as well." Gary, age seventy, told us, "I've basically decided that I don't need other people's company too much. And yet if I'm in a situation where I'm in company – as the wife said – I tend to be the life and soul of the party for some reason." We also heard from self-described extroverts who rely just as heavily as introverts on time in solitude. "I'm someone who can put a little bubble 'round me when I need to and focus on my stuff and not feel too intruded upon by other things," said Monica from England. "And I get a lot from being with people, so that's fine. I get energy from that."

It's important to consider that, even when people call themselves introverts and attribute their love of solitude to that personality trait, there is generally more to it than that. Humans reflexively try to make sense or order out of complexity by categorizing everything around us, but those attempts at simplification often turn out either not to be true or not to be the whole story. Psychologist Fritz Heider proposed "attribution theory" to explain the tendency humans have to interpret and explain behavior (our own and others') by ascribing to it attributes like personality, effort, ability, or even luck.[70] It's natural to do that, but it can be a very limiting way of looking at who we are and what we're capable of. Correlating introversion with a general love of solitude is misleading and gets in the way of answering the question "Who's solitude for?" Ultimately, people who don't consider themselves introverts may assume solitude isn't for them, but it's as much for them as anyone else.

At this moment, researchers don't know whether there is a link between introversion and *enjoyment* of solitude. We and other researchers have not found evidence that introverts necessarily enjoy or gain more benefits from solitude. In fact, in a study of 320 undergraduates (most around age twenty), introverts reported experiencing lonely solitude more frequently than extroverts.[71] Why would people who are assumed to like solitude be more bummed out there? It's a confusing finding that may nonetheless have a simple answer. It may come down to the way introversion is typically defined and measured by researchers.

Introversion is generally defined as being reserved and quiet – and, mainly, *not* extroverted (characterized as being talkative and full of energy).[72] This narrow set of criteria does not capture a lot of "in-between" folks. For now, the simplest way to answer the question "Who's solitude for?" is "Most everybody." Introverts may love solitude, but many extroverts do too. Whether we consider ourselves introverts or extroverts, or we're labeled that by someone else, finding something interesting and meaningful in solitude is more vital to doing well in that space than the personality type we identify with.[66]

That said, it may seem that solitude comes easily to some people and that they are always content there. But solitude doesn't always draw us in because we will feel great, or be focused and curious, within it. Sometimes we may choose to be alone because it can facilitate processing difficult emotions or working through a challenge we have yet to resolve.[69] Even people with a preference for solitude don't always feel shiny and happy when they're there, but that doesn't mean it's not ultimately a positive place for them. One of our study participants, Sheila in England, described solitude as her "therapy time": "Sometimes I'm churning over bad things, be that bad things that have personally happened to me in the past, or the bad things that are happening to the world at the moment and I churn everything over and it gives me . . . that little space that I need to be me," she said.

There's a big difference between that kind of discomfort in solitude and choosing solitude for reasons we'd characterize (not so scientifically) as "not so good." Those "wrong" reasons for choosing solitude are cases in which we feel psychologically forced into solitude, for example, when being "stood up" by someone or excluded from a social event or group. Some people may even choose solitude as a coping mechanism to avoid additional social injury. Others also prefer to spend time on their own because they're feeling socially anxious, depressed, or ostracized.[69,73–75]

It's important to distinguish between having an aversion to others based on social dysfunction and using solitude as a "break" from others. Of course, plenty of kids, as well as adults, choose to "play" or read alone, and happily, for various periods of time and for a variety of positive reasons – and with positive results.[71,76,77] But social exclusion is a different and painful experience that can start at a very young age and may explain why some children withdraw on the playground or in the classroom, and stay withdrawn from society as they age. Many developmental psychologists who study social exclusion in children have demonstrated its impacts on decreased learning motivation at school, in adverse relationships with peers, and on later development of depression and anxiety.[78–81]

Perhaps because of concern for young people who are retreating from the outside world, most of the research on preferring solitude has been done with young people and "emerging" adults (age eighteen to twenty-five years). In those cases, and in the few studies that have been done with adults and older adults, the results have been mixed. Generally, having a preference for solitude either correlated with having negative characteristics like loneliness, social anxiety, and depression or didn't seem either to help or to hurt.[63,82,83] All this research really tells us is that some people prefer to be alone when they feel they don't fit in among others.

On the other hand, and as we've talked about, there is ample and clear evidence that choosing solitude because you find it meaningful is, in fact, a positive thing. That type of motivation is powerful and can overcome a lot of hurdles on the road to acknowledging the potential benefits of solitude. But sometimes, as we'll see next, that requires rising above resistance or overcoming negative messaging associated with solitude.

REFRAMING ALONE TIME

Both time spent alone and time spent in the company of others can sometimes feel lonely, and there's good reason to talk publicly about loneliness. It's important to raise awareness of mental health problems, including depression, anxiety, loneliness, and many others, which, historically, we have kept to ourselves. These conversations help us feel understood and validated by others and encourage people to open up about their own difficult experiences.[84,85] (We look more directly at the implications of loneliness in the coming chapters.) At the same time, focusing on a mistaken assumption that time alone leads to loneliness – which humans have done throughout history and up to the present day – may come at an unintended cost. Conforming to societal norms telling us that spending time with others is paramount, and that solitude is a negative state, can adversely impact anyone's experiences when they are alone, and perhaps especially for those who are forced to be alone. Basically, we know that expecting that we'll be lonely can be a self-fulfilling prophecy in solitude, but can we shift that mind-set?

Two recent studies illustrate how expectations of time alone can affect that space and hint at how reframing our thinking may be possible. In a first-of-its-kind study,[86] 243 participants (age eighteen to seventy-three years) recruited by Harvard University researchers were part of a lab experiment (unlike many US-based psychology studies, nearly half of this sample were participants of color). Each subject reported their mood at the start of the experiment, and then, to understand better how expectations of solitude actually affect that time alone, they read one of three possible descriptions of solitude from a computer screen.

One of those passages, which the researchers called "Solitude Benefits," described time alone as a positive experience with a variety of potential upsides, including that it helps regulate emotions while encouraging creativity and well-being. By comparison, a "Loneliness De-Biasing" passage explained that feelings of loneliness were natural and common, effectively relieving participants of the baggage of feeling that there's something wrong with them for experiencing loneliness. In a final, neutral text, participants read about a topic unrelated to solitude.

After reading their respective descriptions, all participants then sat alone and waited for ten minutes, then again reported their moods. With both the neutral passage and the one that talked about loneliness being natural, participants reported a more negative mood at the end of those ten minutes than when they had started the study. However, those who had been reminded of the benefits of solitude did not experience that drop and instead maintained a positive mood. This study demonstrates that the right expectations can help maintain well-being even during a (pretty uninspiring and) required period of solitude.

A second study[87] – one that we authors did ourselves – also showed that being exposed to negative notions has an impact on solitude. In our version, we gave instructions via video chat to participants in their own homes. To mask the purpose of the study, we asked our subjects a broad range of questions about emotion, but embedded within those were two specific conditions we were most interested in. The first condition was tested in our "Lonely Expectation" experiment, in which participants were told, "For the next part of the study, we will ask you to spend fifteen minutes on your own. First, please find a comfortable, private, and quiet spot in your house. We ask you to sit with your thoughts for this period and avoid doing other activities. *Because nobody else is around, time spent sitting with your thoughts can be challenging and even lonely.* So that you can really sit with your thoughts, please put away and do not check your phone or computer during this time." The second video, like the Harvard study, talked about benefits, and we told participants that solitude can "*give us a chance to get to know ourselves, to explore our wishes, desires, and priorities, and think through any interesting events.*"

Our findings also support the idea that having prior notions about solitude (even ones that are only recently introduced to our thinking)

appears to have at least a modest effect on that time. While the participants who expected to feel lonely when alone felt just as calm sitting
quietly in their homes as did those who expected to benefit, they actually
felt lonelier when it was suggested that they would be. Their expectations
acted like a self-fulfilling prophecy, and they also felt other negative
emotions, such as "distressed" or "irritable," indicating their time alone
was more unpleasant on the whole. The results seem clear-cut, but as
researchers, we have to consider that there could be other factors influencing how people felt, including how lonely they were when they
started the study and how safe their space at home felt. We did not
evaluate those factors directly, so we can only speculate that thinking
that solitude is bad for us makes it unpleasant, but our work provides a
solid foundation for further study.

Our study and others have shown that specifically carrying negativity
into solitude can taint that space, but there are scant data on whether we
can change that mind-set once there and turn time alone into a positive,
meaningful experience. Yet there is anecdotal evidence that it is possible,
at least for some people. Terry, age sixty-eight, from England taught us
about the power of purposefully seeking solitude and setting intentions for
that time. "I think solitude involves a choice, even if it's only a choice to
embrace it. The aloneness may be thrust upon you, but the attitude you
take to it, I think, makes it either loneliness or solitude," she said. Terry has
lived alone for most of her life, while working as a community counselor,
but it was only when she seized her time alone as a place of relaxation, joy,
and discovery that it became just that. "There is something different about
somebody living alone and choosing to embrace the aloneness, and
calling it solitude," she said. "I've felt that embracing it and making it a
special time, which was not just thrust upon me but freely chosen, made it
a better experience. It made the whole experience of being alone better."

In our work, we continue to investigate the impact of past research and
societal norms regarding solitude and our ability to reframe them in our
own lives. So far, we've learned that there is potentially much to be gained
by challenging the dominant narrative that solitude must be lonely. There is
also power in understanding our motivations and intentions when making
the choice to embrace solitude. Moving on, we can consider how and why
well-being hinges on balancing our social and solo needs.

CHAPTER 6

Balancing Solitude with Social Time

BEFORE THE COVID-19 PANDEMIC ENVELOPED the world in early 2020, Colin Foad had always carved out time to be alone, and he valued those opportunities, often on train journeys, to relax and unwind. Although he was often the first to strike up a conversation when friends or colleagues were around, he did his best thinking and reflecting while working on his own. Colin is a psychologist and fellow solitude researcher who described himself as a mix of introvert and extrovert with occasional swings in either direction. For some "together but alone" time, he also played rugby, where he was able to focus his energy on his own experience and enjoyment of the game. All in all, his life felt largely balanced between his time alone and with others.

When the pandemic lockdowns began in England, Colin's firstborn, Freddy, was just one year old, and his daughter Olive was born a bit later. With two babies at home, he had few opportunities to break away for moments of solitude, and like many people, Colin began to struggle. "There's the personal angle of only being three months into the job of full-time dad when the world gets turned upside down, which wasn't easy," he said. When being with his kids was the *only thing* he did with his time, Colin became more depleted than he'd ever been.

Meanwhile, Netta's neighbor Dorothy was having a very different experience. She was ninety-two years old and living alone when the pandemic struck. Before that, she had had trouble walking but still got out often enough to play bridge or meet friends for tea. Her life was a happy balance of social and solo time. During the period when health officials asked vulnerable people to stay home to protect themselves and

109

others from the virus, Dorothy was flung into full-time isolation for the first time in her life and, as a result, was depressed and lonely for a long period.

The pandemic threw off any semblance of balance between alone time and social activity for much of the planet and gave us researchers a rare opportunity to hear from people like Dorothy and Colin about what it meant to be pushed to extremes. It gave us a window into the meaning and value of both solitude and social interactions in our daily lives and what it means to have far too much of either. It also helped us see that the key to contentment may lie in balancing high-quality social relationships with positive experiences in solitude.

For Dorothy and Colin, and many others like them, there were only two ways of experiencing pandemic restrictions: too much time alone/not enough time with others or too much time with others/not enough time alone. In this chapter, we'll get at why neither extreme is ideal, which helps us sort out what balance between solitude and togetherness may look like for each of us, individually.

In our nonpandemic daily lives, we all split our time between interactions with others and time alone, and if we're lucky, we can tweak that balance according to our needs, preferences, and desires. For each individual, contentment generally relies on seriously considering what kind of person we are and honestly assessing our needs.[1] In the grand scheme, we may ask ourselves, Am I a person who needs to be away from people more than I need to be with them, or vice versa? On a more daily basis, we may inquire, Am I going through something and want companionship, or do I need time to myself to sort it out?

Imagine a seesaw, like the kind on playgrounds, balanced when the weight is even on each side. But, if a 60-pound kid sits on one side and a 150-pound adult plunks down on the other, the child is going to have a very unpleasant ride. When we talk about achieving equilibrium between solo and social time, the individual rests on one side and – in theory – their relationships "sit" on the other. If someone is spending all their time alone or, conversely, every minute with others, the seesaw remains weighed down on one side or the other. Only when we begin to sort out how much weight we should put on the side opposite ourselves, and start honoring that, will the seesaw be in balance.

We have heard a lot about balancing solo and social time from our research participants, less as a score being kept and more as a feeling of needing one versus the other at a particular moment. That's sometimes a reaction to having had too much interaction with others and needing "me time." The opposite was also expressed, as an "urge" to get out of one's own orbit and spend time with others. Some people seem to know instinctively when they need a solitude fix, or a game night with friends, but most of us develop an awareness of how to manage those desires over time. And even after recognizing those demands, balancing the solo and social takes active engagement, like exercising muscles. Singer-songwriter Bruce Springsteen put it this way in the 2019 documentary *Western Stars*: "There are two sides of the American character: the solitary side and the side that yearns for connection and community. That's just been a lifetime trip for me, trying to figure out how to get from one to the other, how to reconcile those two things."[2]

As we see it, there's no Team Solitude versus Team Social clash. We don't need to choose to commit ourselves to lives as either hermits or party animals. In fact, we probably shouldn't, according to famed British psychiatrist and writer Anthony Storr (1920–2001). In his work, Storr often challenged the dominant paradigm of psychology by expressing skepticism that relationships were the be-all and end-all of mental well-being and productivity. Storr stressed that being alone can also aid personal growth and achievement. "The happiest lives are probably those in which neither interpersonal relationships nor impersonal interests are idealized as the only way to salvation. The desire and pursuit of the whole must comprehend both aspects of human nature," he wrote.[3] The trick is to have equilibrium between the two: the right amount of social time to fulfill an evolutionary imperative and, alongside it, the ideal amount of solitude to reap its rewards. So how do we do *that*?

PEOPLE NEED PEOPLE

As solitude researchers, you may think we see little value in spending time with other people. But we know that, as great as solitude can be, we need to connect with others to be happy. That's at the heart of human life, and our relationships wield enormous influence over how we think and feel.[4,5] Time with others is how we share parts of ourselves and feelings of intimacy – experiences required to be satisfied with life. In the best of social moments, we can be who we are with others and, therefore, at the center of well-being.[6] Or, as researchers describe it, we exhibit "high-arousal" positive emotions – feelings of joy and excitement – in social situations.[7] Simply put, it's fun to be around others, and we are wired to seek that.

Humans are, in fact, among the most communal mammals – even more so than our highly social ape relatives.[8] We constantly adjust our behavior in exchange for positive social feedback and a sense that we belong.[9] Psychological benefits come with such bonding, and we are rewarded with positive emotions whenever we share resources, provide support, and exchange small talk, even with strangers.[10] Compared to great ape infants, human babies show earlier signs of cooperation and communication with adults. Studies have shown that human children succeed at imitating adults' gazes, actions, intentions, and behaviors at around twelve to sixteen months old, while it takes great ape babies at least a year longer.[8]

Biologists interpret those findings to mean that humans have developed skills to be in tune and connect with others, even those not directly related to us.[8] Human survival is not solely dependent on parents providing food and protection from predators. We must also develop the social and cognitive skills necessary to interact effectively in our communities. Some preliminary evidence suggests that infants' extended reliance on care and attention from adults – aka bonding – helps children gain skills essential to their survival. From a very young age, children imitate and practice those skills with caretakers and other adults (a child following around their parents with a mini cart/trolley of their own while shopping is both adorable and productive).[11]

Based on this understanding of humans as ultrasocial animals, the study of *too much* solitude is the goliath in the literature, examining its risks to our mental and physical health. That work shows us that, from an evolutionary perspective, acting out of sync with the social world can be costly for humans. The (many, many) studies on isolation suggest that most of the damage of being removed from social interaction is explained by the experience of loneliness.[12–14] For reasons we explored earlier in the book, the concepts of isolation, solitude, and loneliness are often conflated,[15] but of all three, loneliness is the most worrisome.

An understanding of what loneliness really is, and why we may experience it, can help us explain the reason solitude may scare us sometimes. We can perceive loneliness as an external state, the lack of another person in our physical orbit, but it's really an internal condition. It also seems entirely subjective; one individual may feel lonely at home while her family is away, but another might relish every minute of that experience.[16] But loneliness is, literally, part of our nature. Recent neuroscience research shows that we have "loneliness neurons" in our midbrains acting like biological alarms warning us when we need more (and more fulfilling) "people time."[17]

This physiological mechanism was particularly important millennia ago, when survival relied upon interdependence. Feeling lonely tells us that our place in the social order is threatened, and it can be useful in small amounts. It clues us in to the fact that our social networks are inadequate. Without that alarm system back then, we might have been lulled into an individual lifestyle (our own hut!), which may have put us at an evolutionary disadvantage (hungry lions!). This knowledge is helpful in motivating us to reconnect with others; it keeps societies cohesive for everyone's benefit.[18] But, just like other physiological reactions that have evolved to help us deal with threats – for example, that cortisol surge we get when we're scared that makes us vigilant and quick to escape predators[19] – loneliness is detrimental in persistent quantities.[18]

In fact, loneliness is experienced in much the same way as physical hunger. Researchers at the Massachusetts Institute of Technology and the Salk Institute for Biological Studies have shown some remarkable results around that idea. In their study, participants fasted in two separate ways – one group was not allowed to eat for ten hours, and the second group was not permitted to interact with (nearly) anyone for ten hours. After that time, those refraining from eating were shown alternating images of food and flowers, while those isolated from social interaction were shown images of flowers and groups of people happily cavorting.[17]

The researchers then scanned the brains of individuals in both groups and focused on the midbrain, an area where impulses for motivation and reward are housed. It's also a region packed with neurons linked to making and processing the neurotransmitter dopamine (which plays a role in feelings of pleasure). The researchers could see in the brain scans of both groups that areas associated with desire were activated in similar ways. The brains of the group forced to be loners (which consisted of young adults who, in general, enjoyed robust social networks outside of the lab) showed a similar response to images of social cues as the food-fasting group did to the images of pasta and berries. The researchers concluded that acute isolation causes a craving for people akin to actual hunger.[17]

Even if loneliness is mainly a relic from a time when our survival as a species depended on banding together, it can have a profound negative impact on our health, mentally and physically. For decades, researchers have been finding evidence linking loneliness and mortality.[20,21] The perception of social isolation is among the most painful of human experiences and has been shown to adversely impact immunity, blood pressure, and vascular health and, ultimately, to cause premature death. Human sensitivity to social rejection is so keen, in fact, that studies have shown that its discomfort is akin to physical pain. A growing body of neuroscience research is accumulating evidence that physical and social pain share common physiological mechanisms. Just as nerves react to touching a hot pan, we get signals from feeling dumped, left out, or overlooked that *something is wrong*.[22]

Anybody who has been picked last for a team in grade school understands the pain of social exclusion, and studies exemplifying the pain of ostracization and human responses to it are also popular in psychology. There are a few main formats many of those studies follow, but they show similar results. Sometimes participants are left out of a conversation among other participants (who are actually researchers pretending to ignore them).[23,24] Or participants play a digital "cyberball" game in which the other participants (again, researchers in disguise) refuse to pass the ball to the research subject.[25] Studies spanning decades and thousands of participants generally show that when people feel like they're being left out, their well-being suffers.[26–28] In recent studies, ostracized "targets" consistently expressed (via online and in-person study questionnaires) that they experienced a drop in fulfillment of basic needs like belonging, self-esteem, and control.[29]

Other work done as part of the Chicago Health, Aging, and Social Relations Study[30] followed 229 people, age fifty to sixty-eight years, for five years to explore the links, if any, between social isolation and health outcomes. Once per year, study participants filled out surveys in the lab that asked them about their time alone, loneliness, and depression, along with evaluating other factors, such as stress. Over time, the researchers statistically tested a chicken-and-egg question: which came first, loneliness or depression (or perhaps something else)? They found that loneliness made people depressed across time, and not the other way around. They also found that the effects couldn't be explained by objective social isolation variables like how many friends people spent time with. This latter finding is significant because it suggests that loneliness relies more on *how one feels* about their social time rather than *how much time* they actually spend in the presence of others.[31]

Even our early human ancestors had to distinguish between good- and poor-quality social setups.[32] Living with any ole hut mate didn't necessarily improve their lot. Understanding who was a true friend versus a dangerous foe was critical to their survival, and modern humans inherited that bias. Spending time with a so-called friend who puts us down, for example, isn't going to fulfill our need for a satisfying relationship; instead, it's likely to make us lonelier.

Without satisfying social time, we can become lonely and depressed, and those feelings make their way into all aspects of our everyday lives, solitude included.[33] But when we do achieve balance between solo and social, that has an altogether different impact. For example, in a study of 330 racially and culturally diverse teens in the greater Washington, DC, area, preferring solitude was related to depression, but only when those people didn't have sufficient social support from others. In cases of adequate support, the effect changed entirely, and there was good evidence that preference for solitude related to *less* depression.[34] Basically, when one perceives oneself as having good friends, one is less depressed in one's preference for solitude than those lacking social support outside of their time alone.

WITH LONELINESS, PERCEPTION IS REALITY

Despite clear evidence that loneliness can harm health, being on our own does not always trigger feelings of loneliness (we wouldn't have written a book about how great solitude can be if it did!). It turns out that perception plays a large part in one's subjective feeling of isolation. When researchers dig deep, they see that loneliness is not caused by spending too much time alone. Instead, when they directly compared *objective time* alone (the amount of time people spent alone per day) to *feeling lonely*, it was clear that perceiving oneself to be isolated had a greater impact than actual physical separation from others.[35] A good example of this phenomenon played out during COVID-19 lockdowns, which thrust the idea of spending too much time alone into the spotlight.

During that time, mainstream media coverage centered around stories of people stuck at home.[36,37] Even we solitude "optimists" reacted to the first UK lockdowns in March 2020 by designing studies to gauge harmful effects like depression, anxiety, and loneliness. In our early research, which tracked more than 800 living-alone adults and older adults in the early months of the pandemic, we didn't even *think* to test positive reactions to additional alone time (relaxation, creativity, and the like). Instead, we thought only of trying to predict which people would suffer mental health problems because of their increased time in solitude.

Our findings,[38] and those from other researchers at the time, surprised us all. Individuals living alone didn't seem to experience the expected drawbacks. On average, across our sample, mental health stayed perfectly steady, neither improving nor deteriorating even though our participants spent more time alone than they had before the movement restrictions. Other labs collected feedback from thousands of participants, and those researchers saw that under nearly all circumstances, people didn't struggle with time alone in the same way.[39] Instead, some did well in solitude, even enjoying it and feeling it was a change they *wanted to hold on to*, whereas others (like Dorothy from the beginning of this chapter) clearly wanted out. The takeaway is that while both popular media and researchers expressed a blanket concern that all people spending time alone would likely experience adverse effects, the reality was more complicated.

In addition to the perception factor, these early findings that lockdowns were not as psychologically harmful as feared could be the result of tracking participants for relatively short periods. In contrast, one large-scale study conducted by researchers at University College London showed that certain "at-risk" groups (young adults, women, people living alone, less educated people, city dwellers, ethnic minorities, and the economically disadvantaged) had a higher risk of experiencing more emotional loneliness than in previous years. Eighteen percent of those surveyed during the pandemic said they "often" felt lonely (compared to 8 percent before).[40] Similarly, a large-scale analysis of thirty-four long-term studies from four continents (with more than 200,000 participants) showed, on average, a 5 percent increase in loneliness during the pandemic.[41] Yet even these latter researchers concluded that the "observed effects were small and heterogeneous," meaning that although a minority felt much lonelier than before, many others did fine or even better than they had previously.

Naturally, any increase in loneliness should be taken seriously, and outreach to "at-risk" groups is critically important. But the researchers felt that "at this point in time, concerns about a 'loneliness pandemic' are likely overblown."[41] These findings tell us two other interesting things: first, people who were vulnerable to loneliness before the pandemic were at greater risk during it; second, solitude wasn't necessarily bad in general, but prolonged, restrictive periods of it may start to drain people of their emotional resources.

However slight the observed increase in loneliness was in the aforementioned studies, the rise fed a widespread assumption that social restrictions would cause universal despair. That may be because, even prior to the onset of the pandemic, loneliness had been cast as a growing "epidemic," a pervasive public health problem to be cured.[37] In 2018, the world's first minister for loneliness was appointed in the United Kingdom and tasked with tackling isolation.[42] In early 2021, Japan also added a minister of loneliness to its government ranks.[43]

It's clear that loneliness affects a sizable portion of humanity, at least at times, but it appears to be far less common than present political rhetoric – and mainstream media coverage of that rhetoric – often indicates. Eric Klineberg, a sociologist and director of the Institute for Public Knowledge at New York University, has studied that mischaracterization. In his book *Going Solo: The Extraordinary Rise and Surprising Appeal of Living Alone*, he talks specifically about how society tends to assume that living-alone adults are missing something they need or want. But now living solo is incredibly common, and it rarely correlates with feelings of social isolation. (More on this in Chapter 10.) As an alternative to cohabitating, Klineberg said, "living alone can offer even greater benefits: the time and space for restorative solitude."[44]

Klineberg believes that true loneliness in modern society may spring from a growing culture of individualism in which "traditional sources of social solidarity," like labor unions, religious groups, and civic associations, have been in steady decline. But even those shifts have not led to epidemic numbers of lonely hearts. "Surprisingly, though, the best data do not actually show drastic spikes in either loneliness or social isolation," wrote Klineberg in an opinion piece in the *New York Times* in 2018 on why it's harmful to characterize loneliness as a health epidemic. "Social disconnection is a serious matter, yet if we whip up a panic over its prevalence and impact, we're less likely to deal with it properly," he wrote.[45]

One of the most influential researchers of loneliness was University of Chicago psychologist John Cacioppo. Some of his work relies on data from the huge, multidecade University of Michigan Health and Retirement Study (HRS),[46] which has surveyed a representative sample of approximately 20,000 Americans and gives a glimpse of loneliness trends over time. "When we look at that survey, it looks like loneliness is around 27, 28 percent. Our best estimates based on that means it's increased anywhere on the order of 3 to 7 percent over the last 20 years," he told the *Atlantic* in 2017.[47] That's not a statistically insignificant shift, but it's far from what many doomsday predictions indicate.

Other researchers, using data from the HRS and the National Social Life, Health, and Aging Project, looked at loneliness in older adults by comparing perceived loneliness in people born between 1948 and 1965 (so-called baby boomers) to those born between 1920 and 1947. The researchers wanted to know, had older adults become lonelier from 2005 to 2016? They concluded in their 2019 paper that, during that ten-year study period, there was no evidence of birth cohort differences in rates of loneliness among US adults over age fifty. They also found that loneliness rates among adults age fifty-seven to eighty-five years remained nearly unchanged during that time.[48]

Why does loneliness dominate headlines despite good science pointing to a modest increase over the past decades? What some sociologists now consider faulty data reported in a 2004 journal article may underlie the initial "evidence" of an alarming rise in social isolation. Those authors replicated a series of questions from the 1985 General Social Survey done by the National Opinion Research Center to measure changes in Americans' core network structures.[49] They basically asked how many confidants, that is, people with whom they would discuss "important matters," the study participants had. In 2004, respondents provided one-third fewer names than the earlier group, and nearly 25 percent (compared to 10 percent in 1985) couldn't come up with anyone at all.[50]

Those dramatic results turned a lot of heads. A 2006 *New York Times* article, "The Lonely American Just Got a Bit Lonelier," called the results "a new installment in the annals of loneliness." "Americans are not only lacking in bowling partners, now they're lacking in people to tell their deepest, darkest secrets. They've hunkered down even more, their inner circle often contracting until it includes only family, only a spouse or, at worst, no one," it said.[51] But the data contained some anomalies, like dozens of instances in which "missing data" cases were miscoded as "percent giving no names," calling into question the veracity of the initial analysis. Overall, the authors of the original study stand by their conclusion of a significant shift in social networks, but they also referenced a number of potential "technical problems" that may have inflated the observed trend.[52]

Despite more recent findings, the initial, erroneous message that loneliness is running rampant endures. If magazine covers shout about a loneliness epidemic among us, we may be swayed by that messaging (even if we're living alone and fine with it!). Feminist scholar Eleanor Wilkinson, at the University of Southampton, has written about the popular conceptualizations conflating loneliness and aloneness. She said that despite the recent emergence of more positive characterizations of being single, stigmatization endures. "Certain attachments, we are told, contain the promise to alleviate loneliness; romantic coupled love is still positioned as the primary way to find meaningful connection. So even while feminist work on single life has reshaped some of these normative life scripts, the specter of loneliness still haunts us. The melancholic figure of the 'tragic loner,' living alone without a partner or family, is still upheld as the cruel fate that potentially awaits us if we do not follow the right path," Wilkinson wrote.[53]

The anxiety over loneliness seems more widespread than the condition itself, and that hyperbole is a disservice to those truly suffering it. If we don't accurately identify who is most affected and how, we're unlikely to arrive at the best ways to address the underlying causes. As a result, preventing loneliness, or mitigating its effects, may be even more elusive. Just as the aforementioned Chicago study of 229 adults showed, having others around doesn't necessarily blunt loneliness. Any one of us can feel intensely lonely even in a crowded room. This was well illustrated in an April 2022 *New York Times* article highlighting instances of loneliness that have persisted even as the world has begun to suspend COVID-19-era social distancing. In the piece, Stephanie Cacioppo, assistant professor of psychiatry and behavioral neuroscience at the University of Chicago, was quoted about college students returning to campus. "Now that students are back, we are hearing so much loneliness and isolation tied to disappointment. College is not what kids expected it to be," she said.[54]

It seems paradoxical that students should feel lonely when they are, again, surrounded by peers. But the state of being alone, or with others, is not the determining factor in our perception of isolation. That's the tricky thing about loneliness – it's not about whether you're around people; rather, it rises and falls based on whether you're getting what you need, or expect to, from those interactions. If you're not, it doesn't matter if you're sitting in a stadium full of people – you're going to feel isolated and lonely. On the flip side, if you feel your relationships are fulfilling, then spending ten hours alone in your room studying is unlikely to elicit crippling loneliness.

Some loneliness research suggests we might reduce that dreaded feeling by balancing sleep, work, exercise, socializing, and "me time."[55] In his book *Together: The Healing Power of Human Connection in a Sometimes Lonely World*, US surgeon general Vivek Murthy, MD, talks about the struggle of emotional isolation.[56] One of his subtler messages: appreciating yourself is key to curbing loneliness. In a recent interview, he said, "Connection to self, it turns out, is the foundation that we need to connect to other people. When we're connected to ourselves we understand that we have self-worth, we understand that we have value to bring to the world. ... What's powerful about solitude is that it gives both the time to quiet the noise around us but it also gives us the opportunity to reflect and to simply be."[57] The idea is to spend time alone to really understand and accept who we are, individually. Other than occasional statements like Murthy's, the importance of me-centered moments to overall happiness is nearly absent from the discussion of loneliness. But we believe that, in some instances, the antidote to loneliness may be – paradoxically – to turn inward, learn to embrace periods of aloneness, and become more resilient in that space (which we talk about in more depth in Chapter 9).

PEOPLE NEED PEOPLE ... BUT NOT 24/7/365

If harsh feelings like loneliness or isolation are even possible, then why, as social animals, should we bother with solitude? Well, as critical as maintaining healthy social connections is, being with people *all the time* doesn't benefit anyone, not the person doing it nor the people they're hanging out with. If we're constantly marinating in others' thoughts and opinions, we can lose track of our own. We've all likely felt this instinctively from time to time, when we're feeling confused, overwhelmed, or simply "maxed out" from other people's input.

We can better understand what's happening while we're engaged with others with help from Frederick ("Fritz") and Laura Perls, German-born psychotherapists and founders of Gestalt therapy. The dominant view in psychotherapy at that time, in the 1940s, was that an expert physician-therapist should simply gather information from a patient and dispense a diagnosis and treatment. But the Gestalt approach turned established psychotherapy on its head in favor of a focus on the importance of fully connecting with the present moment and having rich and genuine interactions with others.[58] Fritz Perls focused on the social world and, in particular, on moments of contact with others. In our daily lives, we experience continuous inputs, feelings, emotions, and responses, and we make what Perls called "creative adjustments" to others, meaning we intuitively, automatically morph to fit our current social contexts.[59] These continuous adaptations go hand in hand with the innate psychological need to connect with others that we have already talked about.

Relating to others and seeking approval and affection are completely natural ways to be human in a social world, but they also have drawbacks. If we are constantly adjusting to others, we can lose sight of ourselves as individuals with discrete needs, emotions, and thoughts.[60] Over time, many sages have weighed in on the importance of stepping away from others, such as influential nineteenth-century writer Ralph Waldo Emerson. "He who should inspire and lead his race must be defended from traveling with the souls of other men, from living, breathing, reading, and writing in the daily, time-worn yoke of their opinions," he wrote in 1860.[61] What Emerson meant is that, while we're busy knowing others, we may neglect our foremost relationship – the one with ourselves. Knowing ourselves is critical to understanding aspects of our being, like what our true beliefs are, where our priorities lie, and what our goals should be. And the person who knows themselves in solitude, Emerson believed, will stay ahead of the crowd. Decades later, philosopher Friedrich Nietzsche (1844–1900) put it this way: "That is why I go into solitude – so as not to drink out of everybody's cistern."[62]

Throughout history, we've seen the high cost of communal thinking and can recognize the importance of stepping away, at least on occasion, from the madding crowd. Christian monk Thomas Merton (1915–68) spent much of his life reflecting on the risks of being overly social. Merton moved into the Abbey of Gethsemani, a monastery in Kentucky, just three days after the United States entered World War II, following the bombing of Pearl Harbor. Then age twenty-six years, he joined the Order of Cistercians of the Strict Observance, more commonly known as the Trappists, a rigid, contemplative order of Roman Catholics. A poet, pacifist, and political activist, Merton had been an orphan for a decade and had been in and out of jail – as well as at Cambridge and Columbia Universities.[63] He poked his finger randomly into the Bible one day while looking for spiritual guidance and selected Luke 1:20: "Behold, you shall be silent."[64]

Fifteen years after entering the monastery, and during the Vietnam War, Merton wrote,[65]

When men are merely submerged in a mass of impersonal human beings pushed around by automatic forces, they lose their true humanity, their integrity, their ability to love, their capacity for self-determination. When society is made up of men who know no interior solitude it can no longer be held together by love: and consequently it is held together by a violent and abusive authority. But when men are violently deprived of solitude and freedom which are their due, the society in which they live becomes putrid, it festers with servility, resentment and hate.

It's an intense sentiment with simple messages: we need time on our own to shut out the collective voices; we need time on our own to access our inner sanctum. Merton did that by living in a monastery, but we don't have to take that extreme step to find our own solitude.

At the same time Merton was writing about the importance of quiet contemplation, social psychologists were motivated by the alarming, post–World War II revelations about how much influence other people can have on us, and often in subtle ways of which we're oblivious. That phenomenon has been thoroughly studied in some now-famous social experiments that examined conformity (Solomon Asch in the 1950s),[66] obedience (Stanley Milgram in the 1960s),[67] and human vulnerability to authority (Philip Zimbardo in the 1970s).[68]

One of the most well-known studies was done by Asch, a researcher interested in how we form impressions and the role of others in molding those opinions. He tested his subjects among groups of clandestine associates – researchers pretending to be participants in the study. Asch showed that when the researcher-participants made obvious errors while comparing the relative lengths of several lines shown side by side, others in the study (the real subjects) made the same errors. The judgments about which lines were longer didn't reflect reality, but the study participants nevertheless conformed their thinking to match that of their compatriots. Asch reasoned that we change our behaviors to accommodate others.[66]

Although many of these older studies on social influence have faced criticism in recent years, the overall point they make resonates today: we are prone to conform and to behave similarly to people around us. Since those experiments were done, most research in the field of social psychology has focused on studying the good and bad of social interactions and group dynamics. Out of that emerged one of the most influential books in the field, *The Social Animal* (1972) by Elliot Aronson,[69] which presented additional evidence that acting in ways that don't reflect who we are is an inescapable human condition and that we are sometimes merely "pawns" in someone else's game. It's tempting to believe that those insights from decades ago are from a time when people were more susceptible to social influence, but they are highly relevant, even now.

Current studies still support the power of social sway. In a large-scale study published in *Nature* in 2012, researchers manipulated the Facebook feeds of nearly sixty-one million people during the 2010 US congressional elections. They showed some social media users an informal message reminding them to vote, while they showed others images of up to six of their friends who had clicked an "I Voted" button. The generic reminder had little influence on whether the users actually went to the polls to cast a vote, but users were highly influenced by their friends having voted. As a result of the researchers' interference, roughly 340,000 additional people were moved to vote, most of them responding to the subtle social pressure of their friends' actions. The effect seemed to cross party lines, and the researchers found no evidence of differences in action among self-described liberals and conservatives.[70] Clearly the social world still influences how we think, feel, and behave just because we are human. (In this instance, the researchers elicited significant action in their subjects, but without malicious intent or result. It's not hard to see, however, how social sway can and has been used to adversely influence others to act in more harmful, even criminal, ways.)

But there is a way to clear the fog and find ourselves again. Luckily, our desire to connect does not have to compromise our authenticity. Research has shown that our needs for autonomy and relatedness are indeed compatible. Throughout adulthood, as we connect and relate to others, and learn to collaborate and cooperate, we constantly negotiate with the social world while still being capable of retaining our individuality and independence. Solitude can play an important part in that dance.

PEOPLE NEED *NO* PEOPLE, AT LEAST SOMETIMES

Solitude offers a chance to be free of external and immediate social demands and expectations, and it can be a crucial time in which to reconnect with ourselves. (As always, we need to remain aware that this opportunity to be free can be thwarted by bringing those concerns with us into solitude.) Emily, a listening coach and journalist whose job is to lead intensive group activities, goes on solitude retreats to spend quality time with herself. We spoke to her soon after a six-day silent retreat in northern England. "I don't go up to *negate* myself, but to *engage* my personal self. In my ideal moments, it was just me in the rolling hills with the newborn sheep. It allows me to be in my own great company, and I find when I return that I am more centered, and I can *respond* instead of *reacting* to others," she said.

In that vein, many of our study participants talked about solitude being essential to their ability to think and reflect. Our research shows that people use solitude to check in with their values and probe personal insights that may have been hidden in the haze of other people's expectations and opinions. We refer to that act as "autonomous functioning," which basically means being in touch with one's values and acting consistently with them (instead of being easily swayed by social pressures). As rewarding as social interactions can be, there are times when a conversation turns sour or we have a heated argument with a relative. Then solitude, absent the constant feedback from our social environment, can provide a space to heal and process negative emotions.

Alicia, age fifty-three, walks to work alone every day and uses that time to transition from one world to the other. "It's also a time to think about, and reflect about, things that have happened, and be able to sort of understand things and try to unpick issues so that they don't, in a way, get into the house," she said. Skye, age twenty-two, from England, shared a similar sentiment. "I enjoy solitude especially if it's been a stressful day or I've had an argument with a friend or something unpleasant has happened to me, I usually end up staying up past bedtime just lying in bed and trying to sort through those feelings on my own," she said. "And I usually end up the next morning in a much better mood because I've had the time to work through whatever has happened and how it's made me feel, and how I can move forward and take actions to either change what's happened or come to peace with whatever happened."

Choosing ourselves over others, at least sometimes, is not a new concept, and, in addition to Emerson, many writers have opined on this idea. (New England in the nineteenth century was steeped in the rhetoric of this type of individuality.) In her poem "The Soul Selects Her Own Society" (1862), Emily Dickinson, self-crowned queen of solitude, succinctly expressed being choosy about whom, if anyone, she spent time with. "The soul selects her own society, Then shuts the door; / On her divine majority, Obtrude no more," she wrote.[71]

American writer Henry David Thoreau also famously embraced the idea of sometimes turning away from society in favor of his inner dialogue; he relished the freedom, independence, and self-determination it afforded him. In *Walden*, his mid-nineteenth-century treatise on the joys of living solo in a shack on the shore of Walden Pond in Massachusetts, he wrote, "I find it wholesome to be alone the greater part of the time. To be in company, even with the best, is soon wearisome and dissipating. I love to be alone. I never found the companion that was so companionable as solitude. . . . Society is commonly too cheap. We meet at very short intervals, not having had time to acquire any new value for each other. We meet at meals three times a day, and give each other a new taste of that old musty cheese that we are."[72]

Nobody wants to be the "old musty cheese" in their relationships, and yet, even today, solitude seekers still earn reputations as cranky recluses because, in the mainstream and in academia, the significance of social ties remains paramount. How often we hang out with friends, how many dates we go on, if we're a "team player" – in short, how big and bright of a social butterfly we are – are often the unofficial indicators of how successful we are in life. The concept of choosing time alone as a holistic act is tough to grasp. How much time we choose to spend alone doesn't rank high in some people's minds as interesting, important, or productive. And, even if we accept that solo time can be beneficial, we tend to view claiming time for ourselves as wasteful, even selfish. But the truth is that the right amount of solitude can improve our inner lives – and even our relationships with others.

THE SYMBIOSIS OF SOLO AND SOCIAL

We've seen some evidence that solitude holds potential advantages for our social selves. While the Perls duo recognized that it's human nature to connect and react to other people, their brand of therapy was designed, in fact, to help people be more self-aware and to use that knowledge to build more real and satisfying relationships. Ideally, those relationships would start with "whole," genuine people who know themselves and can express authentic thoughts and feelings.[59]

We've also found that taking care of ourselves by attending to our needs in solitude gives many of us a greater bandwidth for family, friends, and coworkers. We heard some of our participants talk about exiting alone time with greater reserves of energy and attention available for others and for more "real" connections. "After being alone, it probably helps me authentically interact with people who want to spend meaningful time with me as a person," one study participant told us.

Loneliness researcher John Cacioppo made this point by offering a somewhat conventional, but otherwise helpful example of a couple with a young child: "A new mother with a newborn she loves – loves playing with the baby – that does not mean the husband shouldn't give her a break, let her go off and regenerate, have some time to herself, so that she can return and continue to be absolutely generous and loving and adoring. That time alone enhances social connections, it doesn't contract it," he said.[47] Or, as one of our study participants, nineteen-year-old Tomás from Portugal, put it, "Alone time is for being friends with oneself, relationships start from there."

Being generally more content after spending time in solitude could simply make us easier to be around and, by default, better partners, siblings, colleagues, or friends. "I guess maybe I'm more attentive to other people than maybe I was before, because I'm actually getting my solitude needs met," a woman in her thirties told us. Or perhaps absence simply does make the heart grow fonder. "[Solitude] brings us closer together," one man in his fifties said, because while his wife is away, he prepares a nice meal for her return, for which she is always grateful.

But another force may also be at work. Solitude may boost, or renew, empathy in some people. We have found in our research that people who describe themselves as empathetic or "sensitive," in particular, need time to shut down other people's thoughts and needs. In that way, solitude may simply give them the space to regroup and refill their tanks with empathy. "For me the COVID lockdowns had many unexpected positive effects, effects that I am very keen to maintain going forward. . . .

My extra time alone makes me better as a friend because I have more resources to care for others," Vivian, an Oxford law professor, told us. Or, as Emerson put it in the *Atlantic* in December 1857, "it is not the circumstance of seeing more or fewer people, but the readiness of sympathy, that imports; and a sound mind will derive its principles from insight, with ever a purer ascent to the sufficient and absolute right."[73]

In short, there's a symbiosis at work: solitude may make us better at being social, and vice versa. Results from one of our studies show that the individual differences that make us interact authentically with ourselves and others are the same traits that contribute to the enjoyment of solitude.[74] Other work hints at why that may be. One study of more than 560 Taiwanese junior college students found that agreeableness, which the researchers define as a tendency to promote and maintain an egalitarian relationship with others, increases our capacity for solitude.[75] Think of it as, if you're friendly and cooperative in your relationships, you also enjoy your alone time more. These insights were particularly interesting for Netta, who, remember, was a well-known relationship researcher before coming over to the "solitude side." Surprisingly, the more experimentation we did for our own Solitude Project, the more she could see that many of the things that make us good at relationships are accentuated in solitude – self-connection, doing what we care about and love, openness, and curiosity. The two states seem highly compatible, and striking a balance between the two can make us better, more content people in both spheres.

DEFINING "ALONELINESS"

What happens when we want solitude, but we can't get it? In a scene from the popular TV series *The Kominsky Method*, the title character Sandy (played by Michael Douglas), a Hollywood acting coach in his seventies, attends the wake of his lifelong friend Norman. After spending hours with other mourners, he finds a quiet corner, sinks into a couch, and sighs deeply. Finally, he is alone with his own grief and free to explore his feelings. Sandy imagines conversations with Norman, and those memories bring sadness, amusement, love. But his reminiscences in solitude are interrupted sporadically by others pursuing their own agendas, like Norman's girlfriend and his grandson. Each time, Sandy drags himself back into the present to respond appropriately to the interactions, but he longs to be left alone with his own real, undisrupted emotions and memories, the ones that really matter to him.[76]

The scene illustrates how unsettling it can be when someone needs solitude yet cannot break away from social demands. This concept was recently coined as "aloneliness" by Robert Coplan, a psychologist at Carleton University in Canada, and colleagues. To be "alonely" is to need more solitude than you get.[77] It's based on the researchers' observations of negative feelings related to being unable to spend enough time alone. In a series of studies, the researchers established the role of aloneliness as a "potentially important contributor to our understanding of the psychological costs and benefits of solitude." One of those studies surveyed 379 undergraduate students and found that those who typically preferred to be alone, and said they had been spending less time alone than they intended to in the week prior to the study, were the ones who most strongly endorsed the idea and state of aloneliness. Overall, the findings showed that aloneliness is a discrepancy between how often people want to be alone and how much they get to be.[77]

In our work, we heard from twenty-two-year-old Skye about how honoring someone's need for time alone is essential to any relationship. "I think it's very important to be able to respect people's desires for solitude because you never know why they are asking for that and you never know what the consequences are if people don't get the solitude they need," she said. This feedback very much mirrors the way researchers have described loneliness – a discrepancy between how much social connection one wishes to have and how much one actually has. Thwarting either the desire for solitude or the need for social interactions, it seems, can be stressful.

The fact that new words like "aloneliness" are being created to describe the idea that there is a gap between how much some people want to be alone and how much solitude they actually get is a good indication of how new the field of positive solitude is – and how incomplete the understanding of it remains. But we're now living in a moment with the potential to know it better than ever before. With all the dramatic rhetoric around potential loneliness during the COVID-19 pandemic, for instance, the voices seldom heard came from those who recognized during that time how much they liked having more time alone – and less wasted time on "filler friendships" or other obligatory social interactions. We heard from people who wanted to move forward from lockdown yet not return to the same social treadmill they'd been on for decades prepandemic. Some of them resolved to proactively carve out time for themselves and focus on quality in relationships over quantity (either the number of people in their social sphere or the amount of time spent with them). Alicia, an Italian living in England, told us, "I think potentially what I might want to do is seek more of that time, rather than letting it happen ... like sort of prescribing it in a positive way."

We must recognize that the solo–social balance looks different for each of us. Solitude researchers now suggest that there is a ∩-shaped curve that describes whether time spent in solitude is bad or good for us. On one side of the ∩ is "not enough" solitude, where people getting almost no solitude say they suffer "aloneliness," characterized by stress and other negative emotions, and overall life dissatisfaction. On the opposite side is "too much" solitude, where people may feel lonely and suffer depression and the physical health problems that go along with it. In the middle is ideal – it's the spot where we get enough solitude to feel its benefits.

Although researchers are just starting to explore this question, it's possible that everyone falls somewhere along the ∩, whether they are extroverted or introverted, live in a city or the countryside. But the steepness of the ∩ curve is different for each of us. Some people get to the top of the ∩ with relatively little time alone. Others can have almost endless time before it gets to be too much. It can help each of us to know where our sweet spot is.

Ancient Chinese philosophy describes yin and yang as contrasting forces – lunar and solar – which are ultimately complementary, and interdependent.[78] Borrowing that imagery, we can see our social world as the sun and our solo world as the moon. It feels like warming rays when other people (especially those who are important to us) show they care, when we feel part of a group, or when we have a great conversation. Those social interactions are energizing and joyful. Solitude is more lunar, though equally important. It can regulate our tides and be peaceful and calming. There we reflect, review, relax, and at its best, time alone gives a way to regroup and prepare for the next challenge – or adventure.

CHAPTER 7

Super/Natural Solitude

WHEN JR HARRIS[1–3] WAS A TEENAGER GROWING UP in New York City, his parents worried about him getting caught up in drugs and gang violence in his neighborhood. So, one summer, they sent him out of the city to a Boy Scout camp a few hours north in the Catskill Mountains. Harris hated it at first, being away from his friends and exiled to the "wilderness." But then something unexpected happened. Among the rounded peaks and steep-sided valleys of the ancient Catskills, he found his place.

Harris learned to read a map, start a fire in pouring rain, track animals, and forage for food. And once he had earned three specific merit badges – for cooking, camping, and pioneering – he and the other scouts were allowed to venture beyond the main camp on their own for up to four days. Harris seized the opportunity, picking a campsite on a cliff overlooking a lake, and spent the summer there, returning to "civilization" only to check in with counselors and restock his provisions. He eventually graduated from the Boy Scouts and moved on from the Catskills, but in the six decades since then, Harris has backpacked in some of the most remote and rugged places on the planet – from the Arctic Circle and the Andes to the Amazon – most often alone.

As a boy, Harris was fascinated by early European American pioneers and explorers – especially the mountain men who would disappear into the hills by themselves to trap and hunt with a dog, a couple of pack-horses, their buckskin, and a musket. "That was the lifestyle I always envisioned would be great for me, that was kind of my fantasy, and being alone was part of it," he said. It was a dream played out during those

Catskills summers, but otherwise, Harris was hardly a solitary soul. After university, he began and ran a successful marketing consultancy and raised a family, all in bustling New York. But over the years, he'd escape the city occasionally and pull on his backpack to go walking. Sometimes he had companions, which wasn't bad, just different, but his preference was to go solo.

When Harris talks about his decades of adventuring, he describes two major forces that make those outings consistently compelling – being in nature and being alone. Each of those states offers its own benefits, and his life experiences encapsulate well how the two conditions intersect, overlap, and ultimately complement one another to form a different, or enhanced, state: *solitude in nature*. That third "place" has been little studied up to this point, but with the help of Harris and others, we can begin to understand how powerful it can be.

In past chapters, we talked about the benefits of solitude that we authors have experienced and many others that our research subjects have described. In his own way, Harris echoes many of those – in particular, he loves the autonomy, self-sufficiency, and independence that are hallmarks of his solo adventures. "I like the notion of being completely free, and open. I can eat when I'm hungry, I can rest when I want to, I can go in this direction or that direction. I can go anywhere I want," he said. "I don't have to agree with anybody, I don't have to compromise with anybody. I have total freedom of choice and my life is totally my own."

Of course, solo outings like the ones Harris has built up to in his adult life aren't for everyone, and plenty of people have gotten into trouble in the outdoors, even when they considered themselves experts (the unfortunate misadventures and untimely deaths of bear enthusiast Timothy Treadwell and famed hiker Christopher McCandless come to mind). Solo outings in nature also need not be intense or extreme to reap the rewards that we talk about in this chapter. We've heard from plenty of our study participants about many recuperative, transformative, and even transcendent experiences in "little" wildernesses like back gardens and city parks. What's important isn't the physical distance from other people, necessarily, but how we relate to that green space and our ability to think and act freely in whatever spot we choose.

PRESCRIPTION (℞): NATURE

The idea of human connectedness to nature and the positive effects it has on our well-being have been hot topics for at least the past few decades. And, more recently, the potential of so-called nature therapy has gotten a lot of media play as doctors all over the world have begun writing prescriptions for time outdoors, particularly for patients with chronic conditions like hypertension, diabetes, and mood disorders.[4] But what seems like a new trend is really the renaissance of a way of life once deeply familiar to humans.

Some of the world's oldest belief systems and spiritual practices (later called religions by many) inextricably linked humans with nature. Beginning with Eastern traditions, the most sacred Hindu texts – the four Vedas, which originated in ancient India around 1500 BCE – outline a nature–human relationship based on respect, reverence, and care.[5] Buddhism, from the late sixth century, advises that we live in a universe of energies, in a web of life, where everything has an impact on everything else. Love, respect, and compassion for all life are basic principles of Buddhist philosophy.[6] Taoism (or Daoism) of ancient China, first widely recognized in the fourth and third centuries BCE, posits that humans and animals should live in balance with the Tao, or "the Way" of the universe, a harmonious natural order between humans and our surroundings.[7] In the Western world, there was more of the same in terms of a human–nature link.[8] In animism (a common perspective among Indigenous populations worldwide), animate and inanimate objects alike are equally alive.[9] Pagans (including ancient Celtic, Greco-Roman, Slavic, and Germanic tribes) and polytheists believe that human beings, along with everything else on Earth, are part and parcel of nature and should live in agreement with it.[10,11]

Our predecessors clearly grasped that their survival depended on coexistence with the natural environment,[12] so it makes sense that they would revere and worship nature as sacred and want to live with it in harmony. But that thinking is foreign to many of us in the twenty-first century because of a shift that began a few thousand years ago. Between 2000 and 1700 BCE, the spiritual founder of three major world religions was born (known as Ibrahim in the Qur'an and Abraham in the Bible).

Jews, Christians, and Muslims all think of themselves as spiritual descend-
ants of Ibrahim/Abraham, whom they believe was chosen to spread the
word of monotheism. As Judeo-Christianity rose in Western society, it put
a single "god" at center stage, one believed to exist beyond nature. That
deity, according to biblical texts, also gave followers (at least the right-
eous ones) supremacy over the natural world. To that end, God advised
Adam and Eve to "be fruitful, and multiply, and replenish the earth, and
subdue it: and have dominion over the fish of the sea, and over the fowl
of the air, and over every living thing that moveth upon the earth."[13]

They also believed that God used nature as a "tool of divine justice,"[14]
meaning that the religiously observant were rewarded with rain and sun
to grow their crops, while the heathens got hail and locusts. That contradictory concept – one of many in the Bible, which was cobbled together
over centuries with contributions from various scribes – nonetheless
created a dichotomy between humans and nature that endures today.
(In fairness, some ecologically minded Christian theologians today have
reinterpreted what God told Adam not as a license to strip mine but as a
command to be responsible caretakers of the environment.[15]) In Islam,
which came along a bit later, the Qur'an teaches that "the cosmos exists
to nourish, support, and sustain the process of life – all of life, and in
particular human life," according to historian Syed Nomanul Haq.[16] Like
the similar thesis/antithesis from the Bible, the Qur'an declares that God
has made the natural world "subject to" human beings but, again, that
nature obeys only God. Nonetheless, followers of the Abrahamic religions came away with an understanding that nature was meant to serve
what they believed was the most important life force on Earth –
humanity.

There have been moments over the past few centuries in which
writers and philosophers, and later scientists, have attempted to revive
the pre-Abrahamic beliefs that humans and nature are one and the
same.[17] And many have extolled the conviction, or maybe the intuitive
recognition, that time in nature is good and even essential to human
thriving (see Box 7.1). Like his Romantic predecessors in England,
nineteenth-century writer Ralph Waldo Emerson's insights centered on
a vision of nature intimately tied to the human and the holy. He was an
ordained minister, but, during his own truth quest, Emerson broke with

the Church. He chose instead to hunt for hints about the divine when walking in the woods near his home in Concord, Massachusetts.[18]

Emerson was also keenly attuned to the healing powers of nature. "To the body and mind which have been cramped by noxious work or company, nature is medicinal and restores their tone. The tradesman, the attorney comes out of the din and craft of the street, and sees the sky and the woods, and is a man again. In their eternal calm, he finds himself," he wrote.[19] Emerson was alluding to the idea that beyond the tangible benefits of natural resources (clean water, abundant food, adequate shelter) lie intangible ones that can have a powerful impact on psychological well-being. But it would be a while before that particular concept caught on en masse.

On the other hand, the practical benefits of open space and parks have been a public health concern for nearly two centuries. But back then, beliefs in the beneficial outcomes of having access to green space were based on anecdote alone. The United Kingdom's commons preservation movement was launched in London with an 1865 report asserting that "the necessity of providing Open Spaces for health and recreation has become paramount."[20] It was clear to them that a "sufficiency of open-air lungs," meaning parks and commons, was as important to public health as clean water and sanitary waste disposal. A bit later, Scottish-born and Yosemite-bound naturalist John Muir also preached about a kinship among species and on the tonic of wildness. "Climb the mountains and get their good tidings. Nature's peace will flow into you as sunshine flows into trees. The winds will blow their own freshness into you, and the storms their energy, while cares will drop off like autumn leaves," he wrote.[21]

In addition to male influencers of the time, some insightful female naturalists wrote meaningfully about nature closer to home. American Mary Treat was a rigorous field researcher and popular nature writer in the latter half of the nineteenth century who made significant contributions to the fields of botany and entomology.[22] She and English naturalist Charles Darwin corresponded and collaborated over several years about many ecological topics, including carnivorous plants and the sex of butterflies. In her enthralling and illuminating book *Home Studies in Nature*, she wrote, "A contemplation of Nature, her ways and works, large or small, far or near, in the heavens or on the earth, becomes a source of perennial pleasure, and a true lover of her gracious and un-bounded revelations need not travel far in search of them." Treat referred to her nature studies as the "keenest, most thrilling enjoyment of my life."[23]

BOX 7.1 A CURE FOR BRAINWORKERS

In mid-eighteenth-century America, a condition known as *neurasthenia* was gripping a class of so-called brainworkers whose overthinking in business and other intellectual pursuits was causing anxiety, depression, insomnia, and headaches. Physician Silas Weir Mitchell, a pioneering doctor of such "nervous diseases," devised the "West Cure" for men suffering from the malady – including President Theodore Roosevelt and poet Walt Whitman – requiring them to flee eastern cities and go west to engage in rigorous physical activity like hunting and cattle roping.[24] In his 1871 book *Wear and Tear; or, Hints for the Overworked* (still relevant to many of us today!), Mitchell said that guys could reinforce their nervous systems by engaging in "a sturdy contest with Nature"[25] – and it worked. Men generally returned from their western escapades reinvigorated and refreshed. Mitchell, in fact, prescribed the West Cure for himself, and he went into the wild on annual camping and fishing outings.

There was one group, however, for whom the fine doctor did not recommend the West Cure: women. Instead, he devised for them the "Rest Cure," which required "nervous women, who, as a rule, are thin and lack blood," as Mitchell described them, to take to their beds for six to eight weeks in relative isolation (a nurse was present, but friends and family couldn't visit, and the patient couldn't go outside), overeat tons of protein, get massages, and endure electrotherapy (to prevent muscle atrophy).[26] This treatment plan, which may seem over the top to us now, was very popular with American and British neurologists – for decades. It aimed to discourage women from pursuing roles – like studying or leading creative lives – that were believed to be unsuited to their gender. There is the very real possibility that some women manipulated their way into a Rest Cure session to avoid domestic chores (and we can do little more than applaud that effort), but they were likely in the minority.

Mitchell's powerful cult of personality precluded much vocal opposition to the method (which required some women to eat eighteen or more raw eggs per day), but the historical record is peppered with dissent. Another physician prescribing the "cure," Charles Dana, noted that the "active, keen-witted, intellectual woman ... does not do so well under a method which for a time renders them abulic."[27] That lack of willpower he mentioned did, in fact, cause a major problem for at least one prominent, keen-witted author and champion of women's rights. Mitchell prescribed his misogynistic Rest Cure for writer Charlotte Perkins Gilman, who later penned a fictional though semibiographical short story about her experiences called "The Yellow Wallpaper."[28]

In spring 1887, Gilman spent three months confined to her room soon after giving birth. She later wrote that Mitchell's prescription was to "live as domestic a life as possible. Have your child with you all the time. ... Lie down an hour after each meal. Have but two hours' intellectual life a day. And never touch pen, brush, or pencil as long as you live." She followed his prescription of Gothic torture to the letter and later said she "came perilously near to losing my mind. The mental agony grew so unbearable that I would sit blankly moving my head from side to side." (Other high-profile women decried their rest "cures," including writer Virginia Woolf and social reformer Jane Addams.) There are, of course, many factors that would make the Rest Cure a disaster and the West Cure an antidote (lack of choice and autonomy among them), but another major factor separating the two was *time outdoors*.[28]

Around the same time, landscape architect and open space proponent Frederick Law Olmsted (designer of New York's Central Park and many other public spaces) was an early booster of nature for public health. "It is a scientific fact that the occasional contemplation of natural scenes of an impressive character, particularly if this contemplation occurs in connection with relief from ordinary cares ... is favorable to the health and vigor of men and especially to the health and vigor of their intellect beyond any other conditions which can be offered them, that it not only gives pleasure for the time being but increases the subsequent capacity for happiness and the means of securing happiness," he said in 1865, in a treatise written to preserve California's Yosemite Valley as public land. It wasn't yet "scientific fact," as Olmsted put it, that time in nature improves mental and physical health, but the idea was based on the loose understanding back then of what caused disease – bad air and poor sanitation – and that parks offered an antidote to that.[29]

However influential and sometimes controversial these figures were in their lifetimes, their messages were all but forgotten until the onset of modern environmentalism in the 1960s. Muir's idea that "everything is connected" was revived eloquently by American marine biologist Rachel Carson (1907–64) in her book *Silent Spring*.[30] The work was an urgent plea for understanding that Earth's biodiversity, including people, was being poisoned by chemical pesticides. "In nature nothing exists alone," she wrote. Carson believed if people stopped to revel at the stunning complexity of nature, instead of trying to master it, we might prevent our own destruction – and maybe even thrive. "Those who contemplate the beauty of the earth find reserves of strength that will endure as long as life lasts. There is something infinitely healing in the repeated refrains of nature – the assurance that dawn comes after night, and spring after winter," wrote Carson.[31]

Also in the 1960s, German-born psychologist Erich Fromm coined the term *biophilia* (from the Greek words for life and love). He later defined it as the "passionate love of life and of all that is alive."[32,33] A couple of decades later, American biologist E. O. Wilson further described and popularized biophilia as an "innate tendency to focus on life and lifelike processes," driven by the human imperative to forge harmonious relationships with the larger biosphere. That instinctive preference for nature, and subconscious affiliation for other living things, was believed to reflect millennia of evolutionary bonding with nonhuman organisms.[34] In short, people evolved over millions of years as part of nature, and only recently – since the start of the Industrial Revolution – did we begin moving away from the natural world in a significant way. Now, more than half of the world's eight billion people live in urban areas, and there are twenty-eight "megacities" each exceeding ten million inhabitants.[35]

We may now do most of our foraging in grocery store aisles rather than in forests, but Wilson's biophilia hypothesis, further developed with collaborator Stephen R. Kellert, described a human reliance on nature "that extends far beyond the simple issues of material and physical sustenance to encompass as well the human craving for aesthetic, intellectual, cognitive, and even spiritual meaning and satisfaction."[36,37] That is an aspect that is of great interest to us as researchers of solitude and which we'll talk about in more depth later. Scientists like Wilson had been arguing that our biological link to the natural world has a profound effect on human well-being, but hard data supporting that idea have only come on the scene more recently. There's now a growing body of scientific evidence backing the idea that the human body responds positively to nature.

THE MENTAL AND PHYSICAL UPSIDES OF "SOFT FASCINATION"

Research now shows that nature impacts our brains and our behavior in ways both simple and complex. In recent years, in fact, hundreds of studies have explored the human–nature link and the various nonmaterial contributions nature makes to our well-being. (None of us needs to be alone to reap many of nature's benefits, but, as we talk about later in the chapter, being solo in green spaces has specific upsides.) Investigators at the University of Tokyo recently analyzed more than 300 peer-reviewed scientific papers to pin down how and in what ways nature provides the greatest benefits to humans. They came up with sixteen categories (thirteen positive and three negative) spanning a fascinating array of measured effects. The researchers found that most positive contributions were "regenerative," or those relating to mental and physical health and to subjective well-being. Two of the three negative effects they described included people being irritated by nature (such as having to clean bird excrement off their car) or feeling that it was destructive (like tree roots damaging infrastructure). The third was that some people feel apprehensive, anxious, or fearful in interactions with nature (sometimes expressed as a fear of wild animals but more often as a fear of other people).[38] Concerns over safety and a lack of control in nature aren't the norm, but they shouldn't be swept beneath the rug either (see Box 7.2). Those feelings often result from people having become alienated from nature, or vice versa, and should be taken seriously if there is a chance they could be addressed, for example, with childhood or therapeutic interactions with the outdoors. (In theory, nature lover Heather is in favor of this approach, but in relation to spiders large and small, she is opposed.)

The studies reviewed by the University of Tokyo researchers were mostly focused on urban and semi-urban ecosystems (26.2 percent), forests and woodlands (20.2 percent), inland water (12.5 percent), and coastal areas (8.9 percent). A handful also looked at human well-being in less studied ecosystems, including arctic and mountain tundra, deserts and scrublands, and savannas. Most experiences captured, therefore, were not in remote wilderness locations with zero other people around. In this chapter, in fact, we talk a lot about "solitude in wilderness" experiences, which may conjure up an image of a yeti-like outdoorsperson bushwhacking through trackless backcountry, and that may be accurate in a small number of cases. But it's important to remember that individual perceptions of wilderness – and of solitude – are highly subjective. One person may feel they are in the wild while spying rare birds with a quiet group on a forest plantation in England, whereas another needs to roam alone among wolves in the Alaskan bush. The point is that much of what can be gained by spending time in nature, and spending time alone in the out-of-doors, is accessible almost anywhere, given certain conditions.

University of Michigan researcher Stephen Kaplan made a useful point about this in the mid-1990s, during an uptick in the study of nature's benefits. While outlining the components of restorative environments, he talked about "getting away" versus "being away." We often use the phrase "getting away" as a proxy for escaping to a restorative place like the seaside, the mountains, or a lake, said Kaplan, but that's not the same as "being away." We can *get away* and "still struggle with the old thoughts," he said, meaning that gaining a new environment can be

BOX 7.2 NATURE CAN BITE, LITERALLY

When Heather was a kid, she would spend summer vacations with her mom and siblings engaged in what became known as forced marches. Generally, these took place in US national parks and were imposed regardless of adverse meteorological conditions or general availability of food or water. They trekked through the mosquito-infested Everglades, which left them sunburned and itchy (later they got "I donated blood!" T-shirts in the gift shop). They walked across the scorching sand dunes of Cape Cod National Seashore, with their lips cracked from dehydration and their plastic shoes adhered to blistered feet. (There were also amazing airboat tours of the marsh and sunset campfires by the seashore, but this is a section about the potential downsides of nature.)

This is to say that time in nature is not always the panacea that some research may indicate. In general, to benefit from its soothing and restorative effects, one has to have a sense of ease in one's immediate environment. Confusion and stress – and fear (which can sometimes be exacerbated by gender, race, or sexual orientation) – can blunt positive effects, particularly on solo wilderness forays. Case in point: recently, while hiking in Colorado's Rocky Mountains, Heather and her husband were passed on a trail by a woman solo hiking in the same direction. She whizzed by, headed downhill, with a smile and a chipper "hello!" Ten minutes later, she was heading back up the trail, walking and talking quickly, and looking petrified. She had just come face to snout with a huge black bear and was so terrified that she came back uphill to join forces with her fellow humans. She said that she'd been having a great hike, that she was "in the zone," until she spotted *Ursus americanus*. Ultimately, a group of humans "encouraged" the bear off the trail by making lots of loud sounds and passed without incident. But it was clear that the solo hiker was still shaken (and no wonder, since she'd only ever seen a bear in a zoo prior to that encounter).

Experience, preparedness, and vigilance in the outdoors all have been shown to help people benefit more from solo experiences. That doesn't mean that well-conceived outings won't also sometimes be tough, but it means that there are effective ways to strategize against potential downsides of being alone out of doors.

helpful for restoration but is not necessarily essential. One key to having restorative experiences is that the natural environment "be rich enough and coherent enough to constitute a whole other world," said Kaplan. "A restorative environment must be of sufficient scope to engage the mind. It must provide enough to see, experience, and think about so that it takes up a substantial portion of the available room in one's head."[39] That could be as big as rafting the Colorado River through the Grand Canyon or as small as watching ants racing around on their hills in your backyard.

In that case, said Kaplan, "the sense of being away does not require that the setting be distant. Natural environments that are easily accessible thus offer an important resource for resting one's directed attention." What we're paying attention to, and how, is ultimately what's important. "Directed attention" relates to the way modern humans focus much of the time – with prolonged mental effort, or long and intense periods of concentration, which causes mental fatigue over time. This limitation is likely an evolutionary throwback, and it was helpful for our ancestors to look away from something merely *interesting* in favor of focusing on what was *essential* for their survival. What seems to relieve directed attention fatigue are sessions of what Kaplan calls "involuntary attention" or "soft fascination" (see Box 7.3), which are hallmarks of what's accessible in many natural settings.[40] We seem to know this intuitively on some level when we say that "a change of scenery" will do us good. For some people, that may mean a trip to Ibiza, whereas the authors of this book are generally content just to watch how the light changes with the day or the seasons on a neighborhood walk.

Some participants in our narrative interview studies talked about this type of "soft fascination" leading to peace and tranquility that they didn't experience otherwise. Alice, age forty-eight, from the United States, described her nature walks this way: "I focus on the minutiae so it's almost a meditation for me. I'm watching the grass, the bugs, the birds. I look at it as a place to quiet my mind because my mind doesn't shut up very often and, for whatever reason, having small things to focus on is a way to do that." Ahmad, age thirty-seven, from Iran, described his solo strolls this way: "I tend to notice how it feels to walk outside, the change of temperature between indoors and outdoors. I tend to notice every-thing on the way. I sense the sunlight, the light hitting against my skin."

Other psychological and cognitive benefits of exposure to nature often cited across that body of research are many: decreased stress and depression, elevated mood, lowered anxiety and rumination, and improved memory and cognition. Spending time in parks and woodlands and on beaches, or simply being shown images of nature in some cases, seems to increase energy and vitality and reduce fatigue, restore attention, spur creativity, and encourage a general sense of well-being.[41–47] Studies done by Netta and colleagues have also shown that nature exposure helps people feel more alive (and makes them more caring and generous – a bonus to society).[48]

An important caveat to the research on the mental health effects of nature is that it has a heavily Western bias. University of Vermont researchers recently analyzed a decade of research from the field – including 174 peer-reviewed studies from 2010 to 2020 – and found that study participants were overwhelmingly Caucasian. More than 95 percent of studies were done in high-income westernized nations in North America, Europe, and East Asia – while research on the Global South (except for westernized nations like South Africa) was almost nonexistent.[49] The handful of studies that have considered nonwhite, non-Western experiences also describe health and wellness benefits of immersion in nature, which appear to generalize across different cultural and socioeconomic backgrounds. But, given the scarcity of research on less-westernized nations, it's worth considering that people in other parts of the world could be having some different daily experiences of nature from which we can also learn.

BOX 7.3 ATTENTION RESTORATION THEORY

One clue as to why we're so mentally rejuvenated by nature may lie in the way it influences our attention. Contrast the feeling of standing on a packed street corner in Piccadilly with sitting on a blanket in Regent's Park watching the sunlight filter through the tree canopy. Whereas busy cities with honking taxis tend to sap our energy, natural environments tend to require less, or rather different, attention. It makes sense that spending more time in nature tends to rest, renew, and restore us.

That's not a new idea in science – it was proposed by researchers more than thirty years ago – but the empirical evidence to support it has been growing since then. Rachel and Stephen Kaplan at the University of Michigan launched their influential attention restoration theory (ART) based on the premise that natural spaces and scenes encourage effortless attention, which reboots the brain and gives us a feeling of well-being.[50] ART contends that nature attracts our attention via "soft fascination," compared to the "hard," or directed, attention required to cope with the various demands of nonnatural places. The thinking is that a gentler, indirect focus – the kind used to take in a sunset, bird, or flower – clears our heads of worry and concern, helps us recover from mental fatigue by reducing internal noise, and encourages reflection and restoration.[39]

The claim that nature alters our consciousness is a pretty big one, and since the Kaplans first proposed ART, other researchers have been testing its veracity. One early and creative set of field studies done by researchers at the University of California, Irvine pitted one group vacationing in urban areas against another backpacking in a wilderness setting (a third control group engaged in "passive relaxation" at home). The researchers found that their subjects experienced greater restoration from nature versus the other experiences. The natural environment group had higher rates of "overall happiness," and they also performed better on a proofreading task meant to measure their level of mental restoration.[51] Subsequent studies have shown similar results in groups that simply saw images of restorative environments or had views of nature from their indoor spaces. The positive impacts of nature to insulate and help us recover from stressful life events have also been well studied (some fascinating work has been done, in particular, on the soothing effects of "blue rooms" on prisoners in solitary confinement).[52]

Over time, aspects of ART have also been challenged. One 2018 paper criticized what the researchers saw as a lack of evidence for the idea that humans experience and/or benefit from "soft fascination" in green spaces (that we relax into indirect attention because we have evolved to care about nature).[53] In response, researchers at the University of Michigan (including one of the Kaplans) put soft fascination to the test by asking nearly 400 adults, recruited online, to reflect on four distinct experiences: walking in nature, watching television, hanging out at home, and using a smartphone. Of the four activities, only walking in nature pulled participants' attention forward simply by being interesting, along with encouraging more self-awareness and allowing them to daydream. The researchers concluded that nature alone supported soft fascination.[54] While the mechanism and effects of ART have not been definitively supported, it's a promising concept that warrants more research.

Alongside the possible mental health benefits of nature are its potential physiological benefits. Many studies have shown positive influences of green spaces (or blue ones, in the case of water resources) on our nervous, endocrine, cardiovascular, and immune systems.[55] And in 2018, researchers from the University of East Anglia published a survey of the health benefits of green space exposure compiled in more than 140 studies, including a total of 290 million participants from twenty countries. The British researchers showed evidence that spending time in nature significantly lowered risks for several chronic illnesses. It reduced levels of stress hormones, lowered heart rate, reduced the risk of coronary heart disease, lowered blood pressure, lowered cholesterol, reduced the risk of type II diabetes, and reduced all-cause mortality.[56]

To garner the desired effects of nature therapy, one does not need to be on a multiday solo trek across the Pyrenees. Some research shows that being outside is not even required to get a buzz from nature. Sitting by a window with a view of the sea, sky, or a bird in a tree is enough. But as we'll see, some aspects of being outside are unique to health and healing.

Some of the longest-running research on the physical effects of nature exposure has come from Asia.[57,58] The poetic term *shinrin-roku*, or "forest bathing," was coined by a governmental agency in Japan in 1982 to describe taking in, and connecting with, the forest atmosphere in a leisurely way. Scientific inquiry into the therapeutic effects of forests began not long after that,[59] and since then, studies have shown that "bathing" in the tree canopy lowers stress hormones, including cortisol, adrenaline, and noradrenaline. It also lowers heart rate and blood pressure and decreases sympathetic nerve activity (which controls the body's "fight or flight" response), while increasing parasympathetic nerve activity (which regulates the "rest and digest" functions).[60] Researchers have also found that forest bathing reduces symptoms of anxiety and depression; increases energy, creativity, concentration, and memory; and improves sleep.[61–66]

Findings relating to the effects of forest bathing on immune function are particularly compelling. Beginning in 2005, Qing Li, a medical doctor and researcher in Japan, began plucking adults out of thrumming downtown Tokyo for a three-day, two-night trip into the cedar, beech, and oak woods of northwest Japan. He took blood and urine samples from his subjects in the city, then on days 2 and 3 of the excursion. The results of the change in venue were remarkable, particularly related to "significant differences" (said the researchers) in the number and activity of so-called natural killer (NK) cells in their subjects. On any given day, we all have that type of white blood cell in our bodies. They are soldiers that use killer enzymes to zap tumor cells or ones infected with a virus. Li found that the participants' NK cells were boosted by phytoncides (wood essential oils), which are antimicrobial volatile organic compounds "exhaled" by trees and inhaled by humans.[67–69] Subsequent research has reinforced those findings and has measured other medicinal effects of forest aromatherapy, including modulating blood pressure and blood glucose levels.[70–73]

Forest bathing goes by different names in other parts of the world. *Waldeinsamkeit* is an enduring ideology in Germany, loosely translated as the "solitude of the forest" or the sublime sensation of being alone in the woods.[74] Professor Nikolaus Wegmann, a Germanist and literary historian at Princeton University, told the BBC in 2021 that *Waldeinsamkeit* "represents the soul and deeper psyche of Germany." Although it's long been a cherished condition in Germany (and believed to be a cure for stress), the pandemic years encouraged a forest renaissance there, as in many other parts of the world. Whether in Japan or Germany – or in deep wilderness or a city park – the concept, expectations, and effects of getting up close and personal with trees closely track no matter the locale.[75]

ALONE, BUT IN THE COMPANY OF NATURE

When Naseem Rakha was growing up in Chicago in the 1960s, her family moved from a racially diverse high rise to a three-acre parcel of land in the suburbs adjacent to a forest preserve.[76] Outside the city, life was different in many ways, for better and worse. Rakha, who is half Indian, suffered from racial discrimination for the first time and sought refuge on solo outings, collecting rocks and experiences, in the tree-covered tract near her new home. "I would just observe, observe, observe and spend lots of time in the forest alone ... and that instilled in me, at a young age, a sense of independence and solace, and quiet. I got a sense that I can satisfy my own needs," she said.

Rakha grew up to be a geologist who fell in love with the desert and, along the way, acquired a particular affinity for the Grand Canyon in Arizona. She has found no better place than that 6,000-foot-deep gash in the earth – which bottoms out at the surging Colorado River – "to separate myself from the friction of the world," she said. Like water eroding rock over millions of years, Rakha feels that daily life, with its near-constant flashing and pinging (and bills and politics!), can chafe our spirits. She regularly trades the "chaos of the modern world swirling around" for the basics of rock, river, fossil, flint, and sky. Rakha, like JR Harris (the solo adventurer whom we met at the start of this chapter), has a powerful relationship with nature – and with solitude.

Research on the topic of being *solitary* in nature – as opposed to the effects of simply being in nature – is still very new, and there's relatively little scientific evidence yet to build on. But we can speculate about what may be going on when those two states are combined based on the large amount of data about nature's effects on people. What we've seen in our research on solitude so far, and our own life experiences, also provides some context. In our Solitude Project, we've heard from adventurers of all calibers that the combination of solitude and nature can foster a kind of supercharged state that seems to enhance the benefits of both nature and solitude while conferring entirely new benefits of its own.

One major effect we've observed is that the solo/nature state tends to alter one's outlook. Harris loves stepping away from the rush and rumble of daily city life and into a more basic existence.[1–3] For Rakha, the perspective she gets from nature feels like being part of something bigger than herself and ultimately subordinate to forces greater than herself. "If you're walking in a forest, you're walking on the limbs and twigs and leaves and detritus of things that have passed, and you see the growth that's coming from it. ... When you are in nature, you're constantly reminded that there's a cycle and it's always changing. And so it can give you a sense of hope, renewal, perspective," she said. "It gives you the satisfaction of feeling very small and finite and within something that feels much bigger, and not infinite, but approaching a sense of time that you can't wrap your mind around."[76]

When Harris is in nature, he also feels an innate connection to something larger than himself. "You realize that you need to be a bit humble, and you need to know who you are and where exactly your place is in the universe," he said. Nature has been doing its thing for billions of years, and nothing humans do can improve on that, but he believes we can tap into its greatness. "When you get out in the air, if you can get yourself into that same pace, that same rhythm, that same cadence of nature, and just go with that flow, that's exhilarating for me," he said.[1]

That sense of cosmic vastness is shared by some of our research subjects as well. Sandra likes to walk in the mountains, alone and above the tree line, because of the feeling of grandeur that envelops her there. "It almost feels like being alone on the moon or something sometimes. And it's so comforting because everything is so big and it's been around for so long, that it makes you and all your problems and your whole life seem insignificant. And that's a sort of great feeling, I think. It's just so reassuring," she said. Fiona, age sixty-five, from Scotland, said, "It allows you to think in on yourself, reflect and just take in the beauty of the world, actually." And sometimes that perspective takes on a spiritual or religious vibe, like for Mary, who told us, "Having a belief in some sort of supreme being, supreme soul, whatever you wish to call it, I think that is what I find out somewhere beautiful, somewhere that is a natural part of the earth. Looking at trees or fields or a beautiful sunset, or looking at the sea in particular, I think it's a connection to God really, and just to ongoing life, the living earth."

That connection, or sense of relatedness to nature, is important because it can help fulfill a core psychological need. Remember, as we talked about in earlier chapters, relatedness is key to well-being. We've talked mostly about the need to feel related to other people, but recent research suggests that relatedness may be satisfied, in part, by buddying up to nature. As Muir and Emerson demonstrated, we've long had an inkling that feeling linked to nature breeds well-being. But only in the past decade or so has evidence been mounting to support the idea that feeling a meaningful connection to something bigger than oneself can have a real impact on how one moves through the world.[77] Now, experts who look at the importance of "nature relatedness," or the ways we think about, feel, and experience nature, have found wide-reaching benefits.[78] Canadian researchers observed how feeling like a part of nature affected a sense of well-being in 500 research subjects. They found that positive affect, autonomy, and personal growth were all correlated with a sense of feeling akin to the natural world. "People who are related to nature also reported having a sense of purpose in life, and more self-acceptance," they said.[79]

Experiencing that link to nature, and recovery in its presence, may be possible while gawking at a herd of bison amid a sea of humanity at Yellowstone National Park, but it's arguably easier, or more powerful, without strangers in the mix. Researchers in the Netherlands and Sweden wondered how environment (nature or city) and social context (alone or with company) affects "attentional recovery" (described as regaining the ability to concentrate). They put that to the test by showing a series of images to 106 participants in their lab. After seeing the images, which suggested an hour-long walk through either a forest or an urban center, subjects rated the attractiveness of the environment, both as if they were on their own and as if they were with a friend.

Two interesting findings were recorded. First, the "attractiveness" rating closely correlated with the perceived likelihood of recovery, and second, the subjects found walking in the city more attractive with a friend but felt the restorative effects of the forest would be greater when they were there on their own.[80] In later related work, the Swedish and Dutch researchers were studying the psychological benefits of a brisk walk with parameters similar to the first study. In this one, twenty university students took a series of four outdoor walks each – one with a friend in a city, one with a friend in a park, one alone in a city, and one alone in a park. Again, they observed that when walking in the park, "revitalization" was greater when subjects went solo compared to walking in the city (there the effects were better when the participants had a buddy).[81]

Part of what boosts well-being while alone in nature may be the feeling or understanding that elements of nature are beings, like our own, that may be enhanced in the absence of other humans. Look at a cloud, touch a tree, hear a nightingale sing, talk to a house plant, and you may get the reassuring (we hope) sense that you're not alone. Alex, age thirty-eight, wild-swims in ponds among ducks, swans, and herons to feel akin to that crowd. "You understand that you are a part of nature, so you are not dominating there. So, you're kind of harmonizing with nature as well, you accept nature as it is," he said. "I feel I'm much more positive when I go outside to communicate with nature. I mean even to see animals or squirrels or something like that." Another of our research subjects, Anh, an Asian American in her forties, talked about the basic joy of talking to the African violet house plants she lovingly cultivates. "It's living, it's personification," she said. "That's my companion, I guess you could say." That feeling that they're in a relationship, almost an exchange, with nature gives many people the sense that they are never alone in nature, even when they're in solitude.

"FREEDOM FROM" AND "FREEDOM TO" IN NATURAL SOLITUDE

Researchers have pinpointed several other benefits of being alone in natural settings. Freedom, in many forms, is one perk that often arises in such studies. We divide that sense into what we see as two experiences – "freedom from" and "freedom to." "Freedom from" is expressed by research subjects as a break from all things related to society – noise, expectations, demands. "Freedom to" is what we can fill that newfound space with, once we let go of all the other junk. As we've experienced ourselves, and heard often from others, being in nature connects us to our instincts and senses, emotions, and bodies in a way that is not easily replicated otherwise. The freedom of going solo in an outdoor space (provided one feels safe doing so) can be highly transformative in terms of personal growth, leading people to redefine themselves and their lives through self-connection, -reflection, -discovery, and -confidence.

For JR Harris,[1,2] and many more folks, the "freedom from"/"freedom to" aspect of nature/solitude has had lifelong appeal. From his time in the Boy Scouts and his first cross-country trip to Alaska when he was in his early twenties, Harris has always wanted to see what lay beyond the end of the road, past the next ridge and river. Time in nature gave him the freedom to follow his insatiable curiosity toward growth and self-reflection. "Whenever I took one of these trips, when I came back, I was a different person. It seemed like I was more mature than the guys my age. And as much as I'm finding out about other people and glaciers and caribou migrations, what I'm really learning about is who I am and how I deal with things," said Harris.

As a boy, being at camp was an escape from city life and everything that meant for an African American kid coming of age during the civil rights era. And it offered Harris the "freedom to" discover who he was and to imagine a different life for himself than he'd seen growing up. "Back in the '50s and '60s, there were so many barriers, and so many things that had to be overcome to get an education and really to find out who you are," he said. "But I was able to get away and get up into the mountains and see that there was something different for a young kid, that maybe you could really hope for something better." As he got older, solo wilderness adventures offered Harris new and different freedoms. "All I have to worry about is when I want to eat and where I'm going to find a place to sleep and getting from one place to another safely. And forgetting about the telephones and cars, I can put all of that at a distance. And for the time I'm out there, it is like I am the only person in the world, and I find that very appealing," he said.

Going solo in green spaces, or at least having that perception, has a decluttering, "freedom from" effect for many people like Harris. One early landmark paper published in 1982, from a researcher at the University of Tennessee, looked at the cognitive dimensions of wilderness solitude. It concluded that, among the hundred-plus university-aged wilderness campers it studied, having some control over the information they must process, and the attention required to process it, was key to their enjoyment of that space. Importantly, "wilderness solitude" as defined in this study, and in some others, didn't mean total isolation from others, and most of the campers generally enjoyed the outdoors alongside close friends and family. Most important to benefiting from the relative privacy of the wilderness setting was that the experience allowed for what the researcher called "cognitive freedom." In the case of the wilderness campers in this study, "tranquility and peacefulness" were achieved in three ways: freedom from unwanted intrusions like noise pollution, freedom from the "pressures and tensions of everyday life," and freedom to make choices about where to direct one's attention, what to do, and when to do it.[82]

Another more recent paper, written by researchers in the United Kingdom and South Africa, reinforced these findings.[83] The small but unique study looked at the wilderness experiences of nine university students (age twenty to forty-three years) in Northumberland in northeast England and North Nidderdale in north central England. Study participants first walked and camped in an uninhabited area with a small group, then spent roughly thirty-six hours alone in the wild with no electronic devices or books (though they could write in a journal). The researchers found that the most profound experiences occurred during the solo phase of the experiment, when participants had a strong sense of physical freedom and distance from the distractions of modern life, as well as a feeling of freedom from the responsibilities and obligations of their daily grind. Several months after the field study was done, the researchers interviewed the same participants and found that the experiences had had a meaningful and lasting effect. A third paper focused on a younger group (fourteen- and fifteen-year-olds) also found that the adolescent campers liked the "freedom from the noise of modernity" (though we doubt they put it that way!) afforded by time alone outdoors.[84]

Freedom of that kind is encouraged by alone time in nature, in part because of what it lacks: the prying eyes of other people. The kids at camp perceived solo time as a "break" from societal pressure and being observed by others. That was also true in the Tennessee study from 1982 in which adults said alone time in nature was great because it afforded them freedom from expectations, observations, and societal rules and constraints. It gave them the rare opportunity to be more authentic and somewhat anonymous.[85] Harris put it this way: "Nature doesn't care who you are, or how young or old, it doesn't care how important you think you are, and what you have to do. There's just something very fair, some equity, that out in the wilderness is just, it is what it is."

What links "freedom from" and "freedom to" has been well defined by several researchers writing about transformational experiences in natural solitude.[86,87] When we're able to focus less on what is beyond ourselves, at least in the direct, draining way other people require, we can focus more closely on what lies within us. Self-reflection is a key "freedom to" described by many people enjoying solitude in nature. The adolescent campers said that being alone in nature gave them the freedom to focus on themselves. Several other studies have found that being in nature promotes self-examination and allows people to reconnect and achieve closeness with their own thoughts and needs.[88,89] Many people have reported that nature is a space for them to be still and to reflect on past and future life trajectories, and to gain a better understanding of themselves.[90,91] That's an experience Harris has had countless times in his decades of solo explorations. "It was, and still is, fascinating to me how spending time alone in the wilderness has influenced who I become as a person," he said.

One small but in-depth study looked at the motivations and experiences of four expert North American canoeists to determine if long periods spent alone in nature encouraged personal growth. The paddlers, age forty-five to sixty-eight years, each had at least twenty-five years of experience and already had been on several solo expeditions of at least two weeks in duration. In general, the researchers found that "a self-chosen solo canoe expedition offered an environment for self-actualization, enjoyment, and personal growth." While alone, the canoeists could better observe and explore nature and their place in it. Being alone with one's own thoughts in peace and tranquility and unfettered by time "created the ideal environment for reflection," said the researchers. Participants could contemplate their own beliefs, attitudes, and decisions and maybe even challenge or alter them.[92] (This was also seen in a 2007 in-depth analysis of women who hiked the long-distance Appalachian Trail. One woman, Leslie Mass, movingly described her 2,000-mile solo walk as an opportunity to "shed all the layers that no longer fit."[93]) And with that freedom, the canoeists were able to bring deeper meaning to their experiences. The researchers concluded that "the benefits of time to reflect that emanated from the canoeists were a feeling of renewal, pleasure, satisfaction, and self-awareness."[92]

Even though the canoeists were highly skilled and experienced, the journeys were still challenging to pull off alone. The mental, physical, and emotional demands of paddling through wilderness alone are many, but the return on that investment nevertheless seemed high. One canoeist explained that he was able to successfully confront obstacles because he became more aware of, and sensitive to, his surroundings and his potential and capabilities. Many people who pursue wilderness experiences have reported feeling similarly empowered by the opportunity to be self-reliant. During that time, they may overcome challenges imposed by tricky terrain and shifting weather while not having access to the tools and technologies that they're accustomed to in modern life.

Interestingly, the feeling of self-reliance experienced by testing one's physical and psychological strength during solo wilderness outings often extends to beyond that period of time. In the study of backpackers in Northumberland,[83] the participants returned to "normal" lives feeling more confident in handling life stresses. Think of it as the "I can do anything" effect, by which study subjects reentered their workaday lives with newfound strength and self-esteem. For Harris, that means that sometimes rivers must be crossed when they're high or you get lost and have to find your way back to camp before dark. "I've been afraid so many times out there," he said, but dealing with adversity, even issues of life and death (like grizzlies, lightning, and accidents) in the wilderness, gives him perspective for when he returns to city life and confronts a problem. "I'm like, 'Dude, you walked across Greenland,' and so when I'm at home nothing seems to be that drastic anymore, nothing that I can't handle," Harris said. "Most of all, I don't anticipate. I stay in the present tense. I enjoy what I'm doing and when I don't, I just deal with it. These are the lessons I bring home," he said.

The immense power of rising to a challenge alone in nature is evident in another more recent study including forty adults in Norway, Germany, and New Zealand (age twenty-one to sixty-four years) that pinpointed a host of positive outcomes resulting from their solo outdoor experiences.

The study authors split those aspects of well-being – as psychologists sometimes do – into two categories based on the philosophy of Aristotle. Those are "hedonic" (relating to emotions, engagement, and vitality) and "eudaimonic" (relating to relationships, accomplishment, and meaning). They found that, regardless of age, the experiences were positive, but they also saw some interesting differences between the groups. Younger participants were more likely to cite as positive the eudaimonic factors, including strengthening relationships with nature, other people, and the self (relatedness); the feeling of accomplishment achieved by overcoming challenges (self-reliance); and reflecting on their own values, beliefs, and goals (self-reflection). On the other hand, older participants were more likely to note a boost in positive emotions, fully engaging with the outdoors, and feeling vital and energized after activities and rest in nature.[93]

On a smaller but no less significant scale are everyday triumphs of going solo in nature – they may include spotting a bird in a nearby park you've never seen before or clearing a patch of garden mired in weeds. Either way, you're navigating, making discoveries, and maybe observing something beautiful or inspirational, which all contribute to well-being in nature, and in solitude.

FLOWING WITH NATURE

In our own research on people's experiences in solitude, many of our subjects brought up interactions with nature without being prompted to talk about them. Sometimes our participants preferred interfacing with nature on their own (or with a small, quiet group with whom they could hear their own thoughts), or they simply chose to spend whatever solitude time they had in green spaces. Either way, being alone in nature afforded them some particularly interesting advantages, in addition to those we've already described.

Elizabeth in England talked about the pleasant feeling of being in the moment when walking outdoors and how that heightens her senses and helps her feel more connected to her surroundings. "I think it's something that keeps me rooted, just that sense of the changing seasons and where we are with nature," she said. Harris told us that being alone outdoors increases awareness of his environs. "When I'm out there by myself, my senses seem to get sharper. I seem to see things and hear things and notice things that I don't pick up on even if I'm with just one other person. And so to me there's an aura about being there, alone in nature, that's very satisfying to me ... and I get a sense of inner peace," he said.

That feeling of being entirely absorbed in an activity to the extent of "losing time" while doing it has been described by some researchers as a "flow state."[91,94] Flow has been studied in sports, music, art, and other arenas and is described as the harmony of being in a focused zone, but with effortless attention.[95] But that doesn't mean it comes easily or that it happens when we are engaged in easy (to us) tasks. In a flow state, we must be intrinsically motivated, in control, and feeling that we're taking on a challenge and responding well to it.[96] Hiking alone in nature, for example, can present plenty of opportunities for flow, but only when skill and ability match the task in a way that makes us feel competent.

In one 2003 paper looking at solo hiking experiences, participants described "flow" as a pleasurable psychological benefit of hiking alone. The researchers interviewed twenty hikers (ten women and ten men), age twenty to fifty years, in West Virginia about their experiences of solo trekking. "Participants described this phenomenon as a very relaxing, calming, and peaceful experience that led to personal renewal, a 'revving of the engines,' and even spiritual revitalization," said the researchers. "Solo hikers interviewed for this study described many of the psychological characteristics associated with a flow experience. ... Participants experienced a loss of ego and a centering of attention while hiking alone that allowed them to 'absorb all that's around me' and 'have no distractions.' Participants described this 'flow state' as highly rewarding, using terms like 'refreshing' or 'renewal' or 'relaxing' to describe the emotional and physical rewards of solo hiking."[91]

"Flow" in nature coexists with so-called peak experiences,[97] which we touched on in Chapter 4. While peak experiences can happen anywhere, much of the evidence for achieving them in solitude comes from spending that time in nature. Often that is characterized by having a sense of awe, or even transcendence, from one's surroundings.[98] That may happen if you ever find yourself atop a mountain or deep-sea diving, but peak experiences don't require grandiosity. Gary, age seventy, from the United Kingdom, told us about peak moments he's had in backyard gardens since age twelve. "I've always loved watching nature close up. I mean the pleasure you can get from just walking around – not doing anything – but just watching the bees at work. And simply watching the hover flies sort of buzzing around your head and things like that. It's magical!" he said.

A lack of interaction with other people, accompanied by a closeness and connectedness to nature, may be an ideal recipe for peak experiences, and for general well-being, in solitude. As we speculated earlier, the nature–solitude combination appears to create a supersolitude and/ or supernature experience that cannot otherwise be replicated. Emerson, the nineteenth-century writer, believed that solitude is the only mechanism through which humans can fully tap into nature and all it has to offer. "To go into solitude, a man needs to retire as much from his chamber as from society. I am not solitary whilst I read and write, though nobody is with me. But if a man would be alone, let him look at the stars," he wrote.[99] When a person experiences true solitude, in nature, said Emerson, it "take[s] him away." Harris, who is now mulling a long-desired trek into the High Atlas Mountains of North Africa, is a living embodiment of Emerson's claim, though Harris calls it, simply, "living a dream."

CHAPTER 8

Finding Your Happy Place in Solitude

SEVERAL YEARS AGO, ONE OF OUR RESEARCH SUBJECTS, Lisa, went on a five-day solo retreat in the rolling, heathery moors of Northumberland National Park. The small cabin where she stayed was just a couple of hours inland from her home on the northeast coast of England, but for Lisa, it was like finding a portal to a different dimension. At the time, her hobby was fiction writing, and as sheep grazed nearby and rain clouds crowded the sky, Lisa let her imagination flow. "It was just me in this little cabin with a little open fire, and the dog, and I wrote and wrote, and went for walks, and I ate healthily, and it was just terrific. Later, everyone was like, 'How did you cope? Did you not see anybody for five days?' No, not a soul, and I think about that trip at least once a day since then," she said.

At the cabin, Lisa had no Wi-Fi or cell signal, and after a couple of days, she switched off the music she'd been playing. At that point, she tuned in to birdsong, the splat and patter of raindrops hitting the roof, and the glow of the star-crammed heavens. "It's actually quite shocking how quiet it is. So, it took a bit of getting used to but it's completely and totally dark, and completely and totally silent. It's very odd to say that I miss it, but I really do," she said. "It was amazing just to be completely disconnected. I miss the detachment. I don't know if I could do it long term, but I didn't have a problem with absolute solitude and complete silence. There was nothing. It was just incredible."

As solitude researchers, there's a lot about Lisa's experience and perspective and how she expresses both that we wanted to unpack and examine. We wondered, just as her family and friends had, how she – a busy, forty-four-year-old pastry chef and mother – could unplug so completely from others. What role did setting play in her experience? What value did quiet and stillness have? If our solitude doesn't look like Lisa's, are we doing it wrong? By looking closely at each of these aspects of solo time, as we do in this chapter, we can begin to understand more about what factors really matter in solitude.

SENSORY OVERLOAD

In Lisa's case, nature and solitude seem to be highly compatible because, as we discussed at length in Chapter 7, they offer many people similar and complementary benefits, such as freedom, autonomy, relaxation, and self-reflection. "Returning to nature" is, in many ways, an ancient ritual that reboots us modern humans and improves our overall well-being. Why nature and solitude, whether together or separate, have this effect on many people is explained by what is and isn't happening there and how our attention shifts to match that setting. Research shows that, for better or worse, even subtle shifts in what we sense can make a big difference in our experience of events or spaces. Depending on the setting, our senses can overwhelm us or help us reconnect to parts of ourselves that often lie dormant.

To understand what's going on when we're strolling through a forest versus walking to a café with a colleague or chatting with folks at a cocktail party versus making dinner at home alone, it helps to do the following exercise. Imagine standing by a lake on a still morning. The reflection mirrors the surrounding trees, clouds, and sky. Now, pick up a rock and throw it in the water, and watch the ripples distort the trees, blur the sky. Keep tossing rocks, and the reflection remains fractured, the surface never calms. If the stillness first experienced is our inner world, the rocks represent input from the social interactions we have every day – at work, the grocery store, or even home – which intrude on that inner sanctum. The resulting ripples are what psychologists call "arousal levels," which can be positive or negative, depending on the nature of the event or stimulus we encounter. In its extreme, we can think of it as a "you're hired!" or "you're fired!" variable. This came up in Chapter 4 when we talked about Thuy-vy's experiments on the deactivating effect solitude has on negative emotions. She found that in solitude, people weren't as "excited" as they may be in interactions with others, but they also weren't as stressed or anxious. Being alone had the effect of tamping down both high and low arousal levels.

It makes sense, then, that the best moments of solitude may happen when our internal state reflects those still waters and when that psychological quiet is supported by a mellow environment with little noise or excitement. For Lisa, that was a huge part of the appeal of the isolated cabin in the Northumberland hills. It was quiet, still, and dark. (It's important to note that nature, of course, is not *silent*, but nonanthropogenic sounds like waves crashing and birds tweeting aren't logged in the human brain as "noise" in the same way a train horn is.[1]) Even though Lisa lives in a relatively sleepy seaside village when she's not at the cabin, she can still hear occasional buses rumbling down the high street, neighbors chattering in the streets, and dogs barking in the distance. "You don't realize how noisy the real world is until you're removed from it," she said.

Like Lisa, from the time most of us awake, we're bombarded by sensory information – a chiming alarm (or a chirpy Ed Sheeran tune in Heather's case), airplanes buzzing overhead, kids demanding breakfast, or emails racking up in our inboxes, *ping, ping, ping*. Humans evolved to be hyperaware of our surroundings, and although that's still a helpful way to move through the modern world – like when crossing a busy street safely – it also has drawbacks. The flashing crosswalk signs, honking taxis, people bumping by, and buses and bikes careening through the intersection can leave us feeling like a pinball machine on *tilt*. As many of us know on an instinctual level, near-constant sensory information coming at us every day eventually takes a toll.

People have been perceiving our world as noisy for a very long time. One of the oldest written stories in the world, the *Epic of Gilgamesh* (2100 BCE, from ancient Mesopotamia, now Iraq), begins with a gripe about noise.[2] At a time in which "the world bellowed like a wild bull," complained one god in the poem, "the uproar of mankind is intolerable and sleep is no longer possible by reason of the babel." Their solution? To wipe out humanity. Of course, that was fiction, and people carried on inventing lots and lots of machines – horse-drawn carriages, hand-cranked car engines, Harley Davidsons, supersonic jets – and the sound of that technology has pretty much drowned out everything else our ancestors used to be able to hear. (To get a sense of the start of mass loudening, check out the British Library's "period backgrounds" collection of sound effects, which includes a "Victorian factory" soundbite with the clanging of metal being hammered, the scraping of wood lathes, and the hiss and moan of steam engines.[3] If just two minutes of listening is misery, we can only imagine what a sixteen-hour shift was like!)

In 1859, British nurse and social reformer Florence Nightingale wrote, "Unnecessary noise is the most cruel absence of care that can be inflicted on sick or well."[4] What she understood on a visceral level became the focus of many scientists over the past few decades who have been measuring the health impacts of anthropogenic noise. We know now that humans make cognitive decisions all the time about what to pay attention to in our environment and what to ignore, and noise increases our level of general alertness or our process of activation and attention.[5] As a result, it can impair our cognitive function to some extent – by confusing that process and reducing performance accuracy (including working memory).[6]

Research continues to reveal more about what's happening to our bodies when we're exposed to noise – and when we're not. Researchers in Boston have used positron emission tomography, or PET, to show that transportation noise heightens activity in the amygdala, an area of the brain thought to form the core of a neural system known for processing fearful and threatening stimuli. That activity can trigger stress responses (like inflammation) that can lead to metabolic and cardiovascular diseases.[7] Noise, or unwanted sound, can make us feel exhausted, edgy, and overwhelmed and can increase our risk of anxiety, depression, and dementia. It can also do real damage to our physical health, increasing the risks of heart attack, stroke, and diabetes.[7–9]

A recent survey by researchers in Germany looked at epidemiological and experimental studies from 2007 to 2018 and found that noise from aircraft, road traffic, and rail traffic – and the chronic stress it causes – represents a significant risk factor for the development of cardiovascular disease.[10] A 2018 World Health Organization (WHO) report determined that at least 100 million people in the European Union were affected by road traffic noise and that at least one million healthy years of life are lost every year to traffic-related noise in Western Europe alone.[11] Researchers drilling down on those numbers studied road traffic noise in nearly 750 cities in twenty-five European countries. They found that sixty million adults were exposed to road traffic noise at levels harmful to their health, resulting in more than 3,600 preventable deaths. Based on prior research done by the WHO and the European Environment Agency, the German investigators called road traffic noise "one of the main environmental risks to health and well-being."[12–14]

Chronic noise exposure contributes to 48,000 new cases of heart disease in Europe each year (by promoting the development of vascular dysfunction and high blood pressure) and disrupts the sleep of 6.5 million people (causing an elevation of stress hormone levels and oxidative stress).[7] Researchers at the University of Michigan looking at the sources and levels of noise pollution in the United States found that, due to noise exposure, tens of millions of Americans also suffer a range of adverse health outcomes, including heart disease and hearing loss.[15]

Despite abundant research showing how deleterious the environments we have built can be for us, escaping from the (bleeping!) loud world and its effects can be difficult – but is still possible – and we can use solitude to create that temporary shelter. There are still plenty of ways to find solace on planet Earth – spending time in nature is a great one – because of the changes in our attention it encourages. But, as we'll see, finding or creating a setting in which we can honor our individual senses is most important.

HONORING OUR SENSES

Anyone who has watched a child make a beeline for a huge puddle on a rainy day can see how humans are multisensory creatures, thriving on experiences that fully engage our five major senses. Children may examine their reflection in the puddle, stomp noisily in it, taste and feel the raindrops on their cheeks and tongues, and smell the damp air. Puddle stomping can be a gleeful, all-sensory experience that adults rarely partake in, but we can try to replicate it in some advantageous ways. As we mentioned in Chapter 7, the practice of forest bathing is one way that's been recommended and popular in recent years to engage positively the big five – seeing, hearing, smelling, feeling, and tasting (Netta, for one, can attest to the joys of gorging on wild berries while on a nature walk).

Research has shown how powerful it can be to tune in to our senses, particularly in natural settings. Early on, wilderness researchers looking at the benefits of being in "unimproved" nature heard from their participants that nature experiences create "a unique combination of extreme states of consciousness and increased sensory acuity."[16] Since then, there have been a lot of studies on how *viewing* nature (its colors and shapes, mostly) offers a host of benefits for health and well-being (including, remarkably, altering one's perception of pain).[17-27] But there's likely more to it than just what we see, and some research suggests that stimulating multiple senses concurrently in nature can enhance positive psychological states.[28-30]

One recent study done in Boulder, Colorado, by a group of researchers from several parts of the United States showed that *hearing* more birdsong while walking on a trail improved the hikers' perceived psychological restoration. The researchers played a "phantom chorus" of birdsong from speakers out of sight of trail users, then asked people who hiked those trails – as well as others without the piped-in birdsong – how they felt about their experiences. Those who had heard the enhanced birdsong also had a magnified experience of well-being (the researchers speculated that the result may have been linked to a perception of greater biodiversity in the area).[31]

Many other recent studies have shown how "natural quiet" – including sounds of wind, water, and animals[32-35] – is a major reason people visit and want to protect US national parks.[36] Those sounds, versus anthropogenic noises like traffic and industry, consistently win over listeners. The sounds of rural soundscapes and botanical gardens beat out urban parks and city soundscapes because, researchers posit, they offer a host of restorative effects.[37-43] That's something Netta, who has lived in suburban settings for most of her adult life, deeply identifies with. Whenever she gets away to the countryside, especially somewhere she can escape road noise, the sounds of trees rustling and birds chirping are amplified in her mind. "And my head and my heart feel lighter, and I can breathe easier," she said.

A growing number of studies also suggest that the *tastes* and *smells* of nature could be as important as its sights and sounds. Taste links us immediately and intimately to our surroundings. If you've ever grown your own veggies, you know the superior flavor and sense of self-fulfillment that can be achieved from doing that. And anyone who's ever lived through a summer strike of sanitation workers in New York City (Heather is raising her hand here) can attest to the fact that what we smell can have a major impact on our mood and thinking. The use of smells to promote health, or aromatherapy, is a practice with long historical roots, but it's only more recently that research has shown that pleasant natural odors – like cut grass, blooming flowers, and beeswax – can improve mood and alertness; decrease stress, anxiety, and blood pressure; and increase feelings of happiness and calm.[44-51]

In 2019, UK researchers held workshops with nearly 200 participants in two woodlands in central England to assess the impact, if any, of forest smell. The subjects were asked to record their observations over a one-hour solo "woodland scavenger hunt," and during that time, they made 337 mentions of smells – and, in some cases, the (pleasant) absence of them. Roughly 30 percent of those comments directly linked the smells to well-being and, more specifically, to physical, cognitive, emotional, and spiritual benefits.[52] On the final sense, *touch*, there's very little research on the "hands-on" benefits of nature,[53] but most gardeners with soil-stained fingers – or children running barefoot through grass – may attest to the positive effects of being physically connected to the earth in that way. These benefits have been captured in research on local food production, gardening, and children's nature connections.[54-59] One of our research participants talked about his ritual of collecting bogwood near his home, then spending hours in soothing solitude smoothing and sculpting it into art.

"Favorite place" studies show that many adults find their happy places in natural settings near chirping birds or lapping waves and the like, possibly because of that sensory recalibration.[60] More precisely, research has shown that people from the United Kingdom, United States, Ireland, Scandinavia, and Senegal choose "natural" spaces as their happy places from 50 to 63 percent of the time. The restorative effects of those experiences, like relaxation and self-reflection, seem to be strengthened by how often a person visits their "happy place" in nature.[61–64] Researchers have also found that improvements to mood experienced alone in that natural spot can be both momentary and longer lasting.[65,66] When asked to define solitude in his life, one of our research subjects, sixty-eight-year-old Brian, from England, painted a soothing mental picture that combined time alone, quiet, and nature. "Peace, quiet, on your own, like you're fishing, nobody else around, lovely river, lovely location, fishing away. Peace, quiet, babble of a brook maybe. Just being with nature, lovely, being on your own," he said.

Clearly for folks like Brian and Lisa in Northumberland, an off-the-grid cabin with sheep bleating in the fields constitutes a "happy" place. But while evidence of the positive sensory effects of the outdoors is mounting, particularly when enjoyed alone, most people in the world still live in cities, and not everyone has a green space escape hatch nearby. So, what if you don't have access to a safe spot outdoors, or what if you're generally more content indoors? Does it really matter where you are or what you're doing in solitude?

STEPPING AWAY FROM THE FRAY

In our own research, we have heard from plenty of people whose happy places – and best spots for solitude – are within their homes, in a local library, or at a nearby house of worship. Some major features of those solitude experiences, which seem to make them as good as the nature-based kind for many people, is that they are chosen spaces with no immediate social demands or other distracting external stimuli. One doesn't need to be in a roadless area and miles from "civilization" to reset one's senses. The point is to step away from the fray of our daily interactions and tune in to something that appeals to us. This doesn't mean we have to head to the nearest isolation tank; in fact, studies have long shown that extreme forms of sensory deprivation are detrimental. Instead, it means finding an environment that facilitates focus on our immediate surroundings.

This brings us to an important topic in the settings of solitude: quiet. In our research, we've observed two kinds of quiet that people generally experience – inner and outer. Outer quiet is the literal absence of (man-made) noise and distraction from other people, and inner quiet is a figurative hush that exists when our minds are quiet. Our research subjects talked a lot about the ways they experience this difference in everyday solitude. Some achieve both inner and outer quiet in meditation and mindfulness practices (more on this in Chapter 9), whereas others may escape to outer quiet only to suffer from inner noise, or rumination. That's when, absent outside distractions, negative thoughts circle around in our brains like a whining, single-engine plane that won't land. That creates a mental environment that's not conducive to being alone, and it can be the reason that many people don't like solitude or think they're doing it wrong.

Nearly everyone will struggle in solitude from time to time, regardless of where they are and what they're doing. Most people usually find a work-around (we talk at length about resilience in solitude in Chapter 9). If rumination persists, however, consider spending time with others during those moments instead. That said, solitude need not be a zone just for positive thinking. Several of our study subjects talked about using time alone specifically to process difficult thoughts or emotions. A fight with a friend, a strained financial situation, a marital infidelity, and being overlooked for a promotion were all situations our participants chose to process during their time alone, and ultimately with positive results.

The highly varied experiences of our research subjects have taught us that there is no one-size-fits-all approach to the settings for solitude. What you do and where you do it are all highly customizable. One person's quiet room – or forest – is another's torture chamber. Case in point: twenty-eight-year-old Elliott from Germany loves to step away from his six roommates to an empty room where he can let loose by singing loudly and playing guitar. He's found that this type of alone time is much better for him than the quieter kind out in the woods. In fact, he took a recent solo backpacking trip and disliked most parts of it. While alone in the wilderness, his inner voice was far from quiet. "Why are you out here? You're bored! This camp food stinks!" His favorite part of solitude in the woods was coming home and entertaining his friends with funny stories about his various mishaps. That said, for most of the people we've spoken to, a happy place in solitude means finding a literal quiet spot where they can figuratively hear themselves think. There's now a growing body of research supporting why that's the case.

QUIETUDE (THE LOVE CHILD OF QUIET AND SOLITUDE)

As we talked about way back in Chapter 1, many Western cultures throughout history have often relegated solitude to the fringes and responded to it with suspicion at best or with moral and clinical panic at worst. But in some cultures, the concepts of solitude and quiet are understood as an inextricable pair and are more highly valued for that reason. That includes Finland, where communication ethnographer Donal Carbaugh probed how people there see solitude. He saw it closely linked to another idea – "quietude," or *hiljaisuus* in Finnish, a state in which people are undisturbed in their thoughts and can be "natural with ease." In a journal article, Carbaugh and colleagues described it this way: "A Finnish cultural scene can be set, then, with quietude as its primary mode, silence as its structuring norm, people being directly and knowingly engaged in this."[67]

Carbaugh's study participants described solitude as quiet, undisturbed time when they may be in complete solitude, or perhaps in companionate solitude, such as we described in Chapter 2, where they share personal space with another. One of his subjects said, "I will spend a week in the summer cottage in order to spend time by myself [*omissa oloissaan*]. Those present will include me, and perhaps my friend. The goal is to let other people know you want to be alone without anybody disturbing you. This is a very commonly used [phrase]. It describes a state of mind, when you want to calm down, get away from the hectic life and be alone with your thoughts."[67]

Chinese culture has had a similar relationship with quiet solitude tied to a sense of peacefulness and well-being. The concept was inspired in part by Taoist philosopher Chuang Tzu (aka Zhuangzi or Master Zhuang), who lived during China's violent Warring States period of the fourth century.[68] In his writing, he tells a famous story of the Woman Crookback (a wise female figure is sometimes used to personify the Tao or "Way" itself). In it, she reveals the secret to her contentment and longevity – solitude. "Put the world outside yourself; put things outside yourself; put life outside yourself; you will be able to achieve the brightness of dawn and to see your aloneness," she said.[69] More recently, the first woman of color to win an Academy Award for best director (2021),

Chinese-born Chloé Zhao, spoke about it being "okay to satisfy our primal need for silence." She said, "And in that silence, wonder on your own. Discover on your own. And don't ever be afraid to get to know yourself better."[70]

Beyond anecdotal appreciation of the value of quietude is now a growing body of scientific evidence of its importance. Quiet is a phenomenon that has been well studied in recent decades as it's gotten harder and harder to insulate ourselves from the cacophony of modern life. Those findings, in some cases, echo centuries of lived experiences in certain parts of the world, and most recently, the mounting benefits of quiet have gone mainstream and led to some interesting vacation choices. But first, some background on the science of quiet.

Peter Suedfeld, psychologist at the University of British Columbia in Canada, may have been the first researcher to recognize the value of quietude. His interest in the topic was piqued, he told us, when he examined sensory deprivation studies from the 1960s. In that research, participants deprived of stimulation reported visual and auditory hallucinations. But what others perceived as a lack of stimulation Suedfeld saw as *over*stimulation. Subjects in the studies wore vision-impairing goggles and touch-prohibiting gloves and listened to a constant stream of white noise piped into the lab. Suedfeld believed those sensory extremes threw off the balance of study participants and didn't accurately measure the effects of milder forms of sensory deprivation.[71–75]

Suedfeld decided to do his own experiments and got very different results. He put his participants in darkened and quiet rooms but didn't employ the other sense-depriving techniques. His subjects sometimes spent long periods, even several days at a time, with little stimulation, yet they didn't experience the kinds of mental problems that had been reported in the earlier work. In fact, Suedfeld's subjects voluntarily chose to *stay* in those settings instead of leaving experiments early when given the opportunity, and some participants reported they felt better after time spent in low-stimulation environments. For example, in one study, participants reported feeling less tense, angry, and worn out after the study than their counterparts who stayed in high-stimulation environments, and they were also more likely to feel clear-headed, friendly, and vigorous.[76]

In a recent conversation with Netta, Suedfeld explained his findings from an evolutionary perspective. Humans evolved surrounded by nature and not on busy streets with honking cars and crowds, he said. Those constant sounds, images, and hordes of other people keep us poised for action and wired for interaction. When we return to solitude in quiet spaces, in a way, we're going back to basics. To encourage that return, Suedfeld and his colleagues' research on the topic led to the development of what is called "restricted environmental stimulation therapy" (REST).[76]

REST involves environments that entirely, or almost entirely, lack environmental stimuli, such as noticeable sounds, smells, and tactile and visual cues.[77,78] The basic idea is to give all of the senses a break. Research on REST has been used to help promote better sleep and stabilize mood in people who have bipolar disorder, a psychological disorder where people's moods shift from depressed to manic.[79] In those studies, environmental stimulation could be restricted instead of entirely eliminated so that participants' senses got a reprieve while they could maintain a feeling of connection to the external world. Instead of requiring total darkness, researchers employed a more moderate version of sensory deprivation with amber-colored goggles that blocked out blue light and achieved similar results.[79]

Even if quietude hasn't been a cultural norm up to this point in many places, a lot of people have begun to understand its value and have gravitated toward environments that allow them to achieve it. In the late 1990s, school psychologist Ester Schaler Buchholz wrote meaningfully about her clinical observations of solitude in both children and adults. Even in teeming New York City, she observed the same sense of peaceful quietude that the Finnish seek, but in a very special place – museums. She described museums as places where people go for quiet exploration; for soul searching; or to take in a peaceful, creative atmosphere.[80]

Quietude has also been observed by researchers who studied college campuses in England, Sweden, and Italy. The researchers found that, for students and academics working on-campus, silent places are critical for reflection and recuperation. Historically and today, quietude on English campuses is found within chapels, which were designed, said the researchers, as a "sanctuary for space and time for stillness, prayer, and contemplation." In Italy, students found gardens that helped them to foster that calm. In Sweden, students sought calm, peaceful spaces for reflection as well.[81]

Scientists didn't use to think a whole lot about quiet or silence. Experiments generally used silence as a baseline, or a break, from measuring the effects of other phenomena, such as listening to music. That changed in 2006 when two cardiologists, one Italian and one British, who were studying the effects of music on the cardiovascular system made a couple of surprising discoveries. Interestingly, while the style of music and the preferences of the listener seemed to have no impact on blood pressure, heart rate, or breathing frequency of test subjects, the music's tempo (whether a track was fast or slow) did.[82]

What astonished the researchers most was what happened when the music stopped. The two-minute silence in the middle of the music sequence had a greater impact on reducing blood pressure and heart rate than the slowest-tempo music. "Silence between music had the most profound relaxing effect. In fact, it acted as though it were music with a zero frequency," Bernardi told a medical journal in 2007. He said the effect was similar to the state of relaxation seen in studies of transcendental meditation. Importantly, the impact of silence is heightened by contrasts. "First, you have to concentrate hard, giving your attention to something. Then, when you release the attention, you become very relaxed," said Bernardi.[83]

Like solitude, silence isn't defined by what it's missing, at least according to our brains. Neuroscience research shows that our brains are always active and readily register the difference between noise and quiet, even using a separate network of neurons to do it.[84] We also now know that different areas of the brain are active depending on whether we are engaged with outside stimuli or have broken away from it. When we are in a resting state, being quiet, and maybe in a dark room with our eyes closed, our brains kick into "default mode."[85] That's a network that includes parts of the brain focused on our inner worlds (compared to those activated when we undertake external, goal-related tasks). Provided we don't lapse into rumination, or repetitive negative thinking, it's a chance to shift gears and think about the past and future, and the self and others, without interruption. And it's a golden opportunity to get to know ourselves better.[86]

Now, scientists are beginning to generate more data on how quiet may positively impact health. In addition to the cardiovascular benefits, it seems that a break from noise may reduce cortisol, the body's top stress hormone (which increases the risks of a whole host of health problems). Quiet also appears to improve focus and concentration. In a recent study, Finnish researchers exposed dozens of participants to the sounds of talking, noise, or silence and tested their stress levels and how well they did on tasks requiring concentration. Both listening to speech and listening to noise caused more psychological and physiological stress than silence (speech also caused participants to have to work harder on the assigned cognitive tasks).[87]

In other illuminating experimental work, participants in a study were asked to write two poems in silence. Then two-thirds of them wrote a second poem while enduring an "attention-narrowing stimulation" – an eighty-five-decibel noise blast (a sound at the upper limit of work-acceptable noise) – piped into the lab. The remaining one-third wrote their second poem on the topics of "joy" or "butterfly," once again in silence. Assistants who did not know whether participants had heard the noise judged the creativity and word originality of the poems (they did that simply by counting the number of words that are not typically used to describe joy or butterflies). The subjects who wrote their second poems in quiet were rated to have shown more creativity. Researchers varied the type and frequency of noise and found that unpredictable noise and intelligible speaking, in contrast to white noise, were more harmful to creativity.[88]

Some of the most intriguing findings related to silence and human health are linked to silence's role in improving memory and stimulating brain growth. Ten minutes in a dark, quiet room improved the recall of people with amnesia by 14 to 49 percent (it also improved nonamnesiacs' memory by 10 to 30 percent).[89] Another fascinating finding about the benefits of silence came in 2013 when a team of researchers from the United States and Germany looked at the question "is silence golden?" In that work, mice were exposed to different sounds to assess the neuro-logical effects of those noises and, specifically, if they caused new cell growth in the brain.[90]

The researchers of that study found that all the sounds, including music by Mozart, ambient lab noise, and mouse pup calls, had some short-term neurological effects, but only silence had the desired, lasting effect. Mice that spent two hours per day in silence had new cell development in the hippocampus, the brain region recognized as the memory center, decision maker, and integrator of emotion and cognition. Humans are not mice, of course, but the findings have sparked some speculation that they could be replicated in people and that hippocampus-disabling diseases like depression and dementia may benefit from the therapeutic use of silence.[91]

Perhaps in part due to the mounting evidence of its efficacy, the pursuit of quiet has recently gone mainstream. This has led to some interesting efforts to try to reinstate some peace and quiet in different parts of the world.[92] Within the United Kingdom, quietude has been nurtured by a movement called "Silent Space." It's an initiative developed by a gardener who benefited from time spent in "natural quiet" and then partnered with public gardens in the United Kingdom and beyond to set aside a few hours per week when visitors are encouraged to turn off mobile phones, stop talking, and listen to the sounds of nature. The goal of the project is to foster inspiration and creativity through an appreciation of quiet spots. Silent Space is not entirely new and harkens back to the nineteenth-century reflection gardens we talked about in Chapter 1, managed spaces where people have a chance just to *think*.[93]

Just prior to the onset of the COVID-19 pandemic, silent retreats were getting immensely popular, especially among American tech elites. The *New York Times*,[94] the *Wall Street Journal*,[95] and *Fast Company*[96] all published stories in 2019 about the growing popularity of swapping high-stress, high-volume days for silent, contemplative ones. Switching into "silent mode" was becoming such a sought-after condition that plans were in the works to build new, multimillion-dollar silent compounds in Silicon Valley and farther north in Washington State. Now that the world is returning once again to its prepandemic pace – and volume – in most places, no doubt these types of retreats will once again be popular.

Other therapies now popping up nearly everywhere (and requiring far less time and cash) are the so-called chamber REST sessions recommended by researchers decades ago, in which people lie in a dark room for twenty-four to forty-eight hours, as well as flotation REST. The latter involves bobbing solo in a warm, water-filled tank for thirty-five minutes or more.[77,97] Before storefronts offering silent floats started appearing, researchers constructed flotation REST chambers in labs by making buoyant liquid from water and Epsom salt, turning off the lights, and eliminating all noises. Studies showed a reduction in participants' stress and also recorded their feelings of deep relaxation.[98] One controlled experiment put a group of participants in their twenties and thirties in flotation tanks and compared them to a second group set up in another relaxing condition.[99] Participants in the latter group were asked to sit in a reclined chair in a dim room with little noise. Both did the activity for thirty-five minutes on ten occasions, and the researchers measured their cortisol (stress hormone) before, during, and after treatment.

The results of the study showed that the floaters had lower cortisol than the recliners (who also experienced a notable drop in stress hormones), suggesting that they were more relaxed. In another, very similar experiment, floating reduced blood pressure for fourteen young adults when compared to their age-matched peers in a bland control room.[100] Early studies on flotation REST involved very few participants and therefore had potentially unreliable conclusions, but a recent review of twenty-five existing studies with a total of 449 adults age twenty to forty-five years found good reason to believe that it is helpful for reducing cortisol and for self-reported relaxation and well-being.[78]

The flotation tank experiments also seemed to indicate that there is value in stillness and darkness in solitude. "Noise" can also be more than auditory, of course – it can flood in through our screen-fixed eyeballs. The understanding of the effects of those stimuli has led to another increasingly popular wellness trend – dark therapy.[101] Darkness retreats (which have roots in Tibetan Buddhism and other religious trad-itions[102]) are cropping up in different parts of the world, including Oregon, the Czech Republic, and Guatemala.[103,104] One retreat in the Czech Republic includes a "darkness villa" where visitors spend a week or more alone and in complete darkness (somehow still going about daily routines, though perhaps messily).[105] That type of deprivation is adver-tised to heighten senses, boost creativity, and prevent various disorders and diseases.[105] Thousands of years of anecdote are influential in supporting those results, but the science backing the claims is still thin at this point.

If darkness and silence sound like overly extreme forms of solitude or taking a multiday retreat doesn't float your boat (or suit your budget), you're not alone. But extremes aren't necessary to reap most of the rewards of turning down the volume of the world. We can set up our own hushed and/ or dark sanctuaries – and even our own float baths – to enjoy for an hour or just a few minutes and likely still reap the benefits of stillness and quiet.

Regardless of whether we presently find value in silence or stillness and the settings that encourage them, we have to recognize that they have measurable effects on our selves and on the earth (see Box 8.1). More generally, recalibrating our senses in the way we discussed also has a verifiable value that's critical to keep in mind as we all consider the what, where, when, and how of everyday solitude in our lives. That doesn't mean that achieving positive solitude in any setting or condition necessarily comes easily, and in Chapter 9, we delve into who does well in alone time and why, offering lessons for everyone on resilience in that space.

BOX 8.1 COVID-19 AND QUIET AROUND THE WORLD

Government restrictions during the COVID-19 pandemic ground human activity nearly to a halt in early 2020. During that shift, as we mentioned before, many people realized that they liked staying at home, paring down schedules, and having more "down" time.[106] Many people also recognized the value of solitude like never before and vowed to maintain that experience as societies began to open up again.[107] Similarly, people were able to hear sounds of nature long muffled by the din of human industry and enjoyed quiet where they'd never before experienced it.[108] Senses were recalibrated, new frequencies were tuned in to, and for many people, that helped to craft a kind of insulating barrier between themselves and the horrors of the outside world. It allowed them to see, at least for a time, a silver lining in the storm clouds overhead.[108]

During that time, in fact, the world got historically quiet. The ruckus humans make in nonpandemic times is, of course, significant, and that activity causes vibrations that can be measured as high-frequency seismic waves in the ground.[109] In a 2020 paper in *Science*, an international group of seismologists from thirty-three countries illustrated how the lockdown measures imposed early in the pandemic resulted in a substantial decrease in "seismic noise" worldwide – up to an astonishing 50 percent. During the first months of most everyone staying at home, the researchers could track a "wave of quiet" that first took shape in China and then swept across Europe, the Americas, and the rest of the world.[110]

Acoustic scientists in Singapore, San Francisco, New York, London, and other cities also began to compare prepandemic sound recordings to ones made in the same spots during the height of movement restrictions.[111] With urban streets mostly abandoned, the contrast between recordings is understandably stark. For example, two clips taken as part of a soundscape survey by researchers at University College London in the plaza outside the Tate Modern museum compare midday May 2019 to midday April 2020. In the 2019 clip, loud chatter punctuated by children yelling dominates, whereas the 2020 clip captured only birdsong and a breeze.[112]

A lot of people noticed this seismic shift – this lack of trains rumbling on tracks, planes growling across the sky, and cars and trucks whining ceaselessly over tarmac. For some people, especially in cities, the sound of silence was understandably sad and unsettling, at least in the beginning. But in the midst of immense human suffering, there was, for many people, a newfound peace. Opening a window in a city and hearing birdsong usually drowned out by the crosstown bus signaled hope and offered something palpable about the resilience of nature – and maybe ourselves as part of it.

Lockdowns transformed the aural experience in cities in a matter of days, sound artist Stuart Fowkes told the *Guardian* in 2020. During that time, he heard from a man in Warsaw that he could hear birdsong never before audible near his home. Fowkes, who is also the founder of the Oxford-based, global sound project Cities and Memory, which collects field recordings from around the world, said, "One of the few positives from this situation is that people are starting to reconnect with nature a little bit and starting to notice the sounds that are usually drowned out around them."[113] That sentiment was echoed by Paavo Virkkunen, chief executive of the Finnish tourist board (more than a decade earlier, the tourist board had launched a popular campaign focused on quiet being one of the best things about the country). In an interview with the BBC in 2020, he said, "Silence is one of those values you need to help you separate the essentials from the non-essentials of life. ... When lockdown ends, I'll miss the extra silence we've had."[114]

This loudness "anthropause," as some scientists began referring to it, had measurable effects on the nonhuman animal world as well.[115] Accounts of wildlife "reclaiming" densely settled areas – like deer roaming East London streets and goats traveling in hedge-munching packs in a Welsh village – became a source of fascination and study. The effect on birdlife was particularly profound. Using records of more than 4.3 million birds observed by volunteers from March to May 2017 to 2020 across Canada and the United States, researchers from those countries made some remarkable findings. Of the eighty-two bird species they focused on, 80 percent typically increased in number in urban habitats during lockdowns compared to prepandemic periods.[116]

Seeing nature thrust itself so decisively into spaces vacated by humans had a lasting effect on some people. And simply being able to focus on nature without interference caused others to recognize, or recall, our interconnectedness with the natural world. Ada Limón, the twenty-fourth US Poet Laureate, talked about observing and writing about wildlife during the lockdowns and the experience of being alone – yet not alone – with the natural world. "I think that idea of isolation and aloneness, I really wanted to look at it, interrogate it like, 'Am I alone? I don't know if I'm alone, what does that mean?' Being able to be the watcher but then also realizing that the animals, when you leave the house, are watching you, it's the same three crows and we're having this experience every morning. It started to feel like, oh, I am in community," she said on a recent podcast. Limón spoke about an inner quiet, as well, that allowed her to keep company with others in her mind. "I was in community with these others, and some of the others were ancestors and memories who are with me all the time. And I think I just started to unravel that, being part of something larger. And it felt so refreshing," she said.[117]

Others also used that sudden outer quiet to tap in to an inner silence where they might find the bandwidth to deal with chaos and loss on their paths. Some of them, like writer Thomas McKean, living in New York's East Village, now miss that safe harbor and those moments of calm in the storm. In May 2021, he wrote in the *Nation*, "I feel guilty about it, but I still feel it: There's a part of me that misses the darkest days of the lockdown. . . . I do miss the quiet, the strange peace, the empty streets. . . . This had been the bright light of lock-down in a loud city – the relative quiet: fewer cars and trucks, fewer shrieking-into-cell-phone throngs of bar-hoppers stampeding at all hours. By necessity, we were spending more time at home, so at least our homes really were a refuge (if one ignored that endless stream of ambulances). I could sit in my living room, gazing north at the Empire State Building (my calm watchtower for decades), and after banging pots at 7, feel cocooned in quiet, safe in silence."[118]

CHAPTER 9

Can We Get Better at Being Alone?

I N EARLY APRIL 2020, STREET ARTIST KEVIN KNUTSON,[1] aka "Kreau," walked from his apartment in Seattle's Capitol Hill area to a nearby pub, closed and boarded up. The streets were nearly deserted; the pandemic was still unfamiliar, and everyone was being told to isolate. Within a few weeks, he had watched his neighborhood button up and his neighbors shutter behind closed doors. "There was so much fear and uncertainty," said Kreau.[2]

On that cool, overcast spring morning, Kreau passed dozens of plywood-clad storefronts to one on East Pike Street. He set down his backpack stuffed with spray paint cans and an armful of stencils he'd spent days conceptualizing and cutting. It took him several hours to paint a triptych, and when he was done, the centerpiece image depicted himself as a man sitting on the ground, legs splayed, with arms poking out of a cardboard box covering his head.

A couple of weeks later, Kreau re-created that image, much larger, on another boarded window with the words "Imagination Not Isolation." A thought bubble above the man's head now read, "Don't bother me when I'm in my _____." The mural was meant to be hopeful, and somewhat helpful – rather than feeling confined in solitude, we can see solitude as an opportunity and use it for whatever we choose. That plain ole box – a symbol of childhood comfort and creativity for Kreau – could be much more (time machine, robot, or rocket). "Imagination, or the ability to dream or to abstract thoughts and concepts, is a safe place," he told Heather later. Kreau believed then, as always, that creativity can balance uncertainty in solitude. "Don't despair, be actively doing something else," he said.[2] That inspirational message resonated and, alongside other uplifting murals painted in Seattle in response to pandemic restrictions, was featured in the *Guardian* in April 2020.[3]

Pandemic or not, Kreau is largely content being on his own, but he could see others struggling. "Left to my own devices I would be at home alone most of the time, I don't mind that so much, but I felt my community hurting," he said. That's because solitude is a dynamic space where a lot of thinking happens, which can make it a tough and/or amazing experience. Most people faced some level of uncertainty during that time, and some naturally gravitated toward anxiety-inducing thoughts about health and/or financial insecurity. Knutson wanted them to know that they weren't alone in being alone, that these were mostly shared experiences. "I had the sense that I had to tell the city that there are still people here. Despite it looking like a zombie movie, there's still a heartbeat beyond these walls," said Kreau.

That's when he felt moved to share his works of solidarity, healing, hope, and resilience. For Kreau, the pandemic imposed restrictions around staying home and maintaining distance, but otherwise, there were no rules. It was a chance to do something for himself and his neighbors and a safe space to think and dream in ways that can take one from the mundane to the extraordinary. Kreau wanted to help people break out of their fear and misery, if only for a short time, and encouraged them to use their powers of curiosity and creativity to see solitude as an opportunity rather than a burden.

Being able to create during the pandemic was a privilege, for sure, but also a lifeline for many people. Learning something new, improving skills, or just stretching imagination muscles in general were strategies many employed to counteract feelings of stress, loneliness, and isolation.[4–7] Not all those people were alone (many just felt that way), and having artful ambition was a coping mechanism to turn their lives right side up again. Creative writing, cooking, sewing, learning a new language or how to dance, were all popular pursuits, and with free time, the opportunity to learn whatever one wanted even reawakened a childlike sense of excitement in some people.[8–10]

During that time in our Solitude Project, while other researchers were focused on who was struggling in social isolation, we turned our interest to who wasn't – people, like Kreau, who were doing OK and even flourishing on their own. We wanted to know what made them tick. Looking at what people are doing, who they are by nature, and what mind-sets they have toward and within solitude are all factors affecting their resilience in solitude. In short, those data give us a better idea of who is more likely to have positive experiences in everyday solitude and why, and that may help others who struggle to find a foothold there.

To talk about the factors that encourage resilience in solitude, it helps to look first at what psychological resilience means in general. The term *resilience* originated in the physical sciences (the study of nonliving systems) in the early 1800s, when it was used to describe the quality of elastic substances, those that bounce back after compression or other forms of distortion.[11] Much later, in the 1940s, psychologists and psychiatrists adopted the concept and used it to suggest that people can be "elastic" when subjected to "compression" as well. The idea was that people under stress can also spring back, returning to their prepressure baseline.[12,13]

The earliest researchers of psychological resilience wanted to understand how and why development goes wrong in children. They noticed that not all children responded to tough early life events (like foster care, child abuse, and poverty) in the same ways. Some remained derailed for years compared to development in their peers, whereas others seemed to be able to recover from those adverse conditions – they were resilient in the face of that adversity.[14] The study of resilience has expanded to include all age groups and many different life stressors, but the concept remains the same.[15] It's now defined by the American Psychological Association (APA) as "the process and outcome of successfully adapting to difficult or challenging life experiences, especially through mental, emotional, and behavioral flexibility and adjustment to external and internal demands."[16] The APA also goes a step further, suggesting that resilience is marked by personal growth resulting from overcoming that adversity.

As researchers, when we talk about resilience *in solitude*, we build on that general concept and definition, but with additional context. Suggesting that resilience is required in solitude assumes there is adversity or stress to overcome – and there is, potentially, for some people. We've seen throughout our research that many people seek out time alone for its benefits, whereas others avoid it like the plague. Although we don't know precisely what portion of the population struggles versus thrives in solitude, we do know that no one finds it positive all the time. Knowing that solitude can sometimes be challenging but that there are ways to potentially exercise resilience, we are in a better position to assess how we are doing there and to decide whether it is time to abandon ship (phone a friend!) or to stick with it.

What resources are at our disposal for being resilient in solitude? If we look to the science of resilience, in general, we know that some people are more elastic by nature,[17] though those exact mechanisms are still largely a mystery. We also know that "social determinants" like one's socioeconomic status, level of education, physical environment, extent of social support networks, and more factor into how we rise to meet a challenge.[18] If the stars align and we're born with genetic and/or social advantages, that's terrific, but countless people are not. Do those people still have a shot at greater mental adaptability and fortitude? Fortunately, they do. Studies show that positive adaptation, or greater resilience, can be practiced and cultivated – almost like a muscle that can be bulked up to increase strength and flexibility.

That said, resilience *doesn't* mean gritting your teeth and sticking with it no matter the psychological costs. As researchers, as well as empathetic humans, we embrace the idea of gaining and exercising resilience in solitude realistically and with humility, knowing that pushing through something isn't always a feasible or healthy goal. If a person is suffering from a serious malady like depression, soldiering on in solitude is not advisable. One of the main things that makes people resilient, in general, is the quality of social support we have.[19–22] If being alone feels impossible, it may mean that strengthening social networks is more necessary than sitting by ourselves with ruminative thoughts. Ultimately, spending time in solitude is meant to be an act of self-care. So, if it feels instead like a deeply painful act, that needs to be recognized and resolved.

Of course, being resilient also *doesn't* mean somehow dodging adversity or employing numbness to avoid discomfort or pain. There are times when forging on is what we need to do – and ultimately want to do – to get from a place of risk to one of reward, from seed to sapling. In those instances, we have found in our research that who thrives in solitude aligns in some important ways with what makes folks resilient in general.[23] And what factors and actions encourage and build resilience in solitude also seem to align with what helps people bounce back, in general, in the face of hardship. We touch on a number of those in this chapter, including personality, motivation, mind-set, curiosity, and more. Of course, we're interested in not only *enduring* solitude but also benefiting from it, so we also talk about what we have learned from some solitude superstars about using time alone to boost overall well-being.

WHO FINDS SOLITUDE TOUGH, WHY, AND WHAT CAN THEY DO ABOUT IT?

The most reliable predictor researchers have for resilience in time alone is one's motivation to discover and have positive experiences in that space.[24] But what if someone lacks a strong motivation to spend time in solitude because they generally feel uncertain or unhappy there? Those types of folks are not uncommon, and solitude research – and society in general – is filled with them. That's in large part because the thoughts we can have in solitude are varied and ever changing. Thuy-vy describes time alone in our heads as a "chamber of thoughts echoing in our minds." Those can be positive and self-affirming, or they can be negative and self-defeating, as in the case of worry or rumination.[25–27] In either scenario, our internalized world can amplify those emotions, making solitude amazing for some people and a nightmare for others.

Blaise Pascal, a seventeenth-century mathematician and religious philosopher, observed in his contemporaries a discomfort with idleness and an unease with solitude, and he saw that as the root cause of their discontent. "I have discovered that all the unhappiness of men arises from one single fact, that they cannot stay quietly in their own chamber," he wrote.[28] We can think of Pascal's "chamber" as a literal room or, figuratively, as the mind, as Thuy-vy describes. At the same time, he believed, as we do, that there is value in taking time to probe the potential of that stillness (even if most of us are not working out the modern theory of probability, as Pascal did). To shake off the reluctance many people have and access positive solitude, it's worth trying to understand what undermines the ability to dwell happily in our own "chambers."

Some research suggests possible pitfalls to a particular type of aimless thinking known as mind wandering, or daydreaming, which can be a common occurrence in solitude.[29] When we are alone, it's inevitable that our minds will roam – it is a uniquely human and extremely powerful ability. Is that lack of focus and structure good or bad? Currently the science of the effect of unstructured downtime on well-being gives a mixed answer. That may be because the concepts of boredom, mind wandering, and daydreaming – all kinds of independent thought unrelated to outside stimuli – have gotten blended together in the soup of modern-day psychology and neuroscience.[30] But it's worth highlighting some of those (seemingly) contradictory research findings to get at what concepts and beliefs have been dominating the rhetoric around boredom and mind wandering and which ideas are worth revisiting in the context of solitude.

Pascal's centuries-old claim that an inability to sit with one's own thoughts causes mental "pain" for some people has been supported in several now-famous studies. A 2010 paper titled "A Wandering Mind Is an Unhappy Mind," from Harvard researchers looking at the emotional toll of mind wandering,[31] went viral at the time it was published. For the massive experiment, the researchers developed a smartphone app to do "experience sampling," which means capturing participants' thoughts, feelings, and actions in real time. The project is ongoing, but at the time they published the work, their database had about a quarter million samples from roughly 5,000 people (age eighteen to eighty-eight years) in more than eighty countries. They found that their subjects spent as much as half of their waking hours daydreaming. And regardless of what they were thinking about during that time, being derailed from the task at hand resulted in unhappiness for most people surveyed.

Several years later, another series of boredom studies made headlines around the world.[32] In that work, researchers at the University of Virginia and Harvard University recruited hundreds of undergraduates and community members (age eighteen to seventy-seven years) to take part in eleven different studies. In several rounds, participants were seated in a sparsely furnished lab room with zero external distractions (no cell phones, no pens or paper) for six to fifteen minutes. The individuals were either given prompts about what to think about during that time or told to cogitate on whatever they wanted. Over the first six studies, and in both scenarios, 58 percent of participants rated the difficulty of the task at or above the midpoint of a nine-point scale, and 42 percent said they had an enjoyment level below that same midpoint. In the seventh experiment, all of the conditions were replicated, except that subjects passed that period of downtime in their own homes (32 percent admitted to cheating by seeking outside stimuli). Even though the setting had changed, the results were similar – the experience of being on their own and thinking freely made many people unhappy.[33]

In later rounds, things got interesting. One set of participants was left in a lab room for fifteen minutes, but with one potential source of stimulation – they could push a button that would result in them receiving a mild electric shock. At the beginning of those experiments, all participants had a preview of what the shock felt like, and most had said they'd pay money not to feel it again. Regardless, 25 percent of women (six of twenty-four) and 67 percent of men (twelve of eighteen) chose to zap themselves rather than sit idly and think. (More men are suspected to have opted for shocks, in part, because they are more prone to "thrill seeking" or "sensation seeking" in general.[34] We have to consider that, for some, the mind wandering aspect may have been fine, *and* the shock may have represented "fun" stimulation on some level.)

Why would some people cause themselves pain rather than let their minds wander in time alone? No one really knows for sure, but there are different theories as to why, including that the human mind developed to continuously "scan" the environment for threats and opportunities and may experience discomfort or discontent with nothing to monitor. Other scientists responding to the study suggested that forced inaction may rob us of a sense of meaning and purpose, a key ingredient for well-being. They figured that, however unpleasant, administering a shock to themselves gave individuals in the study something *to do.*[35]

Those findings about the potential downsides of daydreaming are a far cry from the foundation of that research, laid by Jerome Singer in the 1950s and 1960s. When Singer was first studying daydreaming, it was considered pathological by other psychologists, but he suspected there was more to it. He spent his career documenting the risks versus costs of mind wandering, but mostly he studied it as a normal, common human experience that can be hugely positive and productive.[36–43] Some current studies have begun revisiting Singer's work and are rediscovering the richness of his conclusions.

More recently, James Kaufman, a University of Connecticut professor,[44] led the field in understanding that we are creative and imaginative, every day.[45–47] In a recent conversation with Netta, Kaufman also speculated that solitude may aid creativity precisely because time alone allows for mind wandering and idea "incubation." He adds that everyday creativity also doesn't require honing a skill over hundreds of hours of practice; people can do it easily with a little space to think (more on this later).[48]

In the past several years, the science of "spacing out" has gotten more nuanced, and some researchers are now circling back around to the idea that it may indeed serve some important purposes and enhance the experience of being human. For example, researchers from the United States, Germany, and Canada replicated, to some extent, the massive Harvard app experiment. Their 2013 findings largely conformed with those of the earlier study, but their subsequent analyses revealed a "mood benefit of having interesting mind wandering episodes." In short, the participants' moods were positive when they were daydreaming about topics that most engaged them.[49]

Centuries of anecdote suggest that leaving a problem alone for a while and doing something completely different (and significantly easier) can spawn a solution. But it's only in the past decade or so that science has supported that assumption. As we mentioned in Chapter 4, creative incubation takes place in the brain's default network, where mind wandering is also mediated. Moshe Bar, former head of the Cognitive Neuroscience Lab at Harvard Medical School and author of the book *Mindwandering*, has shown in his work how creativity, incubation, and mind wandering rely on one another. Creativity requires incubation, and mind wandering encourages it. Creativity therefore relies on broad, expansive mind wandering, said Bar.[50]

Mind wandering has now been linked with enhanced creativity (including problem-solving ability) in many interesting studies. One study of 145 individuals, age eighteen to thirty-two years, again done by researchers in Germany, Canada, and the United States, showed greatly improved creativity under certain conditions. Participants were given a so-called unusual uses task in which, for example, they needed to come up with as many purposes for a paperclip as possible in two minutes. They then proceeded into one of four conditions – resting, not resting, performing a demanding task, or doing an undemanding task. The subjects who engaged in simple external tasks that allowed their minds to wander far outperformed their peers in creative problem solving.[51] In follow-up research published in 2019, physicists and professional writers who were studied over a one- to two-week period reported that 20 percent of their most significant work-related ideas each day were hatched while their minds were doing "spontaneous, task-independent mind wandering."[52] Another more recent study, by University of Virginia researchers, on the so-called shower effect (the phenomenon of seeming to get great ideas while lathering up) mirrored those earlier findings.[53]

Finally, one of the more profound potential benefits of daydreaming is that, when our heads are in the clouds and less preoccupied with the outside world, we time travel, revisiting the past and picturing the future.[54] During that time, generally, we make ourselves the focus of those thoughts by doing what's called "autobiographical planning," and that process can positively affect well-being. It's during these moments that we derive meaning, make sense out of what we have seen and done, and nurture an understanding of who we are in the world.[55,56]

The bottom line on solitude and idle thinking is that if we choose to daydream and give our woolgathering brains some gentle direction (Bar calls it "directed mind wandering"), we'll have the potential to enhance time alone and combat any numbing boredom or intimidating aimlessness. Then, instead of being a trip through a barren desert, that intentional pause can lead to an oasis of creativity. That's certainly true for the artist Kreau, whom we met at the beginning of the chapter, and for many of our research subjects who turn to solitude to let their minds explore new and uncharted territory in the safety of their own solitude.

WHO'S CONTENT IN SOLITUDE, AND WHY?

The type of solitude most of us experience daily (what we call "everyday solitude") is essentially a neutral state, not inherently good or bad. It's an

CAN WE GET BETTER AT BEING ALONE?

empty vessel waiting to be filled with whatever we decide to fill it with. In that sense, it can't make you feel terrible or great on its own; it simply acts as a mirror reflecting what we bring into it, what we experience there, and what we take away from it.

Why some people experience solitude as a positive space is likely due to a combination of factors. In our work, we have looked at the role of choice (which we talked about in Chapter 5) and motivation, personality and traits, and mind-set. We can see that many of the happiest people in solitude are the ones who want to be alone because they find value there. If we are keen to spend time alone to think through a problem, hone a skill, or simply relax and be quiet, that will most likely be a positive experience.

If we are reluctant to step away from everyone else and feel that there's nothing good for us there, we're more likely to be bored or lonely and less likely to want to return to solitude. But all of that is not written in stone. It may not be an overnight transition, but it seems that some people can shift the way they feel about solitude and within solitude. To understand how to do that, it's essential to look at who does well in solitude, and why.

Is there a solitude personality? A lot of folks think enjoying solitude is an innate attribute. The common stereotype is that introverts, people who are inner focused (versus focused on the outer world of people and events)[57] prefer solitude and possess skills that help them do well there. In reality, the relationship between solitude and introversion is complicated, and the research findings are somewhat contradictory. Some of that has to do with the fact that researchers used to ask subjects about their personalities and experiences in solitude at the same time, which made it difficult to discern what were stable characteristics and what were more fleeting emotions.

What we've seen in our own research is that many people who describe themselves as introverts largely enjoy their alone time, but some also feel energized in interactions with others.[58] On the flip side, extroverts are assumed to despise solitude and do anything to spend all their time around others, but we heard from people who describe themselves as the "life of the party" but also protect and revel in their solitude. So the only thing we know for sure (at this point) about personality and solitude is that one should not trust stereotypes.

As we mentioned in Chapter 5, when we talked to people for our Solitude Project who generally experience alone time as positive about why they think that is, some described a feeling of having been "born to solitude." By that they meant that spending time alone comfortably and enjoyably seems to have always come naturally. Others talked about having adapted to solitude early in life because they were raised around people who treated time alone as a commodity or were encouraged as children to entertain themselves – and that became a lifelong habit and source of enjoyment.

Early exposure to time alone is a factor that seems to set the stage for developing an ability to experience positive solitude later in life, but at the same time, it doesn't portend a life spent apart from others. Some living-alone adults we spoke with maintained that predilection as they aged and have spent decades living on their own, and happily so (while maintaining high-quality social ties as well). Many others who have felt comfortable in solitude for as long as they can remember also have life partners, raise children, and work in professions that rely on daily interaction with others. (While they don't regret living fully integrated lives with others, they often have unmet solitude needs. "Maybe it's only as I've got older that I realized after I'd lost it, how much solitude was really a defining part of me," said Elizabeth, age forty-nine, from England.)

Some people have what we call "agency" in solitude, a kind of confidence to do things they want to do, in the way they want to do them, and feel competent in those tasks. In our own studies with a total of 470 American undergraduate students, age eighteen to twenty-eight years, we found something telling about individuals who had a capacity for "autonomous regulation"[58] (that means they take an interest in their own internal experiences, behave in ways that represent how they truly think and feel, and resist social pressures from others). Through their daily diary entries, we learned that those self-congruent people didn't necessarily *prefer* being in solitude to being with others, but they did spend time alone because they enjoyed it. This finding suggests that the capacity for connecting with and operating from the "self" helped people to get more excited about solitude.

Those people who have cultivated a lifetime capacity for solitude seem to be more resilient during time alone than those who have not.

But that doesn't mean that people who haven't developed that capacity are out of luck. Building that ability for being alone is not like flipping a switch; it takes time,[59] but it's a pursuit we believe is worth the investment. Based on our research, and what we know from a variety of other disciplines, we can speculate about what may help shift time in solitude from something feared to something valued.

BUILDING RESILIENCE IN SOLITUDE

Understanding how to help build resilience in solitude is very much a work in progress for us researchers. But, based on what we've heard from our research subjects, we can speculate about how to develop that capacity by looking at what makes solitude easier and more fruitful for some people. In short, other than having a positive predisposition for it, finding alone time valuable could have something to do with our mind-set toward solitude and what we do while we're there.

The science of mind-set is a complex and fascinating one that is intriguing to consider in regard to resilience in solitude. According to an expert in the field, Alia Crum at the Stanford Mind and Body Lab, mind-sets are "core beliefs or assumptions we have about a domain or category of things that orient us to a particular set of expectations, explanations, and goals."[60] In short, mind-sets help us simplify a complex reality. In more than a decade of work in the field, Crum has also seen that mind-sets orient our thinking, change what we expect will happen to us, and shape our motivations.[61]

There is empirical evidence to support the idea that subjective mind-sets can in general alter objective measurements. The most obvious example of this is the placebo effect – when a pseudo-therapy gives real relief – a phenomenon that scientists have known about on some level for centuries. *Placebo* means "I shall please" in Latin, and the word first appeared in a medical dictionary in 1785.[62] At that time, the definition was "a commonplace method or medicine," which indicates that, even early on, physicians routinely used it as a form of treatment. Later editions of the reference book called it a "make-believe medicine," indicating that it was meant to be an inactive and harmless therapy.[63] For a long time, in modern pharmaceutical studies, placebos were used merely as controls, but then scientists started documenting the profound effects they have on some people. Now they're studied as stand-alone treatments that can evoke both positive and negative effects in some patients (as well as none in others).[64,65]

Crum has also tested the veracity of "belief effects" in experimental work for several years and has shown consistently how what people think about their health and bodies can have clear physiological effects. In her now-famous "milkshake" experiment,[66] nearly fifty participants were given a 380-calorie drink on two separate occasions but were told that it was either a 620-calorie, "indulgent" shake or a 120-calorie, "sensible" version. Despite being served the 380-calorie shake both times, the participants had different metabolic responses depending on which shake they believed they had received. When they drank the shake marked "indulgent," participants had a significantly steeper drop in ghrelin (a hormone that signals the brain about hunger and satiety).[67] Basically, when subjects *thought* they were drinking a fatty shake, their body believed it too, and they were more satisfied physiologically.

So, what do milkshakes have to do with solitude? In short, although we think milkshakes begin and end with their nutritional content (or lack of it!), research shows that they don't. The effects of milkshakes live, in part, in the mind – as does the experience of being in solitude. We may think being alone has everything to do with being physically separate from other people, but the experience really rises and falls based on what's going on in our own heads. That's why we feel it's important to talk about the power and limitations of mind-set in solitude.

In Chapter 5, we described several remarkable mind frame studies in which researchers (including ourselves) suggested to participants either that time alone was a positive experience with a variety of potential benefits or that loneliness was natural. When study participants were told that solitude boosts emotion regulation, enhances creativity, and improves mental well-being, they were less likely to take a hit to their positive mood during that alone time.[68] This idea that believing time alone will be good is also reflected in a qualitative study on the private self by solitude researcher Virginia Thomas.[69] In that work, the individuals who were strong in solitude had intentionally planned for getting the most out of it, and they cultivated that time.

How we think about our level of aloneness while in solitude can also have an impact on that time. When people have good relationships outside of solitude, they carry those connections into their alone time. Researchers call this "high social self-efficacy" – when people feel they *can* and *do* connect with other people to form meaningful social bonds.[70] Having that perception helps people to feel connected, and less isolated, when they are alone as well. In studies looking at maintaining that bond with others even while alone, it's the perception more than the amount of connection that matters.[71,72] Science doesn't yet recommend an ideal number of close contacts that translate into well-being, but anywhere from one to a half dozen may be about right.[73,74] Beyond that, social network size, or how many friends people feel they have, doesn't seem to matter.

Having a positive mind-set in and about solitude is obviously ideal, but what if you find yourself alone for a spell, feeling lonely or intimidated by a lack of outside distractions? We know from our own personal experiences, and those of our study participants, that sometimes it's best to seek quality company when you're mired in negative thinking. But we also know that sometimes those negative thoughts pass or, according to some of our research subjects, negative thinking in solitude can be processed, and/or they can actively shift their inner dialogue to something more positive. Is that true for most people? Can we change the way we feel about solitude – while we're in it – just by thinking differently? There is little empirical evidence at this point to support the conclusion that people can change a negative mind-set about solitude to a positive one, but we have heard a few accounts from participants in our qualitative interviews about how mind-set and solitude interact – and shift – for them. Those experiences of cognitive reappraisal can act as an example of what is possible for the rest of us.

Heidi, age thirty-six, from Germany, used to find being alone depressing, but she "did a lot of work on learning to embrace" being with herself and "sitting with things that aren't great, to turn it around." Now, being in solitude for her "can feel like connection, reflection – and still be really challenging." Although solitude isn't always chockablock with easy, breezy moments for Heidi, she still finds tremendous value in that time "to know your mind," she said. "I think it's one of the benefits of solitude that you have that flexibility to explore approaching things in different ways." Netta had a similar experience when she immigrated to America as a preteen. She was very lonely at first, but in exploring different ways and places to be alone, she learned to love solitude as a peaceful and self-connecting part of her life.

Nineteen-year-old Santiago in Mexico agrees. "Good solitude is getting to know myself and like myself," he said, but arriving at that place in solitude required some adjustment. That didn't mean simply taking a stance always to be jubilant and ignore the tough stuff in that space. To the contrary, he said, that meant "embracing the range of emotions solitude brings; taking the bad with the good is about improving yourself." Daniel, age thirty-eight, from Germany, left home in his early twenties and struggled to find a foothold on his own but learned that solitude was good for "resetting your mind-set" and planning ahead. "It's certainly made me stronger. It's certainly shaped me because it's an either you swim or you drown kind of aspect in the very beginning," he said.

We were particularly interested in those mind-sets and attitudes of our participants that help create positive moments in solitude and appear to encourage resilience in that space. When we asked our study subjects about what they believed made them "good" at being in solitude, they pointed to several factors we want to highlight: *optimism* (having a positive outlook on life); a *growth mind-set* (seeing solitude as an opportunity to reflect and grow); *self-compassion* (being kind to oneself); *curiosity* (exhibiting an openness to learning and experiencing wonder and awe); and being *present in the moment*.[24] That's a lot of possible tactics we could use to build resilience in solitude, so we'll take them one by one.

HOW OPTIMISM ENHANCES RESILIENCE IN SOLITUDE

In our research, we've heard about two different kinds of *optimism* that happen around solitude – people describe themselves as either dispositionally optimistic (meaning being a "glass half full" person by nature) or situationally optimistic (feeling like good things await you in solitude). Some people said they are innately inclined toward optimism, like Linda, age seventy-two, a recent widow living alone in England, who told us, "I always think something good is going to come along. I might be going through a bad time now, but I know it'll get better." Moreover, she said that in most situations, "I know I can make it feel better."

It seems natural that those normally sunny folks would do OK on their own (though that may be a generalization), but what about people, such as James, age thirty-five, who describe themselves as "somewhat but not particularly optimistic" in general? How do they create and maintain positive solitude? James, a British man of Indian descent, told a helpful story. Recently, he experienced a deeply unsettling incident of racism at work. To process the "encounter," he retreated regularly to a bench in his garden apart from his family members. A lot of emotions arose during that time – anger, grief, anxiety – but he chose "a lot more intentionally quiet and intentionally solo" moments to work through his feelings, which he was ultimately able to do. "I don't think I'd be where I am now if I'd not been able to embrace these periods of solitude where I could really process my thoughts," he said.

That was true for Britain-based Gillian, age forty-four, as well. She is recently divorced and living alone for the first time in her life – a massive adjustment. "I didn't really know who I was and what I liked or didn't like in some respects, so I just wanted to learn more," she said. "I guess the solitude that I then found was like this enlightening moment for me because ... it was a really difficult time but at the same time it was really good for me to kind of relearn who I was and find that courage again to be on my own, and figure things out."

HOW A GROWTH MIND-SET SUPPORTS RESILIENCE

Throughout this book, we've touched on the importance of having a growth mind-set like the kind Gillian describes, but it's worth expanding on here. Many of our research subjects talked about using solitude as an opportunity (as opposed to a burden) to check in with themselves, their feelings, and their aspirations and to discover ways to change and grow. We saw this as a device used mainly among participants in their late teens to middle age but also to some extent among older adults we spoke with. (Older adults tend to be more settled in their personas and lot in life and less exploratory in this way, but some still use solitude as a space for emotional calibration and emotion regulation.)

Fiona, a twenty-four-year-old British woman of African descent, told us that solitude "allows me to just reframe how I see the trajectory of my life, and it allows me to speak to myself, understand myself, understand my mind, understand what I'm thinking about, where I'm going, how things fit, and so it really just gives me time to evaluate my thoughts and my feelings and my life. It's actually quite productive." Fiona said that in solitude, "I'm making myself happy with my mind-set," and she resolves to "enjoy every season I'm in."

Ahmad, whom we met in Chapter 4, also talked about using self-reflection as a way to be resilient in solitude: "There are certain traps in solitude that are easily avoided by just being reflective. Like the trap of negativity, or a trap of 'what's wrong with this life?,' of overgeneralizing. Or attributing the discomfort of solitude to something else, or not knowing that something can be easily fixed by just paying attention to it in a different way. So, these traps could be I think – for me at least – they're avoided when I pay attention, when I reflect. When I talk to myself differently."

This proposed "relationship with the self" is a resilience factor first suggested in the 1990s by researchers who described it as a tactic to combat loneliness.[75] Those researchers quite dramatically described the person who develops a relationship with themselves as someone who successfully "survives, conquers, and designs his abandonment." A recent paper by colleague Virginia Thomas updated that work.[69] It described interviews with fourteen American adults, whose average age was fifty, to ask them about their experience of solitude and the skills they used to achieve positive solitude. One of the primary themes to come from those interviews was that participants could connect with the self – enjoy solitary activities, work through their emotions, and reflect – and that being able to do that was key to making solitude a positive experience. We know we've mentioned this a few times already, but it bears repeating: self-reflection is not a pleasurable experience for everybody all the time, and some studies show that reflection in solitude can be related to a lower sense of well-being in some people or under certain circumstances.[76–78] Still, we recommend that all kinds of people give solitude a try to see what benefits they may be able to garner.

HOW SELF-COMPASSION SUPPORTS SOLITUDE

Next, we want to look at the relationship between self-compassion and well-being. Although this is a very new idea in terms of solitude, it is a well-established and clearly linked concept in mainstream psychology.[79] Having compassion for oneself basically means having a healthy attitude about who one is, which seems to affect how difficult we find any given situation. To tolerate and, ideally, enjoy being alone, we need to find meaning and value in our sense of self.[80]

Most of us spend some quiet moments recalling a conversation in which we wish we'd responded differently or a situation in which we wish we'd acted better, and that can be painful – and productive, with a compassionate mind-set. If you're having a tough time in solitude, being aware and accepting of that state – and cutting yourself some slack – could potentially make that time more positive. Our research subjects described it as "befriending oneself" and treating oneself with "patience," "kindness," or "generosity." Reminding yourself that everybody struggles in solitude sometimes and for countless reasons could help you shift what's wrong in that space to what is right for you.

Mathew, age twenty-three, from Hong Kong, explained the importance of self-compassion in his own solitude. For him, being alone hasn't always been easy, because "solitude is sort of like a magnifying glass on how you see yourself, your self-worth and your self-appreciation, or the other, negative side." As a teenager, he'd "pick himself apart" in time alone, but then he practiced self-acceptance (with the simple but wonderful mantra "I love myself") and was able to work through that phase. "Once you reach that point . . . solitude can be really comforting in a way, because you appreciate that person who's there with you," he said.

In some folks, the resilience factors contributing to positive solitude are manifold. For example, Scott, age sixty, from England, lives contentedly with a partner but describes himself as "happy with his own company" because he's a self-declared optimist and curious about everything. Scott spends a lot of "thinking time" in his greenhouse connecting to the "magical" natural world. His descriptions of being curious and seeing things as awe inspiring are particularly interesting for us researchers to consider in regard to resilience in solitude.

CURIOSITY IS KEY

Many of our participants described themselves as "naturally curious," "never bored," always seeking knowledge. This occurred regardless of age, race, gender, nation of origin, socioeconomic status, living arrangement, or relationship status. That is to say that pursuing curiosity, in many different forms, was one of the ubiquitous factors in many people's enjoyment of time alone. Monica, age forty-nine, put it succinctly: "I guess I'm really a curious person and I feel that there's so much more in the world and amongst ourselves to learn and discover." Farah, a thirty-five-year-old Iranian physician living in England, had a deep take (as did some other participants) on pursuing a spirit of inquiry in solitude. "I'm curious about good and bad, truth, and this life, why we are here," she said. In Portugal, Lucas, age twenty-one, said, "When I'm curious, usually I'm happy. I'm intrigued as always, a piece of me wants to know, wants to learn more, so I think it's really connected to happiness."

To understand why it is so powerful for many people, we look to the relatively new study of curiosity. Over time, lots of people have weighed in on the obvious joys, for some, and possible perils, for others, of being inquisitive. Seventeenth-century philosopher Thomas Hobbes referred to curiosity as "lust of the mind,"[81] whereas theoretical physicist Albert Einstein said, "I have no special talent. I am only passionately curious."[82] If he considered it one of his best features (his intuition and persistence weren't too shabby either), then there must be something going on here that's worth noting, right?

Whether we consider ourselves victims of Hobbes's "wonder"-lust or as sharing Einstein's finest attribute, curiosity – the motivation to acquire new knowledge – is something we're all born with. Curiosity drives exploration and innovation, every day, in small and big ways: What's the moon made of? What's at the bottom of the ocean? Curiosity evolved in humans to encourage our ancient predecessors to, for example, seek out data related to sustenance and safety – like where the best berries grew or from where hibernating bears first emerged in the springtime. We learned that this type of information was useful for survival, so we sought it out and retained it, and we still do (Heather retains where the best gelato is sold in Cambridge, for life-and-death reasons, *obviously*).

That "encouragement" is linked to the reward-based system wired into our brains. What's actually happening in the brain when our curiosity is sparked is linked to learning and memory. Several areas of the brain (the substantia nigra, ventral tegmental area, and hippocampus) are activated when we wander down the path of inquiry. How they are connected impacts how and what we learn.[83] From the work of Matthias Gruber and colleagues in the Dynamic Memory Lab at the University of California (UC), Davis's Center for Neuroscience, we know that at the time of peak curiosity – when they are motivated to know more about a question or issue – people get what researchers refer to as a dopamine reward.[84] Dopamine is a neurotransmitter that plays a role in feelings of pleasure, and curiosity seems intrinsically to elicit the same chemical response in anticipation of an answer as do extrinsic items like food or sex.[85] Basically, when we do a good job looking after our needs, our brains congratulate us with a helping of happy hormones.

In a study described in their 2014 paper, the UC Davis scientists presented subjects with a bunch of trivia questions and asked them if they were curious to know the answers. They found that when the participants expressed interest in the topic and wanted to learn more, they were better at retaining that information over a twenty-four-hour period. The researchers also found that once participants' curiosity was aroused, they were better at learning entirely unrelated information as well.[84]

Tapping in to innate curiosity could potentially make time spent in solitude more enjoyable. Maybe you're reading about black holes online or walking outside and wondering how and why tree leaves change color in the fall. Either way, you're fully engaged in wondering, and that process may sustain you for an hour in solitude, and maybe across a lifetime of increased well-being.[86]

Curiosity can often lead to a recognition or realization that surprises or even overwhelms us, ideally in a good way (see Box 9.1). One of our study participants, Linda, whom we met earlier in this chapter, talked about doing something ordinary in solitude that often veers into the extraordinary. She may be walking her dogs or gardening, feeling generally peaceful, but at the same time, she is "observing" and "discovering" and sometimes overcome by a sense of wonder and amazement, of awe.

BOX 9.1 AWE IN SOLITUDE

In solitude, when the mind is not focused on responding to the actions or presence of other people, when we have momentarily shaken off the daily grind of social expectations and obligations, when we are free from thoughts about things that worry or upset us, some people have an opportunity to connect to something larger than themselves. They have a chance to experience wonder and awe.[98]

Awe is another relatively new but increasingly well-studied area of scientific research based on an often overlooked but powerful emotion with a remarkable range of potential positive impacts.[99,100] Pioneering awe researcher Dacher Keltner at UC Berkeley defines it as "being in the presence of something vast and mysterious that transcends your current understanding of the world."[101] People can experience awe on their own or in the presence of others, but in general, it tends to be a very personal and even intimate experience touched by an immensity and complexity that are difficult to comprehend. Awe can be achieved in a moment and doesn't need to be a direct experience; one can feel astonished when looking at an image or video, when reading a story, or through virtual reality.[102]

Everybody's awe button is different, but Keltner and colleagues' research shows that eight categories of events generally elicit awe in humans: moral beauty (seeing other people do good deeds), collective effervescence (like being in a crowd at a football match), nature, music, visual design, spiritual and religious experiences, life-and-death experiences, and epiphanies. Those categories were distilled from work by the UC Berkeley researchers, who surveyed 100 people in each of twenty-six countries and asked them to write their personal stories of awe.[103]

The body of empirical evidence about the psychological and physiological effects of even brief experiences of awe is growing. Michelle Shiota at Arizona State University, another pioneer in the field, has found that awe experiences are so profound that they alter the way we see things and change the way we think about the world around us. Work in her lab has also shown that awe causes a complex bodily response. Specifically, the investigators saw a reduction in the "fight or flight" sympathetic nervous system influence on the heart and a drop in "rest and digest" parasympathetic activity (which relaxes us after periods of danger). This is a dual physiological response very rarely seen in research on emotion (one of the only areas in which it is recorded is research looking at sex immediately after orgasm).[104,105] Researchers have also reported that, in terms of mental health, awe reduces stress, anxiety, depression, and the symptoms of posttraumatic stress disorder.[105] Regarding physical health, it boosts cardiovascular health and reduces inflammation, which improves immune function and longevity.[106]

We don't yet have any idea if feeling awe, wonder, or amazement during our time alone has any real impact on solitude, but based on the findings of general awe research, we can speculate how it may aid resilience in time alone. Overall, the fundamental power of awe may be that those experiences are what psychologists refer to as "self-transcendent," meaning they take us outside of ourselves in a (good) way that makes us feel small, like we're part of something greater.[107,108] We heard this a lot from our participants regarding nature-related experiences of awe in solitude. We are also fortunate to have experienced it many times ourselves. While standing in the shadow of a giant sequoia or witnessing a murmuration of starlings, a process of "unselfing" unfurls, allowing us to put daily stressors into perspective.

Awe also tends to make people feel more generous, humble, and connected to others – all factors linked to resilience and general well-being.[109,110] And it seems to alter our perception of time by planting us firmly in the present moment.[111] That could be another of awe's superpowers that help build resilience in solitude.

This is the same type of feeling that we shared earlier from Scott, who described his greenhouse as "magical." We heard from other participants about being transported to somewhere outside of themselves by experiences like these and how that made their time alone more enjoyable.

BEING PRESENT IN THE MOMENT

We heard from some of our participants that "focusing on the now" or having a "mindful" or "meditative" way of seeing in solitude is one aspect of what makes that time so enjoyable for them. It makes them feel focused and relaxed and boosts their overall sense of well-being. One participant described weightlifting on her own like this: "In the beginning your mind is running and you're thinking about the day, and you're thinking about work … and then, with time, you sort of start to get attuned to your environment and your body, and then a lot of things slide away." Other solitude research has also suggested the possibility that mindfulness enhances solitude with the understanding that, by going there intentionally to be mindful, we can shape our own solitude experience.[87]

For some of our study subjects, mindfulness takes the form of being present in the moment while digging in the garden, drawing a portrait, swimming in a pool, cooking a meal, or, of course, meditating. That's a topic that has gotten a lot of airtime in the past couple of decades with the still-growing popularity of meditation and mindfulness practices. Podcasts, articles, and apps have given guidance on "finding inner peace" and "living in the moment," and elite athletes, lawmakers, and CEOs alike have sung the praises of being fully present observers of their own minds.

The Buddhist-inspired practice of awareness (of thoughts, feelings, surroundings, and bodily sensations) that forms the locus of mindfulness and meditation went mainstream in the Western world initially as a stress reduction technique used in a US medical school in 1979.[88] Since then, thousands of studies have gauged its psychological and physiological effects on nurses, soldiers, kindergarteners, and pretty much everyone in between.[89–94] The science of meditation is far from definitive, and there remain unanswered questions about its efficacy, yet there are copious promising data supporting an array of mental and physical benefits resulting from the practice.

As solitude researchers, we're interested in those data because meditation is a solitary activity millions of people do every day. Some meditators may require total solitude and complete quiet, whereas others may practice in a space with others in public solitude. Regardless, by design, both groups are alone with their thoughts. What can we learn from them about how to be alone, and happily so? Can mental stillness improve resilience in solitude?

Meditation is conscious attention employed to keep us anchored to the present moment. It's about creating a space of acceptance between stimulus and response; it's trying to nonjudgmentally acknowledge a thought, then release it. It can be freeing to know that one can observe a ceaseless stream of mind bubbles but not necessarily be carried away by them. In meditation, as in solitude generally, minimizing external stimuli allows us, little by little, to bring order to internal spaces. Many people find that positive because, as studies have shown, meditation mutes the stressful tendency we humans have to consistently react to incoming information.[95]

That seems to be due to a shift in the way that our brains function while engaged in mindfulness.[96] In short, when it comes to brain function and perceived well-being, less is more. Research has shown that, for longtime meditators, activity in the brain's "default network" quiets down, which means we're less likely to engage in destructive thought patterns like rumination during that time.[97] While doing that, mindfulness practices appear to affect brain function (in the amygdala and prefrontal cortex) in a way that makes us less reactive to stress and able to recover better from stress when we encounter it.[96] After combing through nearly 19,000 meditation studies, researchers from Johns Hopkins University found that mindful meditation can help ease psychological stresses like anxiety, depression, and pain.[98]

As we've shown throughout this book, a lot can happen in time alone. And when we look at all we bring to the threshold of solitude – our personalities, motivations, expectations, moods, and mind-sets – we have a better grasp on how or why we land in that space the way we do. Understanding how all of those factors conspire to shape our time alone, we are in a better position to exercise resilience and exert a positive influence over our thoughts and actions in that space. Those attributes, strategies, and coping mechanisms we bring into solitude can help flip it from tribulation to possibility and provide helpful guideposts on the path to well-being in everyday solitude and – as we'll see in Chapter 10 – across the life span.

CHAPTER 10

Solitude across a Lifetime

A FEW YEARS AGO, on the eve of the COVID-19 pandemic, Bette Ann Moskowitz's husband died. Immense grief became her new, constant companion, and as the pandemic worsened, the physical restrictions that became the norm compounded her loss. There were moments when she wondered if she would survive. But Moskowitz found that a lifetime of loving Marvin had left her with an enduring gift: an appreciation of quiet that was a defining part of his nature.

She hadn't always seen it as a reward. When they'd first married fifty-six years earlier, they hadn't had much in common. "I made noise; he stayed silent . . . I was a show-off; he kept a low profile," she recalled in a recent essay.[1] Marv's "habitual silence" could be taxing, but over time, it bore certain benefits. "Living with a quiet man gave me room – being a noisy person – it made me learn the pleasures of solitude and made me understand its value," Moskowitz told Heather in a recent conversation. "And as I got older, I realized how much everyone needs to be alone with herself, him- or herself, and that living with my husband afforded me that luxury."[2,3]

Moskowitz, age eighty-two, has always drawn a clear distinction between solitude (as good) and loneliness (as bad), but her relationship with being alone has grown and changed over time. "Solitude is a space and a time: room to think, time to think," she said; it is moments in which she confirms her "self" and is not afraid to be alone with her thoughts. When she was busy raising children and running a household, solitude was elusive, and Moskowitz sought it. "I remember being thrilled to take the laundry to the Laundromat where I could sit and think to the hum of the washers and dryers or get lost for an hour in the aisles of the

202

supermarket," she said. But sometimes being alone to think was less desirable and far lonelier, and solitude had to be approached carefully and used intentionally. "I suppose, if I think about it, those years when I was immersed in being a wife and mother while Marv was building his business and traveling a lot, were most lonely. Solitude was necessary for me to maintain who I was."[2,3]

Now, many years later and in mourning, solitude is still extremely important to Moskowitz. Yet, again, that relationship has shifted. She lives on her own and has a ton of solitude, which she actively manages so that it's useful in the way she wants it to be. Since her husband's passing, sitting down to dinner is when Moskowitz feels the loss of her partner and best friend most acutely. That's when her alone time can slump into loneliness, but she's learning to adjust. "It's changed a lot since he died, because that sense of him being there is gone, and I'm very aware of it. But I'm learning now to solve the problem of his lack of presence, and that is to not be afraid to remember, be surrounded by memories," Moskowitz said.[2,3] To cope, she often turns to writing (she is still a prolific author) or baking, walking her dog, or simply sitting for a while and crying. Solitude allows her the freedom to remember and to mourn in her way, by her clock. Then, gradually, she shifts her thoughts to something else and even gets excited for what the future may hold.

As researchers and solitude practitioners, we can appreciate from Moskowitz's experiences the complex relationship most of us will have with time alone over our life spans. We can think of her solitude as a room she's visited and tended to most of her life, a place where she has rearranged the furniture, painted different colors, changed the curtains – all multiple times. As we have seen, depending on what phase of life she has been in, and what events and emotions are influencing that space, when and how Moskowitz has chosen to be in solitude have also shifted.

Solitude is unique to each person, but there are patterns we have observed that we believe shed some light on what kinds of changes we should be aware of and what those mean for well-being in that space during different phases of our lives. Spoiler alert: *how* we spend that time seems to matter quite a bit in terms of our contentment in solitude, as does the nature of our relationships beyond solitude. Through our own research and the work of others on solitude and loneliness, we have learned that we have the option of cultivating alone time. Solitude is like a garden in different seasons: what we sow and what we reap changes over time, and we have to plant what's most likely to grow and thrive.

SOLITUDE THROUGH THE AGES

We began this book talking about solitude through the ages in terms of history and shifting societies. We pointed out that, over time, solitude has been more or less (mostly less!) tolerated as a need or desire of regular people. If we narrow that lens to look at the life span of the individual, we are learning through our research and that of others that the pattern is similar. We also tend to seek and tolerate time alone in a nonlinear way throughout the mortal journey from childhood to older adulthood, meaning that we don't necessarily love or hate it in a consistent way throughout our lives. There seem to be several reasons for that, which we'll dive into in this chapter. Most importantly, knowing that solitude through the ages of any individual will expand and contract can help us mold our relationship with it and direct us toward a higher level of well-being in that space.

In general, how we spend our time, and with whom, changes as we age. As youngsters, we're all about parents, siblings, and friends, whereas as we get older, we clock more hours with partners, offspring, and coworkers. Around age forty, the number of people we interact with also begins to shrink, and we spend more time on our own. In later years, that trend toward solitude deepens. According to the Global Change Data Lab based in Oxford, which looked at trends in America from 2009 to 2019, fifteen-year-olds, on average, spend 200 minutes per day on their own. By the time we hit eighty years of age, that time increases to 500 minutes per day.[4]

At the same time, the number of single-person households has been booming in most parts of the world for decades. In a history of living alone, KDM Snell at the University of Leicester notes that there has been a "historically unprecedented" rise of so-called solitaires throughout the twentieth century, and especially since the 1960s. "The direction and pace of change is staggering, and brings many questions. It is found regardless of country and place," he wrote. Snell looked at the rapid pace of change, in particular in Europe, North America, Japan, and Britain, where just 5 percent of the population lived in one-person households prior to 1911. That rose to about 17 percent in the 1960s and has continued on an unabated ascent since then.[5]

Even if we don't live by ourselves, each of us likely knows at least a handful of people living on their own. Globally, the proportion of living-alone adults varies widely by geography, but it is still significant. The Pew Research Center found that, on average, 16 percent of adults in the 130 countries and territories it studied (from 2008 to 2018) were on their own at home.[6] Although the rise of singleton households is a global phenomenon, the gains are and have always been greater in wealthy nations, where people can better afford to strike out on their own. Whereas as many as 40 percent of people in some Northern European countries may now live solo, those living alone in lower-income nations may still be as low as 1 percent.[7] Of course, this difference comes down to more than economics in some places where culture and religion also play a role (for example, according to Pew, 70 percent of the world's older Hindus live with extended family).

In nations with advanced economies, statistics paint a striking picture of how we live now. In 2021, the proportion of one-member households in the United Kingdom ranged from about 26 percent in London to 36 percent in Scotland.[8] In the United States, the proportion of adults living alone more than doubled from 13 percent in 1960 to 29 percent in 2022.[7] That amounts to a large swath of adults age eighteen or older in the United States who are now living solo – roughly thirty-eight million people.[9–11.] Living alone, either by choice or by circumstance, is especially common for older adults. In Europe, 28 percent of adults age sixty and older live on their own; in the United States, it's a close 27 percent.[6]

There are now more adults choosing to, and succeeding in, being on their own than at any time in history.[12] A major factor in that calculus is the rise in the number of singletons, particularly in the United States. Again, the statistics here are eye-popping: according to the latest US Census, nearly 46 percent of adults (age eighteen years and older), or about 130 million people, are currently single (68 percent never married, 20 percent are divorced, and 12 percent are widowed).[13] In the United Kingdom, the proportions are even higher. In 2020, more than thirty-five million people in England and Wales – or 58 percent of the adult population – were single, compared to twenty-four million who were married.[14] Being single doesn't mean that someone lives alone, or even spends most of their time alone, but the concurrent rise in living-alone adults in most parts of the world is a good indication that many are.

At this pivotal moment in history, it's important to know if all this singleness and alone time is having an impact on quality of life – and quality of solitude. To that end, we have to consider *why* people are single and/or living alone. According to Snell, the "striking growth" in single-adult households of all ages may be "contributing to what is now widely diagnosed as 'an epidemic of loneliness' or a 'loneliness time bomb.'"[5] As we've touched on throughout this book, societal changes leading to more people spending more time alone (during a pandemic, for example) tend to alarm folks who fear that loneliness will spike under those conditions. But Snell cautions against leaping to such conclusions without considering the crucial role of choice.

Many more people can afford to live alone, making going solo much less financially risky than it was before the mid-twentieth century.[15] In many ways, people also don't have to rely on each other in the same ways they did historically. Advances in government services and technologies allow us to connect to wider networks and to access resources without having to depend solely on the family unit.[16] This may be a somewhat cynical take on the statistics, but many of us can point to people in our own lives – if not ourselves – who we know prefer to live on their own and do so because they are able. The challenge is to shift our thinking to match changing demographics and to see those people as more of the rule than the exception to it.

A partial shift in social norms around relationships (for example, acceptance that a woman doesn't have to go from her parents' home to her husband's, which was long the case) has also contributed to more people remaining decoupled. And for women in particular, the ability to achieve economic independence means that marriage is no longer necessary or desirable in the way it had been for most of history. That's led many young women to strike out on their own, intentionally.[17] Being on one's own can also happen without much planning but turn out to be great. Such was the case for twenty-eight-year-old Lily Kaplan, living in

New York City, who wanted to stay in the neighborhood her friends were fleeing for lower rents elsewhere. "I was anticipating feeling lonely or feeling scared to live alone," she told the *New York Times* in 2022, "especially as a young woman."[18] But that feeling never materialized. Despite the common misconception of lonely singles, many living-alone adults maintain strong social ties beyond their immediate families. For them, it's the best of both worlds – a wider network to satisfy their social needs and the freedom to live solo by choice.

For some adults, being alone is a lifestyle, embraced as autonomy and freedom from the obligations and compromises required by being in a couple or a larger family unit. Often, those who purposefully choose to live alone consider the risks associated with that, such as personal safety and financial security, but those risks do not necessarily overshadow the benefits.[19–22] Many who live alone by choice form a positive identity around their lifestyle, expressing the desire to be perceived as whole, active human beings instead of half of a partnership.[23] This may be a difficult concept for some folks to grasp, particularly the ones brought up on films like *Jerry Maguire*, in which the sobbing Dorothy Boyd (Renée Zellweger) exclaims to the beaming title character (Tom Cruise), "You complete me!"[24] But in many recent narratives, it's obvious that living single is by design and even forms a defining part of some people's identity. National Singles Days are popping up around the world to acknowledge and celebrate that conscious status, and a flurry of recent books explain and defend the joys of going solo.[25]

Thus, for a variety of reasons, millions of people now live alone and choose to remain single. But just like for those living coupled or in family units, that doesn't mean solitude is always an illuminating and joyful experience. Whether we're living alone or in a dormitory full of people, contentment in solitude more often results from how we feel and what's going on in our lives than from if we split the rent with someone. As Thuy-vy and colleagues have seen in some recent research they conducted on understanding solitary experiences of living-alone adults, our perceptions of solitude transform with our life experiences.[26] This can make solitude, and life in general, better or worse during certain phases, as context shapes experiences in time alone. It may be challenging when, for example, new parents are forced to abstain from many of their usual social events or interactions because of childcare responsibilities. (It can also be near impossible to find time for themselves, which we've heard many times from research participants – and have experienced ourselves!) For immigrants moving to a new country – which we three authors also have extensive experience with – the first months can be difficult when they are feeling acutely the distance from home and previous social circles. That can be exacerbated by feelings of marginalization and social isolation.[27] Some professions expose people to long hours working alone, which can lead to feelings of isolation, particularly when individuals feel underwhelmed by their role. For those lone workers, solitude might be filled with boredom and frustration.[28]

In our narrative interviews with people from around the world, we heard often about how life circumstances can affect the quality of solitude, positively or negatively. Gillian, whom we met in Chapter 9, was recently divorced but learning to be much happier living on her own than with the misery she'd experienced living with a partner who wasn't right for her. Her perception of solitude was that she finally had the space to take control of her physical and mental health, and even though she was dating on and off, she was in no rush to move in with anyone again. At the time we spoke with Gillian, she gave us a snapshot of her current relationship with solitude. If we had spoken with her ten years ago, or if we were to check back with her ten years from now, that partnership would likely look different in some ways, as we'll see when we look specifically at the impact that age has on time alone.

AGE MATTERS IN LONELINESS AND SOLITUDE

Despite how society may be advancing in accepting ways of living that defy the cookie-cutter version, biases about loneliness and solitude endure – particularly in relation to age and gender. Consider the use of the misogynistic word *spinster* to describe an aging, unmarried woman, versus *bachelor* for a man. The former conjures images of a haggard, lonely old witch who "with a black cat for a pet could still find herself the target of her neighbors' suspicions."[29] (By the way, the United Kingdom only stopped using the term *spinster* in official records in 2005!)[30] And we make assumptions about what a thirty-year-old woman may be "missing" in her life if she's living on her own, compared to a thirty-year-old guy, who may be celebrated for "sowing his wild oats." We also tend to think that older adults living on their own, particularly women, are bereft of companionship most of the time. As Moskowitz's experience of living alone and mourning her husband informed us at the beginning of this chapter,[1-3] in some cases and at certain moments, we may be right in our assumptions, but certainly not often, as a growing body of research also indicates.

Though we are not loneliness researchers, that phenomenon has been studied for longer, and more comprehensively, than anyone has studied positive aloneness, aka solitude. Thus statistics and analyses about loneliness can clarify some aspects of people's experiences in solitude. Consider the work of researchers at the University of Massachusetts–Boston who analyzed data from a large health and retirement study in America. From the in-depth responses of nearly 12,000 adults age fifty years and older, the researchers observed that subjective loneliness and objective social isolation were not well correlated.[31] That means that just because many older people are often alone, they aren't necessarily lonely and experiencing the negative health effects of that state. Older adults living with others may be just as lonely, if not more so, than those on their own, but the true causes of that feeling (like mental illness or bad relationships) may be overlooked or misunderstood in that population, with dire consequences.[32]

Regardless of how society is shifting, and how many more adults are living on their own, loneliness does not seem to be increasing in a significant way. Researchers using data from that same huge, multi-decade University of Michigan Health and Retirement Study as well as from the National Social Life, Health, and Aging Project compared perceived loneliness in people born between 1948 and 1965 (so-called baby boomers) to perceived loneliness in those born between 1920 and 1947 – they wanted to know whether older adults had become lonelier from 2005 to 2016. In short, the answer was no. The researchers observed that age and cohort had little impact on rates of loneliness among adults age fifty-seven to eighty-five years. They concluded that biological age is not the main cause of loneliness; rather, they found that loneliness is often a consequence of underprivileged life circumstances (such as educational level or socioeconomic status), which can make one lonely at any age.[33] These findings from the United States mirror cross-national data in other work. A study that analyzed data from 12,248 adults older than fifty years in more than a dozen European countries showed similar results.[34]

Further findings on loneliness can clue us in to possible trends in how age and life events affect time spent alone and can suggest potential parallels to explore in solitude research. For example, the Community Life Survey, 2019/2020, done by the UK Office of National Statistics, captured a fascinating glimpse of who feels lonely and when.[32] When drilled down to age, the results across responses reveal an illuminating pattern.

The survey split up the responses of participants (age sixteen to seventy-five years and older) into several age brackets. The overall loneliest age group surveyed was sixteen- to twenty-four-year-olds, but beyond that point, loneliness declined significantly until age forty-five. At that stage (in forty-five- to fifty-year-olds), there was a small spike in reported loneliness, and then it dropped again through age seventy-four (sixty-five- to seventy-four-year-olds were, in fact, the least lonely age group). Beyond that, for the seventy-five and older group, loneliness increased slightly across every metric (shown by an increase in "some of the time" and a decrease in "hardly ever"), except for the proportion of people who said they were "never lonely," which remained the same. Other studies have observed that this slight spike in loneliness is maintained in the "oldest old" adults who face adversities, including health issues, financial troubles, and a lack of education. But for elders who don't experience those difficulties, loneliness tends to drop once again at that stage of life.[33,34]

Other key surveys and studies have shown similar results, reinforcing the key idea that there is a nonlinear relationship between age and loneliness. Researchers at the University of California, San Diego and Tulane University surveyed more than 2,800 Americans, age twenty to sixty-nine years, to find out more about what loneliness looks like across that fifty-year span. Their data suggested that loneliness was higher among respondents in their twenties than among those in their sixties, and like the UK survey, the study showed a small but significant rise in loneliness among subjects in their mid-forties.[35]

Researchers in the United Kingdom, Belgium, and the Netherlands looked at *why* loneliness shifts across the life span, which may give insight into when and why solitude may be tougher at certain times.[36] Perceptions of closeness and alienation seem to factor in to whether people of all ages experience loneliness. The researchers observed that in early adolescence (twelve to fifteen years old), the lack of a close friend, nonacceptance by peers, and victimization are all sources of loneliness. In later adolescence and young adulthood (fifteen to twenty-one years old), the desire for intimacy grows, and loneliness is rooted in the lack of a close friend and the lack of a romantic relationship (and possibly rejection). Lack of intimate friendships or romantic relationships again factored in to loneliness in early adulthood and midlife. Those causes were again cited by the fifty plus age group but were accompanied by the experiences of losing a partner, ill health, and reduced social activity.

We've really only scratched the surface of the body of loneliness research, but we can see that concerns about loneliness are justified to some degree, as a portion of the population experiences its deleterious effects at some point during their lives, and those folks need to have access to resources to help them counteract those dips in well-being. At the same time, we can see that simply spending time alone continues to be a poor predictor of loneliness – regardless of age. That fact should be a bigger part of the overall conversation than it currently is so that we're not looking for loneliness in all the wrong places or at the wrong times. Awareness of when and why we may be more vulnerable to loneliness can also help change the conversation on alone time and reduce bias against solitude. If we gain a better idea of when and how to approach time alone over our lifetimes, we can maximize its possible benefits and be more content in everyday solitude.

THE BIG PICTURE ON SOLITUDE

Compared to the study of loneliness, relatively little research has looked at the role of solitude, or positive alone time, across the life span. Researchers tend to focus on children and older adults – the groups believed to be most vulnerable to loneliness – ignoring most people in between. But loneliness and solitude are completely different experiences (which you, reader, well know if you've read this far). Notably, the difference between loneliness and solitude is discerned early in life. Even adolescents, whose ability to grasp nuance we often (wrongly) underestimate, can differentiate between unpleasant isolation and enjoyable solitude.

A group of Greek researchers whose work illustrates that point interviewed 180 second, fourth, and sixth graders (age seven to eleven years) from Athens about their experiences with loneliness. In their replies, over 70 percent made a distinction between being alone and being lonely.[37] They reported that being alone didn't automatically mean they'd be lonely and that a person can feel lonely in the presence of others. Not surprisingly, that awareness increased with age; about 67 percent of nine-year-olds in the fourth grade recognized it, whereas a little over 88 percent of eleven-year-olds in the sixth grade did. The children explained that one may not feel lonely when alone for a variety of interesting and enlightened reasons, including being satisfied with their interpersonal relationships, being occupied with a pleasant activity, making plans for shared future activities, or just wanting to think.

Other solitude research has looked at different siloed age groups and has shown that preadolescents (age eleven or twelve years) may struggle with aloneness, whereas mid-adolescents and teenagers tend to appreciate it more.[38] Further studies have observed that well-being in solitude dips in middle age and that, contrary to popular belief, older adults seem to do better than young people at reaping the benefits of alone time.[39–41] To understand what accounts for this mini roller coaster of well-being in solitude over the life span, we have to answer these questions: How do our emotional needs and values change as we age, and how does that affect our experience of solitude? What can we learn from older adults' experiences in solitude that may be useful for tapping in to well-being in solitude at any age?

One clue about why and how solitude may differ over the lifetime comes from researchers in Israel who asked two groups of people – those in young and middle adulthood (age eighteen to sixty-four years) and older adults (age sixty-five to eighty-five years and older) – about their experiences in positive solitude.[42] Certain benefits were important to people regardless of age, including quiet time and being alone in nature, which respondents said fostered a sense of peacefulness. Having time for hobbies and recreational activities that allowed them to express creativity was another plus enjoyed across all ages. But when the researchers compared the seventeen- to sixty-four-year-olds to the sixty-five years and older group, they observed one distinct difference: for younger participants, solitude was positive because it acted as an escape hatch from daily duties and social engagements; it also helped them regulate emotions and regain a sense of control. None of the older participants approached positive solitude in this way; instead, they emphasized that the freedom to choose to be alone, and to master their own destiny while there, was its defining positive attribute.

This may be because, as Erik Erikson, a psychodynamic theorist (and one of the founders of developmental psychology), suggested, social activity is naturally reduced in older age and replaced with reflections on one's own life narrative.[43] His view that movement away from social spaces is a normal developmental step was echoed later by Elaine Cumming and William E. Henry, who drew a parallel between withdrawal from social interactions and greater satisfaction in later life.[44] This may be true in part because our emotional needs shift as we age. Research examining emotions across the life span, in particular, has drawn some conclusions that challenge the stereotype of the sad, lonely retiree.[45]

For example, in one diary study asking 184 adults (age eighteen to ninety-four years) to record their emotions across a week, researchers found that negative emotions, such as anger, sadness, fear, guilt, shame, frustration, and boredom, declined from age nineteen to age sixty. At sixty, the effect flattened, and up to age ninety-four, people continued to report fewer negative emotions. The results showed that older adults generally have more, not less, well-being in solitude than the average youngster.[46] That's because as we age, we get better at regulating our emotions,[47] and this is particularly true when it comes to downregulating negative emotions based on specific anxieties[48] (that's why it's rare – at least outside of politics! – to see a seventy-five-year-old throw a temper tantrum).

Multiple studies have also shown that older adults often value low-arousal positive emotions, such as feeling calm and peaceful, over high-arousal positive emotions, such as being excited and energized.[49–51] Think of it as a preference for sitting by a fireplace listening to music over rushing the main stage at Glastonbury music festival. This is because as we get older, it takes more effort to recover from high-energy events. That's evidenced in a study of twenty-nine young adults from eighteen to twenty-three years and thirty older adults age sixty to eighty-seven years in which the researchers asked participants to choose film clips they wanted to watch for fifteen minutes. Older participants were more likely to choose segments that were more neutral and lower in arousal, whereas younger participants leaned more toward stimulating and negative film clips.[52]

Some aspect of so-called socioemotional selectivity is likely also at work in accounting for older adults' well-being in solitude.[53] That's a fancy name for a theory that argues that as people age, they start to appreciate more the importance of how they spend their time. Because young people often feel time is limitless, they choose to pursue a larger number of fragmented goals rather than sifting more carefully through priorities. As we age, we shift our attention to pursuing fewer but more satisfying or emotionally meaningful goals. This was described as the "bucket list effect" by Alexandra Freund, who suggested that older adults are freer to engage in more leisure activities and to be more self-focused and relaxed than the child-rearing or career-focused set. Being free of those obligations, while still investing in some social relationships, allowed older adults more physical and mental space to just chill out in solitude.

Because they value creating meaningful experiences, adults also naturally grow to value relationships in terms of *quality* rather than quantity.[54] That means potentially less time spent with others – measured in fewer people or less time with them – but more of that time spent on higher-quality encounters. A group of researchers in the United States and China found that for people in their teens and twenties, one's number of friends mattered most (as measured in health effects). Older than that, and quality of friendship appeared more consequential than quantity. For the oldest adults studied (age sixty-five to seventy-nine years), how often they saw friends mattered little in terms of their overall loneliness. The investigators speculated that older adults may be more content with a few close friends, or less frequent visits, than young people.[54] Researchers at Oslo University Hospital had similar findings when they surveyed nearly 15,000 people in Norway, age eighteen to seventy-nine years, about loneliness and social interactions. Younger people spent the most time with friends, but even though the older age groups had fewer friends or saw them less often, they reported higher levels of satisfaction with the contact they did have.[55]

The benefits of this shift from quantity to quality of social interaction were shown in a unique study that followed 133 people from the time they were undergraduates until midlife.[56] Researchers at the University of Rochester and Brooklyn College looked at social integration, friendship quality, and the psychological effects of the two across thirty years of the participants' lives. Having a large quantity of interactions in their twenties, then downshifting to fewer but higher-quality (defined as intimate and satisfying) connections in their thirties resulted in participants reporting higher levels of well-being at midlife (fifty years old). The study also showed that a high number of social interactions at age thirty had no psychological benefits later in life and that, while meaningful relationships were important at every age, they were more consequential to later health when experienced at age thirty than at age twenty. What this means is that the shift most of us seem to make from being hyper-social in our youth and potentially more anxious in solitude to being happier in solitude as older folks is natural and beneficial – and not necessarily something to be feared. Reducing the number of people in our social networks later in life, by chance or by choice, clearly has fewer negative effects than conventional wisdom suggests. If you perceive that you have meaningful social ties, regardless of how many people that includes, then you are less likely to be lonely in solitude.

At the same time, we must acknowledge the range of experiences possible in solitude, particularly for older people. A review of seventeen papers looking at solitude in older adults concluded that time alone is experienced both positively and negatively (occasionally, at the same moment). In analyzing previous work, the researchers observed that the relationship between solitude and well-being for older adults is a complex one that – as we alluded to earlier – seems to have a lot to do with an individual's personal experiences.[57] We can't escape that as we age, life is marked by losses – of partners, friends, health and mobility, and maybe financial security.

Though no one is immune to the effects of these seismic life shifts, they have a different impact on each individual. Some older adults living alone, or spending most of their days solo, do fine, while others struggle.[26] In some of our most recent research, we have heard a lot from older adults in northern England about "coping with" or "becoming accustomed to" solitude, whether or not those individuals have come into it by choice or by circumstance. They talk about "learning to live with it," but this is not necessarily the same thing as experiencing periods of positive solitude in their daily lives. Again, as we've written about at length in this book already, choice is key to contentment in that space. If we are homebound with no way to get to the activities we once enjoyed doing, then we're going to be less likely to embrace that alone time and mold it into positive solitude.

SHAPING EVERYDAY SOLITUDE

As we've talked about throughout this book, there are aspects of how we feel and what we do in solitude that can make it better or worse. When we look at those factors while also considering age, which we've done in our own work and have seen in other recent research, we begin to see some interesting patterns in what role solitude plays as we age. We also can understand better what role it can, and maybe should, play during different phases of our lives (see Box 10.1). If we dislike being alone in adolescence, does that mean we're going to be lonely in our seventies? Conversely, if we love being alone when we're young, does that mean we'll embrace it in midlife? Knowing the answers to these questions may allow us to maximize the potential of solitude by shifting our expectations, desires, and actions during alone time at eighteen or eighty and everywhere in between.

Few studies have taken a life span view of solitude, but the ones that do offer some interesting findings. In a study of 185 adults in Atlanta, Georgia, age twenty to eighty-one years, researchers set out to better understand how people across the adult life span felt in so-called momentary solitude as they went about their everyday life routines.

BOX 10.1 HUMAN BEING VERSUS HUMAN DOING

Italians have a phrase – *il dolce far niente*, "the sweetness of doing nothing." But for them, it's more nuanced than "nothing," meaning instead that there is delight to be had in a state that's equal parts *being* and *doing*. That's a helpful way to think about the type of balance we may want to strive for in solitude at any age – a happy medium between being in our heads with our thoughts and doing tasks that exist in the world beyond our minds.[58] *Being* gives us time to explore, understand, and develop ideas about ourselves in relation to the world, whereas *doing* allows us to pursue goals and feel good about accomplishments. Finding the right balance between the two conditions can be a way to be more resilient in solitude, and increase overall well-being, at twenty-five or eighty-five years old.

Psychotherapy guru Carl Rogers (1902–87) prized time when he could just *be* and advocated, above all, for self-exploration and self-understanding.[59] But personally, Rogers also enjoyed life most when he was *doing* (writing a book or talking to other people, for example). Even though engagement in external tasks made him happier in general, Rogers understood the immense value of sticking with an internal conversation to see where it could lead, rather than moving on to the next flashy to-do item. More recently, Hadassah Littman-Ovadia, a psychologist at Israel's Ariel University, expanded on that paradigm, describing four types of daily existence: solitary doing, communal doing, solitary being, and communal being. Balancing those conditions in everyday life is "essential for human health and flourishing," she said. Littman-Ovadia focused on two of those modes – being and solitude – as "perhaps stigmatized by their inferior popular image." She said they "can be perceived as under-used muscles that have the potential of facilitating a stronger, more complete life." (We could not agree more!)[58]

Though it's easy to imagine not much is happening physically while we're sitting around just being, brain scan studies show evidence that the default mode network (DMN), which we referenced in Chapter 9, is very active during that time. That high level of neural activity consumes 20 percent of the body's total energy – more energy than any other area of the brain. In fact, according to DMN experts, intrinsic activity accounts for roughly 90 percent of the brain's overall energy use.[60] The takeaway: gaining self-knowledge can be hard work. (As mentioned earlier, we have to be aware that rumination can also happen in the DMN, but that state is distinct from positive being because of *how* we are thinking.) Doing is also ultra-important because it's part of human nature to set goals for ourselves and then pursue them.[61] Doing can be fun, interesting, and satisfying. It's how we feel competent in our lives and how we can become the best versions of ourselves.

We need being and doing to be in balance, but in reality, we don't always have to choose between them. Sometimes they can coexist,[59] such as when we bake a cake with a recipe that we know so well it takes little thought or when we spend time digging in the garden. Those activities are low in what psychologists call "cognitive load" – they don't require careful, focused attention on the present moment – so they allow the mind to wander and explore whatever arises.[60] We heard from some of our research participants about chopping vegetables for dinner or cleaning their apartments almost as a "gateway" activity used as a warm-up for the being and thinking part of solitude.

Our research subjects, and particularly those who are adept at achieving positive solitude, talked to us quite a bit about having focus, purpose, and intention in time alone. That seemed to help orient and direct their time while still allowing for internally focused thoughts. A lot of people like to make a plan for what they will do in solitude because they find it diffuses anxiety they may experience and makes that time easier and more enjoyable. Others embrace the feeling that solitude is a blank slate when they can do and think whatever they want to from moment to moment.

As we've touched on throughout this chapter, what feels right may be a function of age or what we have going on in our lives at present. If you are in your teens and your friend just died in a car accident, you may have more difficulty in time alone with that grief than someone in their eighties might. That doesn't mean that solitude cannot be helpful at certain moments for that eighteen-year-old or that having some company at times would benefit the grieving eighty-year-old; it just means that we have to be in tune with what influence age and context may have on the quality of our alone time.

As research on solitude over the life span suggests, sometimes whether being or doing portends greater contentment in solitude may be guided by age. For younger people, well-being in solitude seems linked to feeling efficacious in that space, so in that case, *doing* something that helps one feel capable is a good choice. As we get older, a mix of *being* and *doing* may mold solitude that is the most useful and interesting – whether in middle age, facing big questions about life and purpose on a mountain hike, or in older age, finding a beautiful seaside spot to just sit, relax, and read. Ultimately, which path any of us decides to tread in solitude – being or doing – may vary by day or mood, but an awareness of those states and desires can help us all find more value and well-being in time alone.

Over a stretch of ten days, participants were "beeped" five times per day, at which point they reported their affect or mood and sometimes also gave salivary samples to measure their cortisol (a stress hormone) level.

Overall, the study participants experienced momentary solitude – when people were truly by themselves and not communicating with anyone else electronically – both positively and negatively. The results indicated that, compared to being with other people, momentary solitude prompted less high-arousal positive affect (feeling alert and active) and more low-arousal negative affect (being bored or depressed) in all age groups.[39] That means that, as we pointed out in Chapter 4, it's not uncommon for solitude to feel less exciting and maybe more boring for some people than spending time with others. Also similar to prior work, this research showed a positive link between solitude and low-arousal positive affect, meaning that participants generally felt more calm and relaxed during those moments ("which may facilitate self-reflection, creative thinking, and emotional renewal," speculated the researchers). They also found no significant association between solitude and high-arousal negative affect (being fearful or anxious).

For those reasons, the researchers called momentary solitude a "double-edged sword," but that sword was not of uniform length or sharpness across the age groups. Compared to younger adults, older adults generally experienced more positive and fewer negative emotions in time alone (and didn't show the cortisol increases that younger participants did). The researchers observed that "spending time alone is thus an experience that is not necessarily negative and that may improve with aging." In general, older people seemed to do better, perhaps, the researchers speculated, because they tend to focus on the positive and are more competent in regulating their emotions in that space. The passing years may give older adults more time to develop a capacity for time alone or a routine or structure that makes it more positive.

In our own research, we have been interested in capturing the experiences of people in as many age groups as possible, both in terms of what we do and how we feel in solitude and how those change over time. During the early days of the pandemic, we recruited more than 2,000 participants from various age groups, including adolescents (age thirteen to sixteen years), adults (age thirty-five to fifty-five years), and older adults (age sixty-five years and older).[62] We wanted to know whether qualities of solitude change depending on age and, if so, how. We asked subjects to write about what had made time spent on their own good or bad in the three months prior and what they had learned. Several prominent themes were evident in their personal narratives of time spent in solitude. We heard most about using solitude to achieve three things: competence, autonomy, and self-growth. *Competence* involved participants feeling efficacious in solitude while engaging in chosen activities and skill building. Solitude that had *autonomy* fostered self-connection, self-reliance, and freedom from outside pressure. And *self-growth* was characterized by reflecting on oneself, developing coping abilities like patience, and engaging with spirituality.

We learned from looking at responses across the three age groups that perceived benefits of solitude tend to shift over the life span. What is most important for adolescents to achieve in solitude differs from what ranks high either with middle-aged or older adults. Competence, growth, and autonomy – in that order – are most consequential to adolescents.

Adults care most about growth, then autonomy, then competence. Older adults are most interested in autonomy (by far the most consequential benefit), then growth, then competence in solitude. In many ways, this reprioritizing in solitude over the life span makes a lot of sense. It's particularly important for adolescents to feel like they are doing well, and improving, on a chosen task (in or out of solitude). Adults spanning middle age tend to be concerned with taking stock and reflecting on their identities and priorities. Meanwhile, many older adults want most to maintain a certain level of self-reliance and freedom from the influence of others.

These findings about what qualities solitude has, and when, gel with our study's other revelation, that is, who enjoys the most peaceful mood when alone. When we looked at narratives from young people, middle-aged folks, and older adults, we tracked a similar nonlinear relationship between well-being in solitude and age that we talked about earlier regarding loneliness. In particular, we saw a drop in perceived well-being in solitude in middle age (the inverse of the spike seen in the loneliness data), a benefit that rebounded in older adults. Despite the prevailing assumption that older adults are destined to suffer in isolation (especially during a pandemic), they reported the most relaxed and least lonely mood in solitude. Seniors also lacked a sense of alienation, or feeling of absence about social connection, which indicated that they drew a clearer distinction between social and alone time (and the upsides of each) than other age groups. Surprisingly, the next most content group were adolescents. Last, despite having the highest self-determined motivation for solitude, were the middle-aged adults in our study, who expressed the least peaceful mood in solitude – perhaps because their self-growth focus in solitude can make that time more challenging in general.

Being cognizant of which benefits prevail among various ages may help steer us toward certain objectives and activities that result in greater contentment in solitude. For example, a teenager who understands that time alone may be more gratifying when they engage in an activity in which they can gain know-how may find greater well-being there. In adulthood, understanding that solitude is a fruitful place for self-growth (which isn't always easy but is often gratifying) can be illuminating. Older adults, who have been in their own company the longest, rely less on needing to feel they are growing or getting better at anything in solitude to make it enjoyable. Spending time alone merely to feel free may be reason enough for many elders to seek and be satisfied in solitude.

All this research on lived experiences of solitude and loneliness illustrates that age and phase of life certainly influence our interest in, and tolerance and enjoyment of, time alone. What we now know about how our developmental and emotional needs evolve as we get older can help us claim and reframe our daily experiences of solitude. It can also be hugely helpful in choosing when and in what ways to harness solitude to our greatest benefit. That's an instrumental part of what makes alone time positive – but it's just one piece.[63]

For as many answers and suppositions as we can offer about the role that solitude plays in our daily lives, we still have many questions. There's a lot more to discover about what's happening to each of us when we're alone, and when we think about future lines of inquiry, certain paths are particularly intriguing to each of us researchers. Netta is curious about which aspect of the experience of being with ourselves is the basic reason we love solitude – are all things autonomy (authenticity, curiosity, choice, interest) the key? Or is it merely the calming lack of others' chatter? Or is it most important that quiet opens the door to being truly with ourselves (something she suspects may be true, as she feels most peaceful when she's free to be with herself in nature)? Netta also wonders about the interaction between culture and solitude and whether autonomy in solitude looks the same despite different perceptions of social acceptance and relationships. Lifestyle raises additional questions; class, for instance, can determine how much time one has to be alone, and location (urban versus rural) may also play an important role.

The fascinating direction of future research for Thuy-vy is not what separates us but rather what unites us. Despite cultural differences, we may share the same way solitude affects our cognition and feelings, and Thuy-vy is interested in learning about the mechanisms that lie beneath nuanced experiences of solitude. Our perceptions and appraisals of the experiences within solitude can differ, depending on our motivation, our attitudes, and the norms that we internalize, but those experiences come from biological and physiological processes that are not yet fully understood. Such activities have been identified for loneliness and social isolation, but will we one day find similar ones for solitude? What universal processes are activated when we are alone? Heather is also curious about the physiology of solitude and whether we experience differences based on gender. She'd also like to know more about the dynamics of solitude in companionate solitude and how understanding and respecting those may improve the quality of intimate relationships.

At this moment in time, when we approach solitude with everything we've talked about in this book – shaking off stigma, understanding the importance of choice, knowing what perks are possible, striking a balance between solo and social, finding our preferred setting and purpose, and embracing our emotional needs at any age – we can see that solitude has the potential to be so many things at once. It can be a proving ground, a refuge, a think tank, an amusement park, a revelation, and more. Throughout life, we may aim for or merely stumble upon solitude, but either way, it's largely what we make of it (see Box 10.2).

BOX 10.2 SOLITUDE CHECKLIST, FOR ALL AGES

Throughout this book, we've been dropping practical hints for how to seize positive solitude whenever and wherever possible and appropriate. In rounding up some of those, we offer these final pointers.

Take your solitude pulse. Check in with yourself and ask, Could I benefit from stepping away? Or, if you fear solitude, ask yourself why you think it's not for you. Challenge your assumptions, and keep yourself open to what you might discover.

Start small, stay mighty. You've likely heard of the power of high-intensity interval training in exercise. Paul Salmon, psychologist at the University of Louisville, suggests trying it with solitude.[64] Especially if you're new to embracing alone time, start with short spurts of it throughout the day and work your way up to wherever you want to go. (On the flip side, there's nothing wrong with a weeklong meditation retreat, if you're "feeling it"!)

Adopt a thoughtful approach. As many meditation teachers and practitioners know, setting an intention for a practice can set the stage

---

for success. Being mindful and nonjudgmental in solitude helps us tap into what our needs are and guides us toward well-being in that space.

Create a framework. For some people, time alone is a span of gaping nothingness. In that case, it's best to make a plan for solitude – maybe there's a new recipe you've been meaning to try or a book that's been sitting on your nightstand unopened. Having an idea of how you want to occupy that time, what you want to rest your attention upon, can make it easier to venture into solitude and maintain a positive relationship with it into the future.

Be curious. This may be the single most powerful secret weapon we all have in solitude. Being open and inquisitive sets a tone of discovery and opportunity (and fun!) versus an expectation of success or failure (*not* fun!).

Opt for a low-sensory environment. Remember all that stuff we said about reducing stimulation and embracing quiet? That doesn't mean you need an isolation tank, just a place where you can focus on your thoughts. (Again, if blasting Metallica works for you instead, then rock on!)

Be open to experimentation. What works for you to find positive solitude may differ based on your phase of life or your mood from one moment to the next. Stay open to the many, many possibilities offered in solitude, and pick those that best suit you at the time.

Believe in belonging. Just because we're not interacting with other people while in solitude doesn't mean we're truly alone. We can balance "me time" with "us time," and help mitigate feelings of isolation or loneliness, by remembering that we have friends and family to lean on.

Practice "integrated emotion regulation." Phew, that's a mouthful, but it basically means engaging your emotions with curiosity instead of judgment.[65] Psychologist and solitude researcher Virginia Thomas suggests that rather than avoiding distressing feelings that may arise in time alone, we can learn to approach and explore them in a neutral way, which can help us self-regulate and destress.[66]

Beware of "sneaky infiltrators." The question of technology use in solitude is a thorny one. The use of social media has been shown to curb boredom and loneliness in solitude, particularly in young people, but it may also distract from one of the key benefits of solitude: time to reflect on ourselves, and in an authentic way. Proceed with caution, and choose what feels right for you.

Plan for and protect periods of solitude. Choose you, intentionally, at least some of the time. Treat time alone as a need you should plan for, while also being on the lookout for impromptu moments of aloneness that you can transform into positive, enjoyable solitude.

Our relationship with solitude is an ongoing, lifelong journey that begins from the time we grasp the difference between lonely and alone, and it grows with us, giving us what we need as long as we choose it. It may allow us the time and space to practice the ukulele, write a letter to an old friend, grieve a loss, or stream *Ted Lasso* episodes – again – (all things we authors have done in solitude) and laugh out loud by ourselves, with ourselves, for ourselves. Whatever we choose to do, and to be, in those priceless solo moments is entirely of our own making, and those decisions are all steps on the path of well-being in solitude and in life.[63]

Acknowledgments

Putting together a book like this does not happen solely with the work of the three names that grace its cover. The authors have many people to thank for their input, inspiration, and guidance. To start, we would like to thank the thousands of subjects who contributed so generously to our research with their thoughts, experiences, and insights, which breathed life into the concepts in this book.

Netta also acknowledges the thoughtful and caring guidance of her two research (and life and psyche) advisors, Rich Ryan and Ed Deci, who springboarded her scientific and personal understanding and growth. With their guidance, she developed the capacity to learn about the world through data and her own experiences. Netta has also had the great luck of working with wonderful colleagues who have ignited her imagination and confidence. That list is far too long to catalog fully here, but she thanks Nicole Legate and Silke Paulmann for helping her to dream big and take a leap into *Solitude* – and, of course, Heather and Thuy-vy, her wonderful collaborators and coauthors, for their wisdom and words, which made for good company in *Solitude*. Finally, she is thankful for her family, including (but not limited to!) her husband, Andy; her parents; her sister Dana; and her two children, Maya and Ari. Each has taught her important lessons about herself and the world and given her the drive to pursue her most important goals. They have inspired her to want to learn more, be better, and know herself.

Thuy-vy thanks her parents and sisters in Vietnam who have supported her through years of pursuing her passion and research on solitude. She'd also like to acknowledge Rich Ryan for saying, early in the pursuit of her PhD, "If you want to study solitude, why do something else?" And Thuy-vy is grateful to Ed Deci for always being there, building up her younger, shyer self, and to Orin Davis for his mentorship and encouragement in her pursuing a research career. She has gotten much guidance from other solitude researchers along the way, including Julie Bowker, Robert Coplan, Bella DePaulo, Sharon Ost Mor, Virginia Thomas, and her coauthors. She is thankful for her husband, Jonathon McPhetres, who always asks her the hard questions; she is a better methodologist because of him. Her best friend, Kaitlyn Werner, has always been there and makes academia a less lonely place. Finally, thank you to the research participants of the "Your Home and Neighborhood" and "Interviews about Time Alone" projects (you know who you are) – your stories gave Thuy-vy the strength and confidence to ask better questions!

Heather thanks her friends and family, especially her husband, Juan Nieto Castro, and sister Alison Baukney for their unflagging love and support (and for leaving her *alone*, when necessary!) throughout the writing of this book. She thanks Netta and Thuy-vy for trusting her to gather and tell these stories of solitude. Heather is forever grateful for having had Ellen Baukney (1941–2018) as her mom – a first grade teacher and encourager of all questions, big and small.

All three authors are thankful for the wise and hardworking group at Cambridge University Press, including Emily Watton, Rowan Groat, Laura Simmons, Janka Romero, Christine Gorman, and Holly Monteith. Your experience and excellence are unparalleled.

References

CHAPTER 1

[1] Guggenheim, D., Osisek, B., & Leckart, S. (Executive Prod.). (2019). *Inside Bill's brain: Decoding Bill Gates* [TV mini series]. Concordia Studio/Netflix.

[2] Asher, S. R., & Paquette, J. A. (2003). Loneliness and peer relations in childhood. *Current Directions in Psychological Science, 12*(3), 75–78.

[3] Margalit, M. (2010). *Lonely children and adolescents: Self-perceptions, social exclusion, and hope.* Springer.

[4] Rotenberg, K. J., & Hymel, S. (1999). *Loneliness in childhood and adolescence.* Cambridge University Press.

[5] Despain, D. (2010). Early humans used brain power, innovation and teamwork to dominate the planet. *Scientific American.* www.scientificamerican.com/article/humans-brain-power-origins/

[6] Hamilton, W. D. (1971). Geometry for the selfish herd. *Journal of Theoretical Biology, 31*, 295–311.

[7] Janis, I. L. (1972). *Victims of groupthink: A psychological study of foreign-policy decisions and fiascoes.* Houghton Mifflin.

[8] Taylor, B. (2009). Separations of soul: Solitude, biography, history. *American Historical Review, 114*(3), 640–51.

[9] Barbour, J. D. (2014). A view from religious studies. In R. J. Coplan & J. C. Bowker (Eds.), *The handbook of solitude: Psychological perspectives on social isolation, social withdrawal, and being alone* (pp. 557–71). Wiley.

[10] Mattson, I. (2013). *The story of the Qur'an: Its history and place in Muslim life* (2nd ed.). Wiley-Blackwell.

[11] Exodus 24:18 (NIV).

[12] Martin, D. L. (1999). The vision of Zoroaster: An essay on the mystical origins of "the Good Vision." *Iran and the Caucasus, 3*(1), 9–32.

[13] Darrow, W. R. (1987). Zoroaster amalgamated: Notes on Iranian prophetology. *History of Religions, 27*(2), 109–32.

[14] France, P. (1996). *Hermits: The insights of solitude.* Chatto & Windus.

[15] Webb, D. (2007). *Privacy and solitude in the middle ages.* Hambledon Continuum.

[16] Landaw, J. (2011). *Prince Siddhartha: The story of Buddha.* Simon and Schuster.

[17] Lopez, D. S., Jr. (2002). *The story of Buddhism: A concise guide to its history and teachings.* HarperCollins.

[18] Ficinus, M., & Kaske, C. V. (1989). *Three books on life* (Vol. 57). Center for Medieval and Early Renaissance Studies, State University of New York.

[19] Telles-Correia, D., & Marques, J. G. (2015). Melancholia before the twentieth century: Fear and sorrow or partial insanity? *Frontiers in Psychology, 6*, 81. https://doi.org/10.3389/fpsyg.2015.00081

[20] Burton, R. (1932). *The anatomy of melancholy* (H. Jackson, Ed., Vol. 1, p. 33). Dent. (Original work published 1631)

[21] Beach, W. (1846). *The American practice of the family physician.* Messrs. Andrews.

[22] Beach, W. (1836). *American practice of medicine.* Legacy.

[23] Yeoman, T. H. (1850). *People's medical journal, and family physician* (p. 3). George Vickers, Strand.

[24] Vincent, D. (2020). *A history of solitude* (p. 22). Polity Press.

[25] Burke, P. (1997). *The Renaissance.* Bloomsbury.

[26] Danford, J. W. (2014). *Roots of freedom: A primer on modern liberty.* Open Road Media.

[27] Ameriks, K., & Clarke, D. M. (2000). *Aristotle: Nicomachean ethics.* Cambridge University Press.

[28] Seneca, L. A. (2016). *Seneca's letters from a Stoic* (p. 2). Dover.

[29] de Montaigne, M., & Hazlitt, W. (1842). *The complete works of Michael de Montaigne* (p. 104). J. Templeman.

[30] Hume, D. (1874). *A treatise of human nature* (Vol. 2, p. 150). Longmans.

[31] Defoe, D. (1719). *Serious reflections during the life and surprising adventures of Robinson Crusoe: With his vision of the angelick world.* W. Taylor.

[32] Zimmermann, M. (1810). *Solitude considered, with respect to its influence upon the mind and the heart.* C. Dilly.

[33] Wordsworth, W. (1849). *The poems of William Wordsworth* (pp. 144–45). E. Moxon.

[34] Emerson, R. W. (1854). *The complete works of Ralph Waldo Emerson: Nature addresses and lectures.* Houghton, Mifflin.

[35] Campbell, G. (2013). *The hermit in the garden: From imperial Rome to ornamental gnome.* Oxford University Press.

[36] Fernandez, L., & Matt, S. J. (2020). *Bored, lonely, angry, stupid: Changing feelings about technology, from the telegraph to Twitter.* Harvard University Press.

[37] Pawlak, M., Zawodniak, J., & Kruk, M. (2020). Approaching boredom from a theoretical angle. In *Boredom in the foreign language classroom* (pp. 1–14). Springer.

[38] Van Tilberg, W. (2020). Leprosy of the soul? A brief history of boredom. *The Conversation.* https://theconversation.com/leprosy-of-the-soul-a-brief-history-of-boredom-144754

[39] Kazin, A. (1980, September 7). Hopper's vision of New York. *New York Times.* www.nytimes.com/1980/09/07/archives/hoppers-vision-of-new-york.html

[40] Tisserand, M. [@m_tisserand]. (2020, March 16). We are all Edward Hopper paintings now [Tweet]. Twitter. www.twitter.com/m_tisserand/status/1239618422079660034

[41] Fischer, C. S. (1988). "Touch someone": The telephone industry discovers sociability. *Technology and Culture, 29*(1), 32–61.

[42] Gans, H. J. (1982). *The Levittowners: Ways of life and politics in a new suburban community.* Columbia University Press.

[43] Sangster, D. (1960, January 2). *Loneliness* (p. 23). Maclean's.

[44] Abbey, E. (1988). *Desert solitaire.* University of Arizona Press.

[45] Krakauer, J. (2009). *Into the wild.* Knopf Doubleday.

[46] Strayed, C. (2013). *Wild: From lost to found on the Pacific Crest Trail.* Knopf Doubleday.

[47] Rodriguez, R. (2021). *The book of hermits.* Hermitary Press.

[48] Averett, S., Argys, L. M., & Hoffman, S. D. (Eds.). (2018). *The Oxford handbook of women and the economy.* Oxford University Press.

[49] Mackay, C. S. (2009). *The hammer of witches: A complete translation of the Malleus Maleficarum* (p. 43). Cambridge University Press. (Original work published 1486)

[50] King, M. H. (1984). *The desert mothers: A survey of the feminine anchoretic tradition in Western Europe.* Peregrina.

[51] Chryssavgis, J. (2008). *In the heart of the desert: The spirituality of the desert fathers and mothers* (Rev. ed., pp. 29–32). World Wisdom.

[52] Ward, B. (1984). *The sayings of the desert fathers: The alphabetical collection* (Rev. ed., p. 196). Cistercian.

[53] Wellesley, M. (2018). *The life of the anchoress.* British Library. www.bl.uk/medieval-literature/articles/the-life-of-the-anchoress

[54] Millett, B. (Ed. & Trans.). (2000). *Ancrene Wisse: A guide for anchoresses based on Cambridge Corpus Christi College MS 402* (p. 56). University of Exeter Press.

[55] Julian of Norwich. (1675). *Revelations of divine love to Mother Juliana, anchorite of Norwich.* www.bl.uk/collection-items/the-long-text-of-julian-of-norwichs-revelations-of-divine-love

[56] Lerner, R. E. (1972). *The heresy of the free spirit in the later Middle Ages.* University of California Press.

[57] Van Mierlo, J., & McDonnell, E. W. (1955). The Béguines and Beghards in medieval culture. With special emphasis on the Belgian scene. *Revue Belge de Philologie et d'Histoire, 33*(3), 671–74.

[58] Simons, W. (2003). *Cities of ladies: Beguine communities in the medieval low countries, 1200–1565.* University of Pennsylvania Press.

[59] Fister, P. (2018). Commemorating life and death: The memorial culture surrounding the Rinzai zen nun Mugai Nyodai. In *Women, rites, and ritual objects in premodern Japan* (pp. 269–303). Brill.

[60] Pullin, N. (2020). *Domestic solitude in early Modern Britain.* https://solitudes .qmul.ac.uk/blog/domestic-solitude-in-early-modern-britain/

[61] Lambert, A. T. d. (1815). *Marchioness de Lambert's advice to her daughter* (p. 26). George Nicholson.

[62] Wollstonecraft, M. (1992). A vindication of the rights of woman. In *Works of Mary Wollstonecraft.* www.su.se/polopoly_fs/1.399226.1536049294!/menu/ standard/file/Kurplanering_Klassikerkurs_MaryWollstonecraft.pdf (Original work published 1792)

[63] Tomalin, C. (1992). *The life and death of Mary Wollstonecraft.* Penguin.

[64] Chopin, K. (2006). *The complete works of Kate Chopin* (p. 120). Louisiana State University Press.

[65] Stanton, E. C., & Ladd, D. M. (2001). *Solitude of self* (p. 372). Paris Press.

[66] Robinson, F., & Smith-Laing, T. (2017). *An analysis of Virginia Woolf's "A room of one's own."* Macat Library.

[67] Woolf, V. (1931). *The waves* (p. 252). United Kingdom: Hogarth Press.

[68] Sarton, M. (1992). *Journal of a solitude* (p. 12). W. W. Norton.

[69] Sarton, M. (1997). *May Sarton: Selected letters, 1916–1954* (p. 364). W. W. Norton.

[70] Arndt, K. L. (2013). A room of one's own, revisited: An existential-hermeneutic study of female solitude [Unpublished doctoral dissertation]. Duquesne University.

[71] Heimtun, B. (2012). The friend, the loner and the independent traveller: Norwegian midlife single women's social identities when on holiday. *Gender, Place, and Culture, 19*(1), 83–101.

[72] www.risamickenberg.com/hermette-magazine

[73] Mickenberg, R. (2022). *The Hermettes are alone and happy.* www.abc.net.au/ radionational/programs/sundayextra/alone-and-proud/13940478

CHAPTER 2

[1] Weinstein, N., Hansen, H., & Nguyen, T. V. (2022). Definitions of solitude in everyday life. *Personality and Social Psychology Bulletin,* 01461672221115941.

[2] Braun, V., & Clarke, V. (2012). Thematic analysis. In H. Cooper, P. M. Camic, D. L. Long et al. (Eds.), *APA handbook of research methods in psychology: Vol. 2. Research designs: Quantitative, qualitative, neuropsychological, and biological* (pp. 57–71). American Psychological Association.

[3] Nguyen, T. V. T., Weinstein, N., & Ryan, R. M. (2021). The possibilities of aloneness and solitude: Developing an understanding framed through the lens of human motivation and needs. In R. J. Coplan & J. C. Bowker (Eds.), *The handbook of solitude: Psychological perspectives on social isolation, social withdrawal, and being alone* (pp. 224–39). Wiley.

[4] James, L. (2019). Incredible story of "last true hermit" who survived 27 years alone in the wild. *The Mirror.* www.mirror.co.uk/news/uk-news/incredible-story-last-true-hermit-18782745

[5] Brown, L. (2022). Pan Macmillan snares "Hermit of the Treig" Ken Smith's "fiercely unique" memoir. *The Bookseller.* www.thebookseller.com/rights/pan-macmillan-snares-hermit-of-the-treig-ken-smiths-fiercely-unique-memoir

[6] Nguyen, T. V. T., Ryan, R. M., & Deci, E. L. (2018). Solitude as an approach to affective self-regulation. *Personality and Social Psychology Bulletin, 44*(1), 92–106.

[7] Gilovich, T., Medvec, V. H., & Savitsky, K. (2000). The spotlight effect in social judgement: An egocentric bias in estimates of the salience of one's own actions and appearance. *Journal of Personality and Social Psychology, 78* (2), 211–22.

[8] Boothby, E. J., Clark, M. S., & Bargh, J. A. (2016). The invisibility cloak illusion: People (incorrectly) believe they observe others more than others observe them. *Journal of Personality and Social Psychology, 112*(4), 589–606.

[9] Mareschal, I., Calder, A. J., & Clifford, C. W. (2013). Humans have an expectation that gaze is directed toward them. *Current Biology, 23*(8), 717–21.

[10] Mangolini, V. I., Andrade, L. H., Lotufo-Neto, F., & Wang, Y. P. (2019). Treatment of anxiety disorders in clinical practice: A critical overview of recent systematic evidence. *Clinics, 74,* e1316.

[11] Durà-Vilà, G., & Leavey, G. (2017). Solitude among contemplative cloistered nuns and monks: Conceptualisation, coping and benefits of spiritually motivated solitude. *Mental Health, Religion, and Culture, 20*(1), 45–60.

[12] Rilke, R. M. (2007). *The poet's guide to life: The wisdom of Rilke* (p. 36). Random House.

[13] Rilke, R. M., & Mood, J. J. L. (1975). *Rilke on love and other difficulties: Translations and considerations of Rainer Maria Rilke* (p. 31). W. W. Norton.

[14] Vincent, D. (2020). *A history of solitude.* Polity Press.

[15] Ratner, R. K., & Hamilton, R. W. (2015). Inhibited from bowling alone. *Journal of Consumer Research, 42*(2), 266–83.

[16] Wrangham, R. (2009). *Catching fire: How cooking made us human.* Profile Books.

[17] Gregersen, S. C., & Gillath, O. (2020). How food brings us together: The ties between attachment and food behaviors. *Appetite, 151,* 104654.

[18] Her, E., & Seo, S. (2018). Why not eat alone? The effect of other consumers on solo dining intentions and the mechanism. *International Journal of Hospitality Management, 70,* 16–24.

[19] Brown, L., Buhalis, D., & Beer, S. (2020). Dining alone: Improving the experience of solo restaurant goers. *International Journal of Contemporary Hospitality Management, 32*(3), 1347–65.

[20] Khot, R. A., Arza, E. S., Kurra, H., & Wang, Y. (2019). Fobo: Towards designing a robotic companion for solo dining. In *Extended abstracts of the 2019 CHI conference on human factors in computing systems* (pp. 1–6). CHI.

[21] Finney, C. (2021, September 19). "Table for one? Yes, please" – the joy of eating alone. *The Guardian.* www.theguardian.com/food/2021/sep/19/table-for-one-the-joy-of-eating-alone

[22] Koponen, S., & Mustonen, P. (2022). Eating alone, or commensality redefined? Solo dining and the aestheticization of eating (out). *Journal of Consumer Culture, 22*(2), 359–77.

[23] Choi, S. H., Yang, E. C. L., & Tabari, S. (2020). Solo dining in Chinese restaurants: A mixed-method study in Macao. *International Journal of Hospitality Management, 90,* 102628.

[24] Chang, Y. Y. C. (2020). Lonely or alone? Solitary dining in Japan and Taiwan. *International Journal of Culture, Tourism, and Hospitality Research, 15* (1), 10–25.

[25] McKeown, J. K., & Miller, M. C. (2020). #tableforone: Exploring representations of dining out alone on Instagram. *Annals of Leisure Research, 23*(5), 645–64.

[26] Brown, L., Buhalis, D., & Beer, S. (2020). Dining alone: Improving the experience of solo restaurant goers. *International Journal of Contemporary Hospitality Management, 32*(3), 1347–65.

CHAPTER 3

[1] Deci, E. L., & Ryan, R. M. (2008). Self-determination theory: A macrotheory of human motivation, development, and health. *Canadian Psychology/ Psychologie Canadienne, 49*(3), 182–85.

[2] Ryan, R. M., & Deci, E. L. (2017). *Self-determination theory: Basic psychological needs in motivation, development, and wellness.* Guilford.

[3] Nguyen, T. V. T., Weinstein, N., & Ryan, R. M. (2021). The possibilities of aloneness and solitude: Developing an understanding framed through the lens of human motivation and needs. In R. J. Coplan & J. C. Bowker (Eds.), *The handbook of solitude: Psychological perspectives on social isolation, social withdrawal, and being alone* (pp. 224–39). Wiley.

[4] Beauchamp, G., Hulme, M., Clarke, L., Hamilton, L., & Harvey, J. A. (2021). "People miss people": A study of school leadership and management in the four nations of the United Kingdom in the early stage of the COVID-19 pandemic. *Educational Management Administration and Leadership, 49*(3), 375–92.

[5] Holt-Lunstad, J. (2021). A pandemic of social isolation? *World Psychiatry, 20* (1), 55–56.

[6] Weinstein, N., Nguyen, T. V., & Hansen, H. (2021). What time alone offers: Narratives of solitude from adolescence to older adulthood. *Frontiers in Psychology, 12,* 714518.

[7] Arnesen, L. (2021). *Skiing into the bright open: My solo journey to the South Pole* (p. 72). University of Minnesota Press.

[8] Arnesen, L. (2021). *Skiing into the bright open: My solo journey to the South Pole* (pp. 8–9). University of Minnesota Press.

[9] Plummer, W. (1995, March 13). Into the great white open. *People Weekly,* 109–10.

[10] Arnesen, L., Bancroft, A., & Dahle, C. (2019). *No horizon is so far: Two women and their historic journey across Antarctica* (p. 13). University of Minnesota Press.

[11] Pausanias. (n.d.). *Description of Greece.* www.perseus.tufts.edu/hopper/text?doc=Paus.+10.24

[12] Plante, T. G. (2010). *Contemplative practices in action: Spirituality, meditation, and health.* ABC-CLIO.

[13] Stabile, S. J. (2012). *Growing in love and wisdom: Tibetan Buddhist sources for Christian meditation.* Oxford University Press.

[14] Heidegger, M. (1962). *Being and time* (J. Macquarrie & E. Robinson, Trans.). Harper & Row. (Original work published 1927)

[15] Sartre, J.-P. (1992). *Being and nothingness: A phenomenological essay on ontology.* Washington Square Press. (Original work published 1948)

[16] de Beauvoir, S. (1970). *The ethics of ambiguity.* Citadel Press. (Original work published 1947)

[17] Kierkegaard, S. (1983). *Fear and trembling and repetition.* Princeton University Press. (Original work published 1843)

[18] Sedikides, C., Slabu, L., Lenton, A., & Thomaes, S. (2017). State authenticity. *Current Directions in Psychological Science, 26*(6), 521–25.

[19] Kernis, M. H., & Goldman, B. M. (2006). A multicomponent conceptualization of authenticity: Theory and research. *Advances in Experimental Social Psychology, 38*, 283–357.

[20] Hopwood, C. J., Good, E. W., Levendosky, A. A., et al. (2021). Realness is a core feature of authenticity. *Journal of Research in Personality, 92*, 104086.

[21] Harter, S. (2002). Authenticity. In C. R. Snyder & S. J. Lopez (Eds.), *Handbook of positive psychology* (pp. 382–94). Oxford University Press.

[22] Day, D. V., Shleicher, D. J., Unckless, A. L., & Hiller, N. J. (2002). Self-monitoring personality at work: A meta-analytic investigation of construct validity. *Journal of Applied Psychology, 87*(2), 390–401.

[23] Wood, A. M., Linley, P. A., Maltby, J., Baliousis, M., & Joseph, S. (2008). The authentic personality: A theoretical and empirical conceptualization and the development of the Authenticity Scale. *Journal of Counseling Psychology, 55*(3), 385–99.

[24] Boyraz, G., Waits, J. B., & Felix, V. A. (2014). Authenticity, life satisfaction, and distress: A longitudinal analysis. *Journal of Counseling Psychology, 61*(3), 498–505.

[25] Debats, D. L., Drost, J., & Hansen, P. (1995). Experiences of meaning in life: A combined qualitative and quantitative approach. *British Journal of Psychology, 86*(3), 359–75.

[26] Gandhi, M. (1911, November 26). Letter to Hermann Kallenbach. In *The collected works of Mahatma Gandhi* (Vol. 12, p. 101). https://gandhiserve.org/c/cwmg.pdf

[27] Slabu, L., Lenton, A. P., Sedikides, C., & Bruder, M. (2014). Trait and state authenticity across cultures. *Journal of Cross-Cultural Psychology, 45*(9), 1347–73, quote on 1347.

[28] Lenton, A. P., Slabu, L., Bruder, M., & Sedikides, C. (2014). Identifying differences in the experience of (in)authenticity: A latent class analysis approach. *Frontiers in Psychology, 5*, 770. https://doi.org/10.3389/fpsyg.2014.00770

[29] Brotheridge, C. M., & Grandey, A. A. (2002). Emotional labor and burnout: Comparing two perspectives of "people work." *Journal of Vocational Behavior, 60*(1), 17–39.

[30] Gino, F., Kouchaki, M., & Galinsky, A. D. (2015). The moral virtue of authenticity: How inauthenticity produces feelings of immorality and impurity. *Psychological Science, 26*(7), 983–96.

[31] Thomas, V. (2022, March 30). Is your solitude authentic? *Psychology Today.* www.psychologytoday.com/us/blog/solitude-in-social-world/202203/is-your-solitude-authentic

[32] Averill, J. R., & Sundararajan, L. (2014). Experiences of solitude: Issues of assessment, theory, and culture. In R. J. Coplan & J. C. Bowker (Eds.), *The handbook of solitude: Psychological perspectives on social isolation, social withdrawal, and being alone* (pp. 90–108). Wiley.

[33] Nguyen, T.-V., Weinstein, N., & Sedikides, C. (n.d.). *Solitude, authenticity and self-consciousness.* Unpublished manuscript.

[34] Weinstein, N., Hansen, H., & Nguyen, T.-V. (n.d.). *Who feels good in solitude: A qualitative interview analysis of the personality and mindset drivers of well-being when alone.* Unpublished manuscript.

[35] Boyraz, G., & Kuhl, M. L. (2015). Self-focused attention, authenticity, and well-being. *Personality and Individual Differences, 87,* 70–75.

CHAPTER 4

[1] Weinstein, N., Hansen, H., & Nguyen, T.-V. (n.d.). *Who feels good in solitude: A qualitative interview analysis of the personality and mindset drivers of well-being when alone.* Unpublished manuscript.

[2] Weinstein, N., Nguyen, T.-V., & Hansen, H. (2023). With myself: Self-determination theory as a framework for understanding the role of solitude in personal growth. In *Handbook of self-determination theory.* Oxford University Press.

[3] Freeman, E., Akhurst, J., Bannigan, K., & James, H. (2017). Benefits of walking and solo experiences in UK wild places. *Health Promotion International, 32*(6), 1048–56.

[4] Jiang, M., & Leberecht, T. (2020). *Living room sessions: A conversation with the writer* [Video]. YouTube. www.youtube.com/watch?v=QfMnpry8LGk

[5] Wheeler, I. (2001). Parental bereavement: The crisis of meaning. *Death Studies, 25*(1), 51–66.

[6] Hammond, C., & Lewis, G. (2016). The rest test: Preliminary findings from a large-scale international survey on rest. In *The restless compendium* (pp. 59–67). Palgrave Macmillan.

[7] Mozart, W. A. (1780). *An Die Einsamkeit* [Song].

[8] Bonney, B., & Martineau, M. (Recorders). (2005). *Die Einsamkeit* [Song]. From *The other Mozart: Franz Xaver Mozart, the songs.* Decca.

[9] Wolff, L. (2008). "Kennst du das Land?" The uncertainty of Galicia in the age of Metternich and Fredro. *Slavic Review, 67*(2), 277–300.

[10] Long, C. R., & Averill, J. R. (2003). Solitude: An exploration of benefits of being alone. *Journal for the Theory of Social Behaviour, 33*(1), 21–44.

[11] Larson, R., Csikszentmihalyi, M., & Graef, R. (1980). Mood variability and the psychosocial adjustment of adolescents. *Journal of Youth and Adolescence*, *9*(6), 469–90.

[12] Strickland, B. R., Hale, W. D., & Anderson, L. K. (1975). Effect of induced mood states on activity and self-reported affect. *Journal of Consulting and Clinical Psychology*, *43*(4), 587.

[13] Russell, J. A. (1980). A circumplex model of affect. *Journal of Personality and Social Psychology*, *39*(6), 1161–78.

[14] Nguyen, T. V. T., Ryan, R. M., & Deci, E. L. (2018). Solitude as an approach to affective self-regulation. *Personality and Social Psychology Bulletin*, *44*(1), 92–106.

[15] Hipson, W. E., Kiritchenko, S., Mohammad, S. M., & Coplan, R. J. (2021). Examining the language of solitude versus loneliness in tweets. *Journal of Social and Personal Relationships*, *38*(5), 1596–610.

[16] Beaty, R. E., Kenett, Y. N., Christensen, A. P., et al. (2018). Robust prediction of individual creative ability from brain functional connectivity. *Proceedings of the National Academy of Sciences*, *115*(5), 1087–92.

[17] Zabelina, D. L., & Andrews-Hanna, J. R. (2016). Dynamic network interactions supporting internally-oriented cognition. *Current Opinion in Neurobiology*, *40*, 86–93.

[18] Swift, T. (Dir.). (2020). Folklore: The Long Pond Studio sessions [Documentary]. Long Pond Studio.

[19] Graf, K. (2011). The Library chronicle of the University of Texas at Austin, 1970–1997 online. *Archivalia*, 13.

[20] Fassler, J. (2014, March 11). "I Don't Believe in Writer's Block." *The Atlantic*. www.theatlantic.com/entertainment/archive/2014/03/i-dont-believe-in-writers-block/284354/

[21] Balakrishnan, G. (2003, February). *Introducing Ernest Hemingway*. www.lsj.org/literature/essays/hemingway

[22] Fassler, J. (2014, February 4). What great artists need: Solitude. *The Atlantic*. www.theatlantic.com/entertainment/archive/2014/02/what-great-artists-need-solitude/283585/

[23] Schwartz, E. I. (2004, September 13). *What Steve Wozniak learned from failure*. https://hbswk.hbs.edu/archive/what-steve-wozniak-learned-from-failure

[24] Mozart, W. A. (1825). Letter of W. A. Mozart, to the Baron V. In *The Harmonicon* (No. XXXV, pp. 198–99). https://books.google.nl/books?id=9jFDAAAAcAAJ&dq=harmonicon

[25] De Saint-Exupéry, A. (1943). *Le Petit prince* [The little prince]. Reynal & Hitchcock.

[26] O'Keeffe, G., Goodrich, L., & Bry, D. (1976). *Georgia O'Keeffe*. Viking Press.

[27] O'Keeffe, G. (1974, March 4). Georgia O'Keefe's vision. *New Yorker*. www .newyorker.com/magazine/1974/03/04/the-rose-in-the-eye-looked-pretty-fine

[28] Smith, C. (2009, February 22). *Interview with Agnes Martin (1997)* [Video]. YouTube. www.youtube.com/watch?v=_-JfYjmo5OA

[29] Martin, A. (1997). *With my back to the world* [Series of paintings].

[30] Opinion of the week: At home and abroad, ideas and men. (1960, July). *New York Times*, p. E9.

[31] Wallas, G. (1926). *The art of thought* (Vol. 10). Harcourt, Brace.

[32] Einstein, A. (1931). What I believe. In *Forum and century (1930)* (Vol. 84). https:// archive.org/details/sim_forum-and-century_1930-10_84_4/page/n27/

[33] Bowker, J. C., Stotsky, M. T., & Etkin, R. G. (2017). How BIS/BAS and psycho-behavioral variables distinguish between social withdrawal subtypes during emerging adulthood. *Personality and Individual Differences, 119,* 283–88.

[34] Mercier, M., Vinchon, F., Pichot, N., et al. (2021). COVID-19: A boon or a bane for creativity? *Frontiers in Psychology, 11,* 601150.

[35] Jaiswal, A., & Arun, C. J. (2020). *Unlocking the COVID-19 lockdown: Work from home and its impact on employees.* Unpublished manuscript.

[36] Privette, G. (2001). Defining moments of self-actualization: Peak performance and peak experience. In *The handbook of humanistic psychology: Leading edges in theory, research, and practice* (pp. 160–82). SAGE.

[37] Maslow, A. H. (1958). A dynamic theory of human motivation. In C. L. Stacey & M. DeMartino (Eds.), *Understanding human motivation* (pp. 26–47). Howard Allen.

[38] Maslow, A. H. (1943). A theory of human motivation. *Psychological Review, 50* (4), 370–96.

[39] McLeod, S. (2007). Maslow's hierarchy of needs. *Ardian.* https://ardian.id/ ruang-kelas/psikologi-industri/maslows-hierarchy-of-needs/

[40] Chambers, C. (2013, December 6). Was Nelson Mandela the pinnacle of human psychology? *The Guardian.* www.theguardian.com/science/head-quarters/2013/dec/06/was-nelson-mandela-the-pinnacle-of-human-psychology

[41] World Bank. (2022, November 30). *Poverty overview.* www.worldbank.org/ en/topic/poverty/overview

[42] Davis, J., Lockwood, L., & Wright, C. (1991). Reasons for not reporting peak experiences. *Journal of Humanistic Psychology, 31*(1), 86–94.

[43] McDonald, M. G., Wearing, S., & Ponting, J. (2009). The nature of peak experience in wilderness. *Humanistic Psychologist, 37*(4), 370–85.

[44] Byrd, R. E. (1984). *Alone: The classic polar adventure* (pp. 3–4). Island Press.

[45] Armstrong, H. E. (1934, August 19). Byrd's lonely vigil was a mental test. *New York Times*. www.nytimes.com/1934/08/19/archives/byrds-lonely-vigil-was-a-mental-test-in-his-long-isolation-in-a.html

[46] Byrd, R. E. (1984). *Alone: The classic polar adventure* (p. 85). Island Press.

[47] Byrd, R. E. (1984). *Alone: The classic polar adventure* (p. ix). Island Press.

[48] Byrd, R. E. (1984). *Alone: The classic polar adventure* (pp. 295–96). Island Press.

[49] De Saint-Exupéry, A. (1943). *The little prince* (K. Woods, Trans., p. 70). Harcourt, Brace & World.

CHAPTER 5

[1] Interview with Jennifer Pharr Davis (2022, April 6).

[2] National Park Service. (n.d.). *Appalachian National Scenic Trail*. www.nps.gov/appa/index.htm

[3] Appalachian Trail Conservancy. (n.d.). *Weather hazards*. https://appalachiantrail.org/explore/plan-and-prepare/hiking-basics/safety

[4] Ryan, R. M., & Deci, E. L. (2006). Self-regulation and the problem of human autonomy: Does psychology need choice, self-determination, and will? *Journal of Personality, 74*(6), 1557–86.

[5] Deci, E. L., & Ryan, R. M. (2008). Facilitating optimal motivation and psychological well-being across life's domains. *Canadian Psychology/Psychologie Canadienne, 49*(1), 14–23.

[6] Stephens, N. M., Fryberg, S. A., & Markus, H. R. (2011). When choice does not equal freedom: A sociocultural analysis of agency in working-class contexts. *Personality and Social Psychology Science, 2*(1), 33–41.

[7] Savani, K., Stephens, N., & Markus, H. R. (2011). The unanticipated interpersonal and societal consequences of choice: Victim-blaming and reduced support for the public good. *Psychological Science, 22*(6), 795–802.

[8] Savani, K., Markus, H. R., Naidu, N. V. R., Kumar, S., & Berlia, N. (2010). What counts as a choice? US Americans are more likely than Indians to construe actions as choices. *Psychological Science, 21*(3), 391–98.

[9] Stephens, N., Hamedani, M., Markus, H., Bergsieker, H. B., & Eloul, L. (2009). Why did they "choose" to stay? Perspectives of Hurricane Katrina observers and survivors. *Psychological Science, 20*, 878–86.

[10] Savani, K., Markus, H., & Conner, A. L. (2008). Let your preference be your guide? Preferences and choices are more tightly linked for North Americans than for Indians. *Journal of Personality and Social Psychology, 95*(4), 861–76.

[11] L'Engle, M. (2008). *The young unicorns: Book three of the Austin family chronicles* (p. 202). Farrar, Straus and Giroux.

[12] Harper, K. (2021, October 30). Igjugaarjuk, the shaman. *Nunatsiaq News*. https://nunatsiaq.com/stories/article/igjugaarjuk-the-shaman/

[13] Rasmussen, K. (1927). *Across Arctic America: Narrative of the 5th Thule Expedition*. Putnam.

[14] Rasmussen, K. (1930). *Observations on the intellectual culture of the Caribou Eskimos: Iglulik and Caribou Eskimo texts* (pp. 54–56). Gyldendalske Boghandel.

[15] Thoreau, H. D. (2004). *Walden*. Princeton University Press. (Original work published 1854)

[16] Howard League (n.d.). *Solitary confinement*. https://howardleague.org/legal-work/solitary-confinement/

[17] Pullen-Blasnik, H., Simes, J. T., & Western, B. (2021). The population prevalence of solitary confinement. *Science Advances*, 7(48), 1–9.

[18] Resnik, J., Albertson, S., Li, G., & Taylor, J. (2022). *Time-in-cell: A 2021 snapshot of restrictive housing based on a nationwide survey of US prison systems*. Available at SSRN.

[19] Méndez, J., Papachristou, A., Ordway, E., Fettig, A., & Shalev, S. (2016). *Seeing into solitary: A review of the laws and policies of certain nations regarding solitary confinement of detainees*. United Nations.

[20] Smith, P. S. (2006). The effects of solitary confinement on prison inmates: A brief history and review of the literature. *Crime and Justice*, 34(1), 441–528.

[21] Haney, C. (2018). Restricting the use of solitary confinement. *Annual Review of Criminology*, 1, 285–310.

[22] Kral, V. A., Pazder, L. H., & Wigdor, B. T. (1967). Long-term effects of a prolonged stress experience. *Canadian Psychiatric Association Journal*, 12(2), 175–81.

[23] Gawande, A. (2009, March 30). Hellhole: The United States holds tens of thousands of inmates in long-term solitary confinement. Is this torture? *New Yorker*. www.newyorker.com/magazine/2009/03/30/hellhole

[24] Zigmond, M. J., & Smeyne, R. J. (2020). Use of animals to study the neurobiological effects of isolation. In *Solitary confinement: Effects, practices, and pathways toward reform* (pp. 221–42). Oxford University Press.

[25] McCall-Smith, K. (2016). United Nations standard minimum rules for the treatment of prisoners (Nelson Mandela Rules). *International Legal Materials*, 55(6), 1180–205.

[26] Meranze, M. (1984). The penitential ideal in late eighteenth-century Philadelphia. *Pennsylvania Magazine of History and Biography*, 108(4), 419–50.

[27] UK Parliament (n.d.). *John Howard and prison reform.* www.parliament.uk/
about/living-heritage/transformingsociety/laworder/policeprisons/over
view/prisonreform/

[28] Masur, L. P. (1991). *Rites of execution: Capital punishment and the transformation of American culture, 1776–1865* (p. 81). Oxford University Press.

[29] Inventing solitary. (2022, June 8). *Philadelphia Inquirer.* www.inquirer.com/
news/inq2/more-perfect-union-philadelphia-solitary-prison-population-incar
ceration-20220608.html

[30] Eastern State Penitentiary. (n.d.). *Timeline.* www.easternstate.org/research/
history-eastern-state/timeline

[31] Dickens, C. (1842). *American notes for general circulation* (p. 40). Harper.

[32] Rubin, A. T. (2021). *The deviant prison: Philadelphia's Eastern State Penitentiary
and the origins of America's modern penal system* (pp. 1829–913). Cambridge
University Press.

[33] Kashatus, W. (1999). "Punishment, penitence, and reform": Eastern State
Penitentiary and the controversy over solitary confinement. *Pennsylvania
Heritage.* http://paheritage.wpengine.com/article/punishment-penitence-
reform-eastern-state-penitentiary-controversy-solitary-confinement/

[34] Lessner, J. (2017, November 19). A cruel and unusual burden: The case for the
unconstitutionality of solitary confinement [Blog post]. *Columbia Graduate Law
Review.* https://blogs.cuit.columbia.edu/culr/2017/11/19/a-cruel-and-unusual-
burden-the-case-for-the-unconstitutionality-of-solitary-confinement/#_ftn5

[35] Mandela, N., & Cartwright, J. (1961). *Long walk to freedom* (pp. 364–65).
Royal New Zealand Foundation for the Blind.

[36] Queen Mary University of London. (2020, October 22). *Queen Mary teams up
with Lambeth Palace for podcast on solitude.* www.qmul.ac.uk/media/news/2020/
hss/queen-mary-teams-up-with-lambeth-palace-for-podcast-on-solitude.html

[37] Sakhi, S. (2020, April 27). Self isolation as imprisonment? *Solitudes.* https://
solitudes.qmul.ac.uk/blog/self-isolation-as-imprisonment/

[38] Frankl, V. E. (1946). *Man's search for meaning: Gift edition* (p. 62). Beacon.

[39] Kim, H. H. S., & Jung, J. H. (2021). Social isolation and psychological
distress during the COVID-19 pandemic: A cross-national analysis. *The
Gerontologist, 61*(1), 103–13.

[40] Pietrabissa, G., & Simpson, S. G. (2020). Psychological consequences of
social isolation during COVID-19 outbreak. *Frontiers in Psychology, 11*, 2201.
https://doi.org/10.3389/fpsyg.2020.02201

[41] Bu, F., Steptoe, A., & Fancourt, D. (2020). Who is lonely in lockdown?
Cross-cohort analyses of predictors of loneliness before and during the
COVID-19 pandemic. *Public Health, 186*, 31–34.

[42] Groarke, J. M., Berry, E., Graham-Wisener, L., et al. (2020). Loneliness in the UK during the COVID-19 pandemic: Cross-sectional results from the COVID-19 Psychological Wellbeing Study. *PLoS One, 15*(9), e0239698.

[43] Jia, R., Ayling, K., Chalder, T., et al. (2020). Mental health in the UK during the COVID-19 pandemic: Cross-sectional analyses from a community cohort study. *BMJ Open, 10*(9), e040620.

[44] Luchetti, M., Lee, J. H., Aschwanden, D., et al. (2020). The trajectory of loneliness in response to COVID-19. *American Psychologist, 75*(7), 897–908.

[45] Heron, P., Spanakis, P., Crosland, S., et al. (2022). Loneliness among people with severe mental illness during the COVID-19 pandemic: Results from a linked UK population cohort study. *PLoS One, 17*(1), e0262363.

[46] Hansen, T., Nilsen, T. S., Yu, B., et al. (2021). Locked and lonely? A longitudinal assessment of loneliness before and during the COVID-19 pandemic in Norway. *Scandinavian Journal of Public Health, 49* (7), 766–73.

[47] Parlapani, E., Holeva, V., Nikopoulou, V. A., et al. (2021). A review on the COVID-19-related psychological impact on older adults: Vulnerable or not? *Aging Clinical and Experimental Research, 33*(6), 1729–43.

[48] Bu, F., Steptoe, A., & Fancourt, D. (2020). Loneliness during lockdown: Trajectories and predictors during the COVID-19 pandemic in 35,712 adults in the UK. *medRxiv*, 1–9.

[49] Chao, R. C. L. (2012). Managing perceived stress among college students: The roles of social support and dysfunctional coping. *Journal of College Counseling, 15*(21), 5–21.

[50] Cohen, S., & Willis, T. A. (1985). Stress, social support, and the buffering hypothesis. *Psychological Bulletin, 98*(2), 310–57.

[51] Field, R. J., & Schuldberg, D. (2011). Social-support moderated stress: A nonlinear dynamical model and the stress buffering hypothesis. *Nonlinear Dynamics, Psychology, and Life Sciences, 15*(1), 53–85.

[52] Raffaelli, M., Andrade, F. C., Wiley, A. R., et al. (2013). Stress, social support, and depression: A test of the stress-buffering hypothesis in a Mexican sample. *Journal of Research on Adolescence, 23*(2), 283–89.

[53] Saltzman, L. Y., Hansel, T. C., & Bordnick, P. S. (2020). Loneliness, isolation, and social support factors in post-COVID-19 mental health. *Psychological Trauma: Theory, Research, Practice, and Policy, 12*, 55–57.

[54] Blake, H., Bermingham, F., Johnson, G., & Tabner, A. (2020). Mitigating the psychological impact of COVID-19 on healthcare workers: A digital learning package. *International Journal of Environmental Research and Public Health, 17*(9), 2997. https://doi.org/10.3390/ijerph17092997

[55] Cole, D. A., Nick, E. A., Zelkowitz, R. L., Roeder, K. M., & Spinelli, T. (2017). Online social support for young people: Does it recapitulate in-person social support; can it help? *Computers in Human Behavior, 68*, 456–64.

[56] Lechner, W. V., Laurene, K. R., Patel, S., et al. (2020). Changes in alcohol use as a function of psychological distress and social support following COVID-19 related university closings. *Addictive Behaviors, 110*, 106527.

[57] Tindle, R., Hemi, A., & Moustafa, A. A. (2022). Social support, psycho-logical flexibility and coping mediate the association between COVID-19 related stress exposure and psychological distress. *Scientific Reports, 12*(1), 1–11.

[58] Very Lonely Luke [@VeryLonelyLuke]. (2020, March 22). *I was social distancing before it was cool* [Tweet]. Twitter. https://twitter.com/verylonely luke/status/1241699170664288256

[59] Isolophile. (2020). In *Urban dictionary.* www.urbandictionary.com/define .php?term=Isolophile

[60] Bennett, J., Jones, D., & Strzemien, A. (2020, June 17). Alone. *New York Times.* www.nytimes.com/2020/05/13/style/coronavirus-modern-love-living-alone.html

[61] Adler, P. A., & Adler, P. (2005). Self-injurers as loners: The social organiza-tion of solitary deviance. *Deviant Behavior, 26*(4), 345–78.

[62] Hojat, M. (1983). Comparison of transitory and chronic loners on selected personality variables. *British Journal of Psychology, 74*(2), 199–202.

[63] Wang, J. M., Rubin, K. H., Laursen, B., Booth-LaForce, C., & Rose-Krasnor, L. (2013). Preference-for-solitude and adjustment difficulties in early and late adolescence. *Journal of Clinical Child and Adolescent Psychology, 42*(6), 834–42.

[64] Burger, J. M. (1995). Individual differences in preference for solitude. *Journal of Research in Personality, 29*(1), 85–108.

[65] Nguyen, T. V. T., Ryan, R. M., & Deci, E. L. (2018). Solitude as an approach to affective self-regulation. *Personality and Social Psychology Bulletin, 44*(1), 92–106.

[66] Nguyen, T. V. T., Weinstein, N., & Ryan, R. M. (2022). Who enjoys solitude? autonomous functioning (but not introversion) predicts self-determined motivation (but not preference) for solitude. *PLoS One, 17*(5), e0267185.

[67] Ryan, R. M., & Deci, E. L. (2000). Intrinsic and extrinsic motivations: Classic definitions and new directions. *Contemporary Educational Psychology, 25*(1), 54–67.

[68] Vallerand, R. J. (2000). Deci and Ryan's self-determination theory: A view from the hierarchical model of intrinsic and extrinsic motivation. *Psychological Inquiry, 11*(4), 312–18.

[69] Thomas, V., & Azmitia, M. (2019). Motivation matters: Development and validation of the Motivation for Solitude Scale–Short Form (MSS-SF). *Journal of Adolescence, 70,* 33–42.

[70] Heider, F. (1958). *The psychology of interpersonal relations.* Wiley.

[71] Long, C. R., Seburn, M., Averill, J. R., & More, T. A. (2003). Solitude experiences: Varieties, settings, and individual differences. *Personality and Social Psychology Bulletin, 29*(5), 578–83.

[72] Carrigan, P. M. (1960). Extraversion-introversion as a dimension of personality: A reappraisal. *Psychological Bulletin, 57*(5), 329–60.

[73] Killen, M., Rutland, A., & Jampol, N. S. (2011). Social exclusion in childhood and adolescence. In *Handbook of Peer Interactions, Relationships, and Groups* (pp. 249–66). Guilford Press.

[74] Ren, D., Wesselmann, E. D., & van Beest, I. (2021). Seeking solitude after being ostracized: A replication and beyond. *Personality and Social Psychology Bulletin, 47*(3), 426–40.

[75] Wesselmann, E. D., Williams, K. D., Ren, D., & Hales, A. H. (2021). Ostracism and solitude. In R. J. Coplan & J. C. Bowker (Eds.), *The handbook of solitude: Psychological perspectives on social isolation, social withdrawal, and being alone* (pp. 209–23). Wiley.

[76] Coplan, R. J., Ooi, L. L., & Nocita, G. (2015). When one is company and two is a crowd: Why some children prefer solitude. *Child Development Perspectives, 9*(3), 133–37.

[77] Goossens, L. (2013). Affinity for aloneness in adolescence and preference for solitude in childhood: Linking two research traditions. In R. J. Coplan & J. C. Bowker (Eds.), *The handbook of solitude: Psychological perspectives on social isolation, social withdrawal, and being alone* (pp. 150–56). Wiley.

[78] Saylor, C. F., Williams, K. D., Nida, S. A., et al. (2013). Ostracism in pediatric populations: Review of theory and research. *Journal of Developmental and Behavioral Pediatrics, 34*(4), 279–87.

[79] Rudert, S. C., Janke, S., & Greifeneder, R. (2021). Ostracism breeds depression: Longitudinal associations between ostracism and depression over a three-year-period. *Journal of Affective Disorders Reports, 4,* 100118.

[80] Nida, S. A., & Saylor, C. F. (2016). Ostracism in children and adolescents. In *Ostracism, exclusion, and rejection* (pp. 202–16). Routledge.

[81] Williams, K. D., & Nida, S. A. (2022). Ostracism and social exclusion: Implications for separation, social isolation, and loss. *Current Opinion in Psychology,* 101353.

[82] Coplan, R. J., & Weeks, M. (2010). Unsociability and the preference for solitude in childhood. In *The development of shyness and social withdrawal* (p. 64). Guilford Press.

[83] Endo, K., Ando, S., Shimodera, S., et al. (2017). Preference for solitude, social isolation, suicidal ideation, and self-harm in adolescents. *Journal of Adolescent Health, 61*(2), 187–91.

[84] Vidourek, R. A., & Burbage, M. (2019). Positive mental health and mental health stigma: A qualitative study assessing student attitudes. *Mental Health and Prevention, 13*, 1–6.

[85] Shattell, M. M., McAllister, S., Hogan, B., & Thomas, S. P. (2006). "She took the time to make sure she understood": Mental health patients' experiences of being understood. *Archives of Psychiatric Nursing, 20*(5), 234–41.

[86] Rodriguez, M., Bellet, B. W., & McNally, R. J. (2020). Reframing time spent alone: Reappraisal buffers the emotional effects of isolation. *Cognitive Therapy and Research, 44*(6), 1052–67.

[87] Weinstein, N., & Scott, A. (n.d.). *Effects of framing solitude expectations on emotions and cognitions during time spent alone.* Unpublished manuscript.

CHAPTER 6

[1] McKenzie, J. (2016). Happiness vs contentment? A case for a sociology of the good life. *Journal for the Theory of Social Behaviour, 46*(3), 252–67.

[2] Springsteen, B., & Zimny, T. (Dir.). (2019). *Western stars* [Documentary]. Columbia.

[3] Storr, A. (1998). *Solitude: A return to the self* (p. 202). Free Press.

[4] Baumeister, R. F., & Leary, M. R. (1995). The need to belong: Desire for interpersonal attachments as a fundamental human motivation. *Psychological Bulletin, 117*, 497–529.

[5] Ryan, R. M., & Deci, E. L. (2000). Self-determination theory and the facilitation of intrinsic motivation, social development, and well-being. *American Psychologist, 55*(1), 68–78.

[6] Lenton, A. P., Bruder, M., Slabu, L., & Sedikides, C. (2013). How does "being real" feel? The experience of state authenticity. *Journal of Personality, 81*(3), 276–89.

[7] Demir, M., & Özdemir, M. (2010). Friendship, need satisfaction and happiness. *Journal of Happiness Studies, 11*(2), 243–59.

[8] Tomasello, M. (2020). The adaptive origins of uniquely human sociality. *Philosophical Transactions of the Royal Society B, 375*(1803), 20190493.

[9] Turner, J. C. (1991). *Social influence.* Thomson Brooks/Cole.

[10] Sandstrom, G. M., & Dunn, E. W. (2014). Social interactions and well-being: The surprising power of weak ties. *Personality and Social Psychology Bulletin, 40*(7), 910–22.

[11] Hrdy, S. B. (2017). Comes the child before man: How cooperative breeding and prolonged postweaning dependence shaped human potential. In *Hunter-gatherer childhoods* (pp. 65–91). Routledge.

[12] de Jong Gierveld, J., & Havens, B. (2004). Cross-national comparisons of social isolation and loneliness: Introduction and overview. *Canadian Journal on Aging/La Revue Canadienne du Vieillissement, 23*(2), 109–13.

[13] Cacioppo, J. T., & Cacioppo, S. (2018). The growing problem of loneliness. *The Lancet, 391*(10119), 426.

[14] Park, C., Majeed, A., Gill, H., et al. (2020). The effect of loneliness on distinct health outcomes: A comprehensive review and meta-analysis. *Psychiatry Research, 294*, 113514.

[15] Vincent, D. (2020). *A history of solitude*. Polity Press.

[16] Cacioppo, J. T., & Patrick, W. (2008). *Loneliness: Human nature and the need for social connection*. W. W. Norton.

[17] Tomova, L., Wang, K. L., Thompson, T., et al. (2020). Acute social isolation evokes midbrain craving responses similar to hunger. *Nature Neuroscience, 23*(12), 1597–605.

[18] Cacioppo, J. T., Cacioppo, S., & Boomsma, D. I. (2014). Evolutionary mechanisms for loneliness. *Cognition and Emotion, 28*(1), 3–21.

[19] Taborsky, B., English, S., Fawcett, T. W., et al. (2021). Towards an evolutionary theory of stress responses. *Trends in Ecology and Evolution, 36*(1), 39–48.

[20] House, J. S., Landis, K. R., & Umberson, D. (1988). Social relationships and health. *Science, 241*(4865), 540–45.

[21] Holt-Lunstad, J., & Smith, T. B. (2015). Loneliness and social isolation as risk factors for mortality: A meta-analytic review. *Perspectives on Psychological Science, 10*, 227–37.

[22] Kross, E., Berman, M. G., Mischel, W., Smith, E. E., & Wager, T. D. (2011). Social rejection shares somatosensory representations with physical pain. *Proceedings of the National Academy of Sciences, 108*(15), 6270–75.

[23] Williams, K. D. (1997). Social ostracism. In *Aversive interpersonal behaviors* (pp. 133–70). Springer.

[24] Chotpitayasunondh, V., & Douglas, K. M. (2018). The effects of "phubbing" on social interaction. *Journal of Applied Social Psychology, 48*(6), 304–16.

[25] Williams, K. D., & Jarvis, B. (2006). Cyberball: A program for use in research on interpersonal ostracism and acceptance. *Behavior Research Methods, 38*(1), 174–80.

[26] Williams, K. D. (2007). Ostracism. *Annual Review of Psychology, 58*, 425–52.

[27] Rudert, S. C., Janke, S., & Greifeneder, R. (2020). The experience of ostracism over the adult life span. *Developmental Psychology, 56*(10), 1999–2012.

[28] Leary, M. R. (1990). Responses to social exclusion: Social anxiety, jealousy, loneliness, depression, and low self-esteem. *Journal of Social and Clinical Psychology, 9*(2), 221–29.

[29] Ren, D., Wesselmann, E. D., & van Beest, I. (2021). Seeking solitude after being ostracized: A replication and beyond. *Personality and Social Psychology Bulletin, 47*(3), 426–40.

[30] Cacioppo, J. T., & Cacioppo, S. (2018). The population-based longitudinal Chicago Health, Aging, and Social Relations Study (CHASRS): Study description and predictors of attrition in older adults. *Archives of Scientific Psychology, 6*(1), 21–31.

[31] Cacioppo, J. T., Hawkley, L. C., & Thisted, R. A. (2010). Perceived social isolation makes me sad: 5-year cross-lagged analyses of loneliness and depressive symptomatology in the Chicago Health, Aging, and Social Relations Study. *Psychology and Aging, 25*(2), 453–63.

[32] Moffett, M. W. (2013). Human identity and the evolution of societies. *Human Nature, 24*(3), 219–67.

[33] Peplau, L. A. (1985). Loneliness research: Basic concepts and findings. In *Social support: Theory, research and applications* (pp. 269–86). Springer.

[34] Barstead, M. G., Smith, K. A., Laursen, B., et al. (2018). Shyness, preference for solitude, and adolescent internalizing: The roles of maternal, paternal, and best-friend support. *Journal of Research on Adolescence, 28*(2), 488–504.

[35] Cacioppo, J. T., Hawkley, L. C., Norman, G. J., & Berntson, G. G. (2011). Social isolation. *Annals of the New York Academy of Sciences, 1231*(1), 17–22.

[36] Sweet, J. (2021). The loneliness pandemic. *Harvard Magazine*. www .harvardmagazine.com/2021/01/feature-the-loneliness-pandemic

[37] Wright, R. (2020, March 23). How loneliness from coronavirus isolation takes its own toll. *New Yorker*. www.newyorker.com/news/our-columnists/how-loneliness-from-coronavirus-isolation-takes-its-own-toll

[38] Weinstein, N., & Nguyen, T. V. (2020). Motivation and preference in isolation: A test of their different influences on responses to self-isolation during the COVID-19 outbreak. *Royal Society Open Science, 7*(5), 200458.

[39] Luchetti, M., Lee, J. H., Aschwanden, D., et al. (2020). The trajectory of loneliness in response to COVID-19. *American Psychologist, 75*(7), 897–908.

[40] Bu, F., Steptoe, A., & Fancourt, D. (2020). Who is lonely in lockdown? Cross-cohort analyses of predictors of loneliness before and during the COVID-19 pandemic. *Public Health, 186*, 31–34.

[41] Ernst, M., Niederer, D., Werner, A. M., et al. (2022). Loneliness before and during the COVID-19 pandemic: A systematic review with meta-analysis. *American Psychologist, 177*(5), 660–67.

[42] John, T. (2018). How the world's first loneliness minister will tackle "the sad reality of modern life." *Time.* https://time.com/5248016/tracey-crouch-uk-loneliness-minister/

[43] Skopeliti, C. (2021). Japan appoints "minister for loneliness" after rise in suicides. *Independent.* www.independent.co.uk/news/world/asia/japan-minister-loneliness-suicides-tetsushi-sakamoto-b1807236.html

[44] Klinenberg, E. (2013). *Going solo: The extraordinary rise and surprising appeal of living alone* (p. 18). Penguin.

[45] Klinenberg, E. (2018, February 9). Is loneliness a health epidemic? *New York Times.* www.nytimes.com/2018/02/09/opinion/sunday/loneliness-health.html

[46] Health and Retirement Study (2022). https://hrs.isr.umich.edu/about?_ga=2.246358723.6566966.1653074630-808340557.1653074630

[47] Khazan, O. (2017, April 6). How loneliness begets loneliness. *The Atlantic.* www.theatlantic.com/health/archive/2017/04/how-loneliness-begets-loneliness/521841/

[48] Hawkley, L. C., Wroblewski, K., Kaiser, T., Luhmann, M., & Schumm, L. P. (2019). Are US older adults getting lonelier? Age, period, and cohort differences. *Psychology and Aging, 34*(8), 1144–57.

[49] National Opinion Research Center. (1985). *General Social Survey.*

[50] Fischer, C. S. (2009). The 2004 GSS finding of shrunken social networks: An artifact? *American Sociological Review, 74*(4), 657–69.

[51] Fountain, H. (2006, July 2). The lonely American just got a bit lonelier. *New York Times.* www.nytimes.com/2006/07/02/weekinreview/02fountain.html

[52] Pew Research Center. (2022). *Appendix B: The GSS controversy.* www.pewresearch.org/internet/2009/11/04/appendix-b-the-gss-controversy/

[53] Wilkinson, E. (2022). Loneliness is a feminist issue. *Feminist Theory, 23*(1), 23–38.

[54] Leland, J. (2022, April 20). How loneliness is damaging our health. *New York Times.* www.nytimes.com/2022/04/20/nyregion/loneliness-epidemic.html

[55] Bruce, L. D., Wu, J. S., Lustig, S. L., Russell, D. W., & Nemecek, D. A. (2019). Loneliness in the United States: A 2018 national panel survey of demographic, structural, cognitive, and behavioral characteristics. *American Journal of Health Promotion, 33*(8), 1123–33.

[56] Yale School of Medicine. (2020). *Together: The healing power of human connection.* https://medicine.yale.edu/news/yale-medicine-magazine/article/together-the-healing-power-of-human-connection-in/

[57] Hidden Brain. (2022, November 14). *Relationships 2.0: An antidote to loneliness.* https://hidden-brain.simplecast.com/episodes/relationships-20-an-antidote-to-loneliness-ZfvXgcym

[58] Shepard, M. (2014). *Fritz.* Open Road Media.

[59] Lobb, M. S. (2001). The theory of self in Gestalt therapy: A restatement of some aspects. *Gestalt Review, 5*(4), 276–88.

[60] Ryan, R. M. (2005). The developmental line of autonomy in the etiology, dynamics, and treatment of borderline personality disorders. *Development and Psychopathology, 17*(4), 987–1006.

[61] Emerson, R. W. (1860). Culture. Atlantic Monthly, p. 350.

[62] Nietzsche, F. (1997). *Daybreak* (p. 201). Cambridge University Press.

[63] Higgins, M. W. (2014). *Thomas Merton: Faithful visionary.* Liturgical Press.

[64] Jacobs, A. (2018, December 28). Thomas Merton, the monk who became a prophet. *New Yorker.* www.newyorker.com/books/under-review/thomas-merton-the-monk-who-became-a-prophet

[65] Merton, T. (1999). *Thoughts in solitude* (p. xii). Farrar, Straus, and Giroux. (Original work published 1956)

[66] Asch, S. E. (1956). Studies of independence and conformity: I. A minority of one against a unanimous majority. *Psychological Monographs: General and Applied, 70*(9), 1–70.

[67] Milgram, S. (1963). Behavioral study of obedience. *Journal of Abnormal and Social Psychology, 67*(4), 371–78.

[68] Zimbardo, P. (2011). *The Lucifer effect: How good people turn evil.* Ebury.

[69] Aronson, E. (2003). *The social animal.* Worth. (Original work published 1972)

[70] Bond, R. M., Fariss, C. J., Jones, J. J., et al. (2012). A 61-million-person experiment in social influence and political mobilization. *Nature, 489* (7415), 295–98.

[71] Dickinson, E. (1890). *Poems by Emily Dickinson* (p. 26). Roberts Brothers. (Original work published 1862)

[72] Thoreau, H. D. (1854). *Walden* (p. 213). Houghton, Mifflin.

[73] Emerson, R. W. (1857, December). Solitude and society (p. 229). *The Atlantic.* https://cdn.theatlantic.com/media/archives/1857/12/1–2/131866140.pdf

[74] Nguyen, T. V. T., Weinstein, N., & Ryan, R. M. (2022). Who enjoys solitude? Autonomous functioning (but not introversion) predicts self-determined motivation (but not preference) for solitude. *PLoS One, 17*(5), e0267185.

[75] Lin, P. H., Wang, P. Y., Lin, Y. L., & Yang, S. Y. (2020). Is it weird to enjoy solitude? Relationship of solitude capacity with personality traits and physical and mental health in junior college students. *International Journal of Environmental Research and Public Health, 17*(14), 5060. https://doi.org/10.3390/ijerph17145060

[76] Lorre, C., Higgins, A., & Javerbaum, D. (2018). *The Kominsky method.* Chuck Lorre Productions & Warner Bros. Television.

[77] Coplan, R. J., Hipson, W. E., Archbell, K. A., et al. (2019). Seeking more solitude: Conceptualization, assessment, and implications of aloneliness. *Personality and Individual Differences, 148,* 17–26.

[78] Wang, R. R. (n.d.). *Yinyang (Yin-yang).* https://iep.utm.edu/yinyang/

CHAPTER 7

[1] Interview with JR Harris (2022, May 31).

[2] jrinthewilderness. (n.d.). www.jrinthewilderness.com/

[3] Harris, J. (2017). *Way out there: Adventures of a wilderness trekker.* Mountaineers Books.

[4] Kondo, M. C., Oyekanmi, K. O., Gibson, A., et al. (2020). Nature prescriptions for health: A review of evidence and research opportunities. *International Journal of Environmental Research and Public Health, 17*(12), 4213. https://doi.org/10.3390/ijerph17124213

[5] Kapur, K. (2013). *Hindu Dharma – A teaching guide.* Xlibris.

[6] Ross, N. W. (2011). *Buddhism: Way of life and thought.* Vintage.

[7] Mair, V. H., & Tzu, L. (2012). *Tao Te Ching: The classic book of integrity and the Way.* Bantam.

[8] Kellert, S. R., Farnham, T. J., & Farnham, T. (2002). *The good in nature and humanity: Connecting science, religion, and spirituality with the natural world.* Island Press.

[9] Harvey, G. (2014). *The handbook of contemporary animism.* Routledge.

[10] Cameron, A. G. (2011). *The last pagans of Rome.* Oxford University Press.

[11] Hicks, R. D. (1972). *Diogenes Laertius, lives of eminent philosophers* (Book VII, Chap. 1). Harvard University Press.

[12] Shultz, S., Opie, C., & Atkinson, Q. (2011). Stepwise evolution of stable sociality in primates. *Nature, 479,* 219–22.

[13] Genesis 1:29 (NIV).

[14] Kay, J. (1989). Human dominion over nature in the Hebrew Bible. *Annals of the Association of American Geographers, 79*(2), 214–32.

[15] Van Dyke, F. H., Mahan, D. C., Sheldon, J. K., & Brand, R. H. (1996). *Redeeming creation: The biblical basis for environmental stewardship.* InterVarsity Press.

[16] Haq, S. N. (2001). Islam and ecology: Toward retrieval and reconstruction. *Daedalus.* www.amacad.org/publication/islam-and-ecology-toward-retrieval-and-reconstruction

[17] Thoreau, H. D. (2004). *Walden.* Princeton University Press. (Original work published 1854)

[18] Hart, J. D., & Leininger, P. (1995). *The Oxford companion to American literature*. Oxford University Press.

[19] Emerson, R. W. (1849). *Nature* (p. 14). J. Munroe.

[20] Lefevee, S. (1894). *English commons and forests: The story of the battle during the last thirty years for public rights over the commons and forests of England and Wales*. Cassell.

[21] Muir, J. (1901). *Our national parks* (p. 56). Houghton Mifflin.

[22] *History of American Women*. (n.d.). Mary Treat [Blog post]. www.womenhistoryblog.com/2014/08/mary-treat.html

[23] Treat, M. L. A. A. (1885). *Home studies in nature* (p. 11). Harper.

[24] Stiles, A. (2012). Go rest, young man. *Monitor on Psychology, 43*(1), 32.

[25] Mitchell, S. W. (1871). *Wear and tear; or, Hints for the overworked* (p. 8). JB Lippincott.

[26] Mitchell, S. W. (1878). *Fat and blood: And how to make them* (p. 9). JB Lippincott.

[27] Dana, C. L. (1904). *Text-book of nervous diseases and psychiatry: For the use of students and practitioners of medicine* (p. 594). W. Wood.

[28] Gilman, C. P. (1935). *The living of Charlotte Perkins Gilman: An autobiography of Charlotte Perkins Gilman* (p. 96). D. Appleton-Century.

[29] Olmsted, F. L., & Roper, L. W. (1952). The Yosemite Valley and the Mariposa big trees: A preliminary report (1865). *Landscape Architecture, 43* (1), 12–25, quote on 17.

[30] Carson, R. (1962). *Silent spring* (p. 51). Houghton Mifflin Harcourt.

[31] Carson, R. (1965). *The sense of wonder* (p. 88). Harper & Row.

[32] Fromm, E. (1964). *The heart of man: Its genius for good and evil*. Harper & Row.

[33] Fromm, E. (1992). *The anatomy of human destructiveness* (p. 406). Henry Holt.

[34] Wilson, E. O. (1984). *Biophilia* (p. 1). Harvard University Press.

[35] World Bank. (2022, October 6). *Urban development overview*. www.worldbank.org/en/topic/urbandevelopment/overview

[36] Kellert, S. R., & Wilson, E. O. (Eds.). (1993). *The biophilia hypothesis* (p. 20). Island Press.

[37] Wilson, E. (1993). *Biophilia and the conservation ethic*. In S. R. Kellert & E. O. Wilson (Eds.), *The Biophilia hypothesis* (pp. 31–41). Island Press.

[38] Huynh, L. T. M., Gasparatos, A., Su, J., et al. (2022). Linking the nonmaterial dimensions of human–nature relations and human well-being through cultural ecosystem services. *Science Advances, 8*(31), eabn8042.

[39] Kaplan, S. (1995). The restorative benefits of nature: Toward an integrative framework. *Journal of Environmental Psychology, 15*(3), 169–82.

[40] Basu, A., Duvall, J., & Kaplan, R. (2019). Attention restoration theory: Exploring the role of soft fascination and mental bandwidth. *Environment and Behavior, 51*(9–10), 1055–81.

[41] Cox, D. T., Shanahan, D. F., Hudson, H. L., et al. (2017). Doses of neighborhood nature: The benefits for mental health of living with nature. *BioScience, 67*(2), 147–55.

[42] Bratman, G. N., Daily, G. C., Levy, B. J., & Gross, J. J. (2015). The benefits of nature experience: Improved affect and cognition. *Landscape and Urban Planning, 138*, 41–50.

[43] Bratman, G. N., Hamilton, J. P., Hahn, K. S., Daily, G. C., & Gross, J. J. (2015). Nature experience reduces rumination and subgenual prefrontal cortex activation. *Proceedings of the National Academy of Sciences, 112*(28), 8567–72.

[44] Takayama, N., Korpela, K., Lee, J., et al. (2014). Emotional, restorative and vitalizing effects of forest and urban environments at four sites in Japan. *International Journal of Environmental Research and Public Health, 11*(7), 7207–30.

[45] Atchley, R. A., Strayer, D. L., & Atchley, P. (2012). Creativity in the wild: Improving creative reasoning through immersion in natural settings. *PLoS One, 7*(12), e51474.

[46] Berman, M. G., Jonides, J., & Kaplan, S. (2008). The cognitive benefits of interacting with nature. *Psychological Science, 19*(12), 1207–12.

[47] White, M. P., Alcock, I., Grellier, J., et al. (2019). Spending at least 120 minutes a week in nature is associated with good health and wellbeing. *Scientific Reports, 9*, 7730. https://doi.org/10.1038/s41598-019-44097-3

[48] Ryan, R. M., Weinstein, N., Bernstein, J., et al. (2010). Vitalizing effects of being outdoors and in nature. *Journal of Environmental Psychology, 30*(2), 159–68.

[49] Gallegos-Riofrío, C. A., Arab, H., Carrasco-Torrontegui, A., & Gould, R. K. (2022). Chronic deficiency of diversity and pluralism in research on nature's mental health effects: A planetary health problem. *Current Research in Environmental Sustainability, 4*, 100148.

[50] Kaplan, R., & Kaplan, S. (1989). *The experience of nature: A psychological perspective.* Cambridge University Press.

[51] Hartig, T., Mang, M., & Evans, G. W. (1991). Restorative effects of natural environment experiences. *Environment and Behaviour, 23*, 3–26.

[52] Berto, R. (2005). Exposure to restorative environments helps restore attentional capacity. *Journal of Environmental Psychology, 25*(3), 249–59.

[53] Joye, Y., & Dewitte, S. (2018). Nature's broken path to restoration. A critical look at attention restoration theory. *Journal of Environmental Psychology, 59*, 1–8.

[54] Basu, A., Duvall, J., & Kaplan, R. (2019). Attention restoration theory: Exploring the role of soft fascination and mental bandwidth. *Environment and Behavior, 51*(9–10), 1055–81.

[55] White, M. P., Elliott, L. R., Gascon, M., Roberts, B., & Fleming, L. E. (2020). Blue space, health and well-being: A narrative overview and synthesis of potential benefits. *Environmental Research, 191*, 110169.

[56] Twohig-Bennett, C., & Jones, A. (2018). The health benefits of the great outdoors: A systematic review and meta-analysis of greenspace exposure and health outcomes. *Environmental Research, 166*, 628–37.

[57] Hansen, M. M., Jones, R., & Tocchini, K. (2017). Shinrin-yoku (forest bathing) and nature therapy: A state-of-the-art review. *International Journal of Environmental Research and Public Health, 14*(8), 851. https://doi.org/10.3390/ijerph14080851

[58] Song, C., Ikei, H., & Miyazaki, Y. (2016). Physiological effects of nature therapy: A review of the research in Japan. *International Journal of Environmental Research and Public Health, 13*(8), 781. https://doi.org/10.3390/ijerph13080781

[59] Miyazaki, Y., & Motohashi, Y. (1996). Forest environment and physiological response. *New Frontiers in Health Resort Medicine, 26*(2), 67–77.

[60] Park, B. J., Tsunetsugu, Y., Kasetani, T., Kagawa, T., & Miyazaki, Y. (2010). The physiological effects of Shinrin-yoku (taking in the forest atmosphere or forest bathing): Evidence from field experiments in 24 forests across Japan. *Environmental Health and Preventive Medicine, 15*(1), 18–26.

[61] Li, Q., Ochiai, H., Ochiai, T., et al. (2022). Effects of forest bathing (shinrin-yoku) on serotonin in serum, depressive symptoms and subjective sleep quality in middle-aged males. *Environmental Health and Preventive Medicine, 27*, 44. https://doi.org/10.1265/ehpm.22-00136

[62] Ochiai, H., Ikei, H., Song, C., et al. (2015). Physiological and psychological effects of a forest therapy program on middle-aged females. *International Journal of Environmental Research and Public Health, 12*(12), 15222–32.

[63] Farrow, M. R., & Washburn, K. (2019). A review of field experiments on the effect of forest bathing on anxiety and heart rate variability. *Global Advances in Health and Medicine, 8*, 1–7.

[64] Park, B. J., Tsunetsugu, Y., Kasetani, T., et al. (2007). Physiological effects of shinrin-yoku (taking in the atmosphere of the forest) – using salivary cortisol and cerebral activity as indicators. *Journal of Physiological Anthropology, 26*(2), 123–28.

[65] Park, B. J., Tsunetsugu, Y., Ishii, H., et al. (2008). Physiological effects of Shinrin-yoku (taking in the atmosphere of the forest) in a mixed forest in Shinano Town, Japan. *Scandinavian Journal of Forest Research, 23*(3), 278–83.

[66] Takayama, N., Korpela, K., Lee, J., et al. (2014). Emotional, restorative and vitalizing effects of forest and urban environments at four sites in Japan.

International Journal of Environmental Research and Public Health, 11(7), 7207–30.

[67] Li, Q. (2010). Effect of forest bathing trips on human immune function. *Environmental Health and Preventive Medicine, 15*(1), 9–17.

[68] Li, Q., Morimoto, K., Kobayashi, M., et al. (2008). Visiting a forest, but not a city, increases human natural killer cell activity and expression of anti-cancer proteins. *International Journal of Immunopathology and Pharmacology, 21*(1), 117–27.

[69] Li, Q., Kobayashi, M., Wakayama, Y., et al. (2009). Effect of phytoncide from trees on human natural killer cell function. *International Journal of Immunopathology and Pharmacology, 22*(4), 951–59.

[70] Park, B. J., Tsunetsugu, Y., Lee, J., Kagawa, T., & Miyazaki, Y. (2012). Effect of the forest environment on physiological relaxation – the results of field tests at 35 sites throughout Japan. *Forest Medicine*, pp. 55–65.

[71] Yu, C., Lin, C., Tsai, M., Tsai, Y., & Chen, C. (2017). Effects of short forest bathing program on autonomic nervous system activity and mood states in middle-aged and elderly individuals. *International Journal of Environmental Research and Public Health, 14*(8), 897. https://doi.org/10.3390/ijerph14080897

[72] Thangaleela, S., Sivamaruthi, B. S., Kesika, P., et al. (2022). Essential oils, phytoncides, aromachology, and aromatherapy – a review. *Applied Sciences, 12*(9), 4495. https://doi.org/10.3390/app12094495

[73] Antonelli, M., Donelli, D., Carlone, L., et al. (2021). Effects of forest bathing (shinrin-yoku) on individual well-being: An umbrella review. *International Journal of Environmental Health Research, 32*(8), 1842–67.

[74] MacEacheran, M. (2021, March 15). *Waldeinsamkeit: Germany's cherished forest tradition.* BBC. www.bbc.com/travel/article/20210314-waldeinsamkeit-germanys-cherished-forest-tradition

[75] Peterfalvi, A., Meggyes, M., Makszin, L., et al. (2021). Forest bathing always makes sense: Blood pressure–lowering and immune system–balancing effects in late spring and winter in Central Europe. *International Journal of Environmental Research and Public Health, 18*(4), 2067. https://doi.org/10.3390/ijerph18042067

[76] Interview with Naseem Rakha (2022, June 7).

[77] Rudd, M., Vohs, K. D., & Aaker, J. (2012). Awe expands people's perception of time, alters decision making, and enhances well-being. *Psychological Science, 23*(10), 1130–36.

[78] Nisbet, E. K., Zelenski, J. M., & Murphy, S. A. (2009). The Nature Relatedness Scale: Linking individuals' connection with nature to environmental concern and behaviour. *Environment and Behavior, 41*, 715–40.

[79] Nisbet, E. K., Zelenski, J. M., & Murphy, S. A. (2011). Happiness is in our nature: Exploring nature relatedness as a contributor to subjective well-being. *Journal of Happiness Studies, 12*(2), 303–22, quote on 310.

[80] Staats, H., & Hartig, T. (2004). Alone or with a friend: A social context for psychological restoration and environmental preferences. *Journal of Environmental Psychology, 24*(2), 199–211.

[81] Johansson, M., Hartig, T., & Staats, H. (2011). Psychological benefits of walking: Moderation by company and outdoor environment. *Applied Psychology: Health and Well-Being, 3*(3), 261–80.

[82] Hammitt, W. E. (1982). Cognitive dimensions of wilderness solitude. *Environment and Behavior, 14*(4), 478–93.

[83] Freeman, E., Akhurst, J., Bannigan, K., & James, H. (2017). Benefits of walking and solo experiences in UK wild places. *Health Promotion International, 32*, 1048–56.

[84] Sweatman, M. M., & Heintzman, P. (2004). The perceived impact of outdoor residential camp experience on the spirituality of youth. *World Leisure Journal, 46*(1), 23–31.

[85] Hammitt, W. E. (1982). Cognitive dimensions of wilderness solitude. *Environment and Behavior, 14*(4), 478–93.

[86] Naor, L., & Mayseless, O. (2020). The wilderness solo experience: A unique practice of silence and solitude for personal growth. *Frontiers in Psychology, 11*, 2303. https://doi.org/10.3389/fpsyg.2020.547067

[87] Ellison, M., & Hatcher, T. (2007). *Wilderness solitude and transformational change: Implications for the workplace* [Paper presentation]. International Conference on Human Resources Development and Practice across Europe.

[88] Huynh, T., & Torquati, J. C. (2019). Examining connection to nature and mindfulness at promoting psychological well-being. *Journal of Environmental Psychology, 66*, 101370.

[89] Kell, S., & Harney, C. (2019). Outdoor solo time: What do elementary students think? *Physical and Health Education Journal, 85*(2), 1–12.

[90] Kaplan, R. (1984). Impact of urban nature: A theoretical analysis. *Urban Ecology, 8*(3), 189–97.

[91] Coble, T. G., Selin, S. W., & Erickson, B. B. (2003). Hiking alone: Understanding fear, negotiation strategies and leisure experience. *Journal of Leisure Research, 35*(1), 1–22.

[92] Swatton, A. (1998). The personal growth of outstanding canoeists resulting from extended solo canoe expeditions. *Pathways: The Ontario Journal of Outdoor Education, 9*(6), 13–16.

[93] Coburn, M. J. (2006). Walking home: Women's transformative experiences in the wilderness of the Appalachian Trail [Unpublished doctoral dissertation]. Institute of Transpersonal Psychology.

[94] Petersen, E., Bischoff, A., Liedtke, G., & Martin, A. J. (2021). How does being solo in nature affect well-being? Evidence from Norway, Germany and New Zealand. *International Journal of Environmental Research and Public Health, 18*(15), 7897. https://doi.org/10.3390/ijerph18157897

[95] Jackson, S. A., & Marsh, H. W. (1996). Development and validation of a scale to measure optimal experience: The Flow State Scale. *Journal of Sport and Exercise Psychology, 18*(1), 17–35.

[96] Csikszentmihalyi, M. (1990). *Flow: The psychology of optimal experience.* Harper & Row.

[97] Privette, G. (1983). Peak experience, peak performance, and flow: A comparative analysis of positive human experiences. *Journal of Personality and Social Psychology, 45*(6), 1361–68.

[98] Bethelmy, L. C., & Corraliza, J. A. (2019). Transcendence and sublime experience in nature: Awe and inspiring energy. *Frontiers in Psychology, 10,* 509. https://doi.org/10.3389/fpsyg.2019.00509

[99] Emerson, R. W. (1849). *Nature* (p. 5). J. Munroe.

CHAPTER 8

[1] Buxton, R. T., Pearson, A. L., Allou, C., Fristrup, K., & Wittemyer, G. (2021). A synthesis of health benefits of natural sounds and their distribution in national parks. *Proceedings of the National Academy of Sciences, 118*(14), e2013097118.

[2] George, A. (Trans.). (1972). *The epic of Gilgamesh* (p. 108). Penguin Classics.

[3] https://sounds.bl.uk/Environment/Sound-effects/027M-1CD0126081X2-3300V0

[4] Nightingale, F. (1859). *Notes on nursing* (p. 508). Dover.

[5] Shinn-Cunningham, B. G., & Best, V. (2008). Selective attention in normal and impaired hearing. *Trends in Amplification, 12*(4), 283–99.

[6] Basner, M., Babisch, W., Davis, A., et al. (2014). Auditory and non-auditory effects of noise on health. *The Lancet, 383*(9925), 1325–32.

[7] Dutchen, S. (2022). The effects of noise on health. *Harvard Medicine.* https://hms.harvard.edu/magazine/viral-world/effects-noise-health

[8] Langguth, B. (2011). A review of tinnitus symptoms beyond "ringing in the ears": A call to action. *Current Medical Research and Opinion, 27*(8), 1635–43.

[9] Bosker, B. (2019, November). Why everything is getting louder. *The Atlantic.* www .theatlantic.com/magazine/archive/2019/11/the-end-of-silence/598366/

[10] Hahad, O., Kröller-Schön, S., Daiber, A., & Münzel, T. (2019). The cardiovascular effects of noise. *Deutsches Ärzteblatt International, 116*(14), 245–50.

[11] World Health Organization. (2018). *WHO environmental noise guidelines for the European region.* www.euro.who.int/en/health-topics/environment-and-health/noise/environmental-noise-guidelines-for-the-european-region

[12] Khomenko, S., Cirach, M., Barrera-Gómez, J., et al. (2022). Impact of road traffic noise on annoyance and preventable mortality in European cities: A health impact assessment. *Environment International, 2*, 107160.

[13] World Health Organization (2018). *WHO environmental noise guidelines for the European region.* www.euro.who.int/en/health-topics/environment-and-health/noise/environmental-noise-guidelines-for-the-european-region

[14] European Environmental Agency. (2020). *Environmental noise in Europe – 2020.* www.eea.europa.eu/publications/environmental-noise-in-europe

[15] Hammer, M. S., Swinburn, T. K., & Neitzel, R. L. (2014). Environmental noise pollution in the United States: Developing an effective public health response. *Environmental Health Perspectives, 122*(2), 115–19.

[16] McDonald, B. L., & Schreyer, R. (1991). Spiritual benefits of leisure participation and leisure settings. In B. L. Driver, P. J. Brown, & G. L. Peterson (Eds.), *Benefits of leisure* (pp. 179–94). Venture.

[17] Soga, M., Evans, M. J., Tsuchiya, K., & Fukano, Y. (2021). A room with a green view: The importance of nearby nature for mental health during the COVID-19 pandemic. *Ecological Applications, 31*(2), e2248.

[18] Mintz, K. K., Ayalon, O., Nathan, O., & Eshet, T. (2021). See or be? Contact with nature and well-being during COVID-19 lockdown. *Journal of Environmental Psychology, 78*, 101714.

[19] Velarde, M. D., Fry, G., & Tveit, M. (2007). Health effects of viewing landscapes – landscape types in environmental psychology. *Urban Forestry and Urban Greening, 6*(4), 199–212.

[20] Ulrich, R. S. (1979). Visual landscapes and psychological well-being. *Landscape Research, 4*(1), 17–23.

[21] Moore, E. O. (1981). A prison environment's effect on health care service demands. *Journal of Environmental Systems, 11*(1), 17–34.

[22] Laumann, K., Gärling, T., & Stormark, K. M. (2001). Rating scale measures of restorative components of environments. *Journal of Environmental Psychology, 21*(1), 31–44.

[23] Tennessen, C. M., & Cimprich, B. (1995). Views to nature: Effects on attention. *Journal of Environmental Psychology, 15*(1), 77–85.

[24] Jacobs, K. W., & Suess, J. F. (1975). Effects of four psychological primary colors on anxiety state. *Perceptual and Motor Skills, 41*(1), 207–10.

[25] Ulrich, R. S. (2002, April). *Health benefits of gardens in hospitals* [Paper presentation]. Plants for People International Exhibition Floriade.

[26] Valdez, P., & Mehrabian, A. (1994). Effects of color on emotions. *Journal of Experimental Psychology: General, 123*(4), 394.

[27] Guilford, J. P., & Smith, P. C. (1959). A system of color-preferences. *The American Journal of Psychology, 72*(4), 487–502.

[28] Hunter, M. D., Eickhoff, S. B., Pheasant, R. J., et al. (2010). The state of tranquility: Subjective perception is shaped by contextual modulation of auditory connectivity. *Neuroimage, 53*(2), 611–18.

[29] Dijk, E., & Weffers, A. (2010). Breathe with the ocean: A system for relaxation using audio, haptic and visual stimuli. *EuroHaptics,* pp. 47–60.

[30] Hedblom, M., Gunnarsson, B., Iravani, B., et al. (2019). Reduction of physiological stress by urban green space in a multisensory virtual experiment. *Scientific Reports, 9*(1), 1–11.

[31] Ferraro, D. M., Miller, Z. D., Ferguson, L. A., et al. (2020). The phantom chorus: Birdsong boosts human well-being in protected areas. *Proceedings of the Royal Society B, 287*(1941), 20201811.

[32] Franco, L. S., Shanahan, D. F., & Fuller, R. A. (2017). A review of the benefits of nature experiences: More than meets the eye. *International Journal of Environmental Research and Public Health, 14*(8), 864. https://doi .org/10.3390/ijerph14080864

[33] Pijanowski, B. C., Farina, A., Gage, S. H., Dumyahn, S. L., & Krause, B. L. (2011). What is soundscape ecology? An introduction and overview of an emerging new science. *Landscape Ecology, 26*(9), 1213–32.

[34] Kaplan, S. (1995). The restorative benefits of nature: Toward an integrative framework. *Journal of Environmental Psychology, 15*(3), 169–82.

[35] Fisher, J. A. (1999). The value of natural sounds. *Journal of Aesthetic Education, 33*(3), 26–42.

[36] Mace, B. L., Bell, P. A., & Loomis, R. J. (2004). Visibility and natural quiet in national parks and wilderness areas: Psychological considerations. *Environment and Behavior, 36*(1), 5–31.

[37] Carles, J. L., Barrio, I. L., & De Lucio, J. V. (1999). Sound influence on landscape values. *Landscape and Urban Planning, 43*(4), 191–200.

[38] Zhang, M., & Kang, J. (2007). Towards the evaluation, description, and creation of soundscapes in urban open spaces. *Environment and Planning B: Planning and Design, 34*(1), 68–86.

[39] Irvine, K. N., Devine-Wright, P., Payne, S. R., et al. (2009). Green space, soundscape and urban sustainability: An interdisciplinary, empirical study. *Local Environment, 14*(2), 155–72.

[40] Payne, S. R. (2013). The production of a perceived restorativeness soundscape scale. *Applied Acoustics, 74*(2), 255–63.

[41] Purcell, T., Peron, E., & Berto, R. (2001). Why do preferences differ between scene types? *Environment and Behavior, 33*(1), 93–106.

[42] Van den Berg, A. E., Koole, S. L., & van der Wulp, N. Y. (2003). Environmental preference and restoration: (How) are they related? *Journal of Environmental Psychology, 23*(2), 135–46.

[43] Alvarsson, J. J., Wiens, S., & Nilsson, M. E. (2010). Stress recovery during exposure to nature sound and environmental noise. *International Journal of Environmental Research and Public Health, 7*(3), 1036–46.

[44] Weber, S. T., & Heuberger, E. (2008). The impact of natural odors on affective states in humans. *Chemical Senses, 33*(5), 441–47.

[45] Lorig, T. S., Herman, K. B., Schwartz, G. E., & Cain, W. S. (1990). EEG activity during administration of low-concentration odors. *Bulletin of the Psychonomic Society, 28*(5), 405–8.

[46] Bentley, P. R., Fisher, J. C., Dallimer, M., et al. (2023). Nature, smells, and human wellbeing. *Ambio, 52*(1), 1–14.

[47] Diego, M. A., Jones, N. A., Field, T., et al. (1998). Aromatherapy positively affects mood, EEG patterns of alertness and math computations. *International Journal of Neuroscience, 96*(3–4), 217–24.

[48] Haze, S., Sakai, K., & Gozu, Y. (2002). Effects of fragrance inhalation on sympathetic activity in normal adults. *Japanese Journal of Pharmacology, 90*(3), 247–53.

[49] Kawakami, K., Kawamoto, M., Nomura, M., et al. (2004). Effects of phytoncides on blood pressure under restraint stress in SHRSP. *Clinical and Experimental Pharmacology and Physiology, 31*, S27–28.

[50] Weber, S. T., & Heuberger, E. (2008). The impact of natural odors on affective states in humans. *Chemical Senses, 33*(5), 441–47.

[51] Glass, S. T., Lingg, E., & Heuberger, E. (2014). Do ambient urban odors evoke basic emotions? *Frontiers in Psychology, 5*, 340. https://doi.org/10 .3389/fpsyg.2014.00340

[52] Bentley, P. R., Fisher, J. C., Dallimer, M., et al. (2023). Nature, smells, and human wellbeing. *Ambio, 52*(1), 1–14.

[53] Franco, L. S., Shanahan, D. F., & Fuller, R. A. (2017). A review of the benefits of nature experiences: More than meets the eye. *International Journal of Environmental Research and Public Health, 14*(8), 864. https://doi .org/10.3390/ijerph14080864

[54] Heckman, J. R. (2012). Human contact with plants and soils for health and well-being. In *Soils and human health* (pp. 227–40). CRC Press.

[55] Bharucha, Z. P., Weinstein, N., Watson, D., & Boehm, S. (2020). Participation in local food projects is associated with better psychological well-being: Evidence from the East of England. *Journal of Public Health, 42* (2), e187–97.

[56] Spano, G., D'Este, M., Giannico, V., et al. (2020). Are community gardening and horticultural interventions beneficial for psychosocial well-being? A meta-analysis. *International Journal of Environmental Research and Public Health, 17*(10), 3584. https://doi.org/10.3390/ijerph17103584

[57] Wood, C. J., Pretty, J., & Griffin, M. (2016). A case–control study of the health and well-being benefits of allotment gardening. *Journal of Public Health, 38*(3), e336–44

[58] Global Action Plan. (2021). *United in compassion: Bringing young people together to create a better world.* www.globalactionplan.org.uk/united-in-compassion

[59] Noone, S., Innes, A., Kelly, F., & Mayers, A. (2017). "The nourishing soil of the soul": The role of horticultural therapy in promoting well-being in community-dwelling people with dementia. *Dementia, 16*(7), 897–910.

[60] Korpela, K., & Hartig, T. (1996). Restorative qualities of favorite places. *Journal of Environmental Psychology, 16*(3), 221–33.

[61] Jorgensen, A., Hitchmough, J., & Dunnett, N. (2007). Woodland as a setting for housing-appreciation and fear and the contribution to residential satisfaction and place identity in Warrington New Town, UK. *Landscape and Urban Planning, 79*(3–4), 273–87.

[62] Korpela, K. M., Hartig, T., Kaiser, F. G., & Fuhrer, U. (2001). Restorative experience and self-regulation in favorite places. *Environment and Behavior, 33*(4), 572–89.

[63] Newell, P. B. (1997). A cross-cultural examination of favorite places. *Environment and Behavior, 29*(4), 495–514.

[64] Korpela, K. M., & Ylén, M. P. (2009). Effectiveness of favorite-place prescriptions: A field experiment. *American Journal of Preventive Medicine, 36*(5), 435–38.

[65] Korpela, K. M. (2003). Negative mood and adult place preference. *Environment and Behavior, 35*(3), 331–46.

[66] Regan, C. L., & Horn, S. A. (2005). To nature or not to nature: Associations between environmental preferences, mood states and demographic factors. *Journal of Environmental Psychology, 25*(1), 57–66.

[67] Carbaugh, D., Berry, M., & Nurmikari-Berry, M. (2006). Coding personhood through cultural terms and practices: Silence and quietude as a

Finnish "natural way of being." *Journal of Language and Social Psychology, 25* (3), 203–20.

[68] Koch, P. J. (1989). Solitude in ancient taoism. *Diogenes, 37*(148), 78–91.

[69] Balcom, D. (2004). *The greatest escape: Adventures in the history of solitude* (p. 92). iUniverse.

[70] Mount Holyoke College [@mtholyoke]. (2021, May 23). *"It's okay to satisfy our primal need for silence... and in that silence, wonder on your own, discover your own path. And don't ever be afraid to get to know yourself better..." – Chloé Zhao'05 to #MountHolyoke2021* [Tweet]. Twitter. https://twitter.com/mtholyoke/status/1396488879063117837

[71] Suedfeld, P., & Vernon, J. (1965). Stress and verbal originality in sensory deprivation. *Psychological Record, 15*(4), 567–70.

[72] Suedfeld, P., Glucksberg, S., & Vernon, J. (1967). Sensory deprivation as a drive operation: Effects upon problem solving. *Journal of Experimental Psychology, 75*(2), 166–69.

[73] Suedfeld, P. (1968). The cognitive effects of sensory deprivation: The role of task complexity. *Canadian Journal of Psychology/Revue Canadienne de Psychologie, 22*(4), 302–7.

[74] Suedfeld, P. (1975). The benefits of boredom: Sensory deprivation reconsidered: The effects of a monotonous environment are not always negative; sometimes sensory deprivation has high utility. *American Scientist, 63*(1), 60–69.

[75] Suedfeld, P. (1982). Aloneness as a healing experience. In L. A. Peplau & D. Perlman (Eds.), *Loneliness: A sourcebook of current theory, research and therapy* (pp. 54–67). Wiley.

[76] Suedfeld, P., Metcalfe, J., & Bluck, S. (1987). Enhancement of scientific creativity by flotation REST (restricted environmental stimulation technique). *Journal of Environmental Psychology, 7*(3), 219–31.

[77] Suedfeld, P., John, W., Jr., & Fine, T. H. (2012). *Restricted environmental stimulation: Theoretical and empirical developments in flotation REST.* Springer Science & Business Media.

[78] van Dierendonck, D., & Te Nijenhuis, J. (2005). Flotation restricted environmental stimulation therapy (REST) as a stress-management tool: A meta-analysis. *Psychology and Health, 20*(3), 405–12.

[79] Phelps, J. (2008). Dark therapy for bipolar disorder using amber lenses for blue light blockade. *Medical Hypotheses, 70*(2), 224–29.

[80] Buchholz, E. S. (2000). Echoes of quietude: Alonetimes in museums. *Journal of Museum Education, 25*(1–2), 3–8.

[81] Su, F., Wood, M., Alerby, E., Da Re, L., & Felisatti, E. (2022). "When the hurley-burley's done, when the battle's lost and won": Exploring the value

and appropriation of silence and quietude in academia. *European Journal of Higher Education, 12*(3), 277–92.

[82] Alerby, E., & Bergmark, U. (2016). *Student participation and influence in education: Possibilities and challenges.* www.diva-portal.org/smash/get/diva2:1059304/FULLTEXT01.pdf

[83] Bernardi, L., Porta, C., & Sleight, P. (2006). Cardiovascular, cerebrovascular, and respiratory changes induced by different types of music in musicians and non-musicians: The importance of silence. *Heart, 92*(4), 445–52.

[84] Scholl, B., Gao, X., & Wehr, M. (2010). Nonoverlapping sets of synapses drive on responses and off responses in auditory cortex. *Neuron, 65*(3), 412–21.

[85] Ekhtiari, H., & Paulus, M. (2016). *Neuroscience for addiction medicine: From prevention to rehabilitation – methods and interventions.* Elsevier.

[86] Moran, J. M., Kelley, W. M., & Heatherton, T. F. (2013). What can the organization of the brain's default mode network tell us about self-knowledge? *Frontiers in Human Neuroscience, 7*, 391. https://doi.org/10.3389/fnhum.2013.00391

[87] Radun, J., Maula, H., Rajala, V., Scheinin, M., & Hongisto, V. (2021). Speech is special: The stress effects of speech, noise, and silence during tasks requiring concentration. *Indoor Air, 31*(1), 264–74.

[88] Kasof, J. (1997). Creativity and breadth of attention. *Creativity Research Journal, 10*(4), 303–15.

[89] Dewar, M., Garcia, Y. F., Cowan, N., & Sala, S. D. (2009). Delaying interference enhances memory consolidation in amnesic patients. *Neuropsychology, 23*(5), 627–34.

[90] Kirste, I., Nicola, Z., Kronenberg, G., et al. (2015). Is silence golden? Effects of auditory stimuli and their absence on adult hippocampal neurogenesis. *Brain Structure and Function, 220*(2), 1221–28.

[91] Yamada, J., & Jinno, S. (2021). Potential involvement of perineuronal nets in brain aging: An anatomical point of view. In *Factors affecting neurological aging* (pp. 163–72). Academic Press.

[92] Booi, H., & Van den Berg, F. (2012). Quiet areas and the need for quietness in Amsterdam. *International Journal of Environmental Research and Public Health, 9*(4), 1030–50.

[93] Silent Spaces. (2021). https://silentspace.org.uk/

[94] Osten Gerszberg, C. (2019, December 9). My week of "Noble Silence." *New York Times.* www.nytimes.com/2019/12/06/travel/silent-meditation-retreat.html

[95] Hrabi, D., & Chen, D. (2019, May 30). Silent meditation retreats: Are you up for the challenge? *Wall Street Journal.* www.wsj.com/articles/silent-meditation-retreats-are-you-up-for-the-challenge-11559240150

[96] Selby, B. (2019, April 13). Silent mode: Why the stars of Silicon Valley are turning to silent meditation retreats. *Fast Company*. www.fastcompany .com/90334124/from-hacking-the-mind-to-punishing-ennui-techs-brightest-are-taking-to-silent-retreats

[97] Barabasz, A., Barabasz, M., Dyer, R., & Rather, N. (1993). Effects of chamber REST, flotation REST and relaxation on transient mood state. In *Clinical and experimental restricted environmental stimulation* (pp. 113–20). Springer.

[98] Jacobs, G. D., Heilbronner, R. L., & Stanley, J. M. (1984). The effects of short term flotation REST on relaxation: A controlled study. *Health Psychology*, *3*(2), 99–112.

[99] Turner, J. W., & Fine, T. H. (1983). Effects of relaxation associated with brief restricted environmental stimulation therapy (REST) on plasma cortisol, ACTH, and LH. *Biofeedback and Self-Regulation*, *8*(1), 115–26.

[100] Jacobs, G. D., Heilbronner, R. L., & Stanley, J. M. (1984). The effects of short term flotation REST on relaxation: A controlled study. *Health Psychology*, *3*(2), 99–112.

[101] Malůš, M., Kupka, M., Dostál, D., & Kavková, V. (2017). Restricted environmental stimulation and psychopathology. In *PhD existence 2017: VIII. česko-slovenská psychologická konference (nejen) pro doktorandy ao doktorandech*. Univerzita Palackého v Olomouci. www.researchgate .net/publication/324727475_restricted_environmental_stimulation_and_ psychopathology

[102] Lowenthal, M. (2003). *Dawning of clear light: A Western approach to Tibetan dark retreat meditation* (p. 197). Hampton Roads.

[103] Hermitage Retreats. (n.d.). www.thehermitageretreats.com/

[104] Dark Retreats. (n.d.). https://darkretreats.com/

[105] Childs, M. (2018, July 6). A week of darkness, for your health. *The Atlantic*. www.theatlantic.com/health/archive/2018/07/darkness-therapy-czech-republic/564365/

[106] Güzel, P., Yıldız, K., Esentaş, M., & Zerengök, D. (2020). "Know-how" to spend time in home isolation during COVID-19; restrictions and recreational activities. *International Journal of Psychology and Educational Studies*, *7* (2), 122–31.

[107] Easter, M. (2021). Don't forget how to be alone. *The Medium*. https:// forge.medium.com/embrace-these-last-moments-of-solitude-f501f0fa3bfa

[108] leBrasseur, R. (2020). How COVID-19 shutdowns are allowing us to hear more of nature. *The Conversation*. https://theconversation.com/how-covid-19-shutdowns-are-allowing-us-to-hear-more-of-nature-136139

[109] Lovatt, S. (2021). *Birdsong in a time of silence*. Penguin.

[110] Lecocq, T., Hicks, S. P., Van Noten, K., et al. (2020). Global quieting of high-frequency seismic noise due to COVID-19 pandemic lockdown measures. *Science, 369*(6509), 1338–43.

[111] https://soundproofist.com/2022/11/28/silent-cities-project/

[112] Bui, Q., & Badger, E. (2020, May 22). The coronavirus quieted city noise. Listen to what's left. *New York Times*. www.nytimes.com/interactive/2020/05/22/upshot/coronavirus-quiet-city-noise.html

[113] Bakare, L. (2020, March 31). Art project captures sound of cities during coronavirus outbreak. *The Guardian*. www.theguardian.com/world/2020/mar/31/art-project-captures-sound-of-cities-during-coronavirus-outbreak

[114] Sims, J. (2020, June 17). Will the world be quieter after the pandemic? *BBC Future*. www.bbc.com/future/article/20200616-will-the-world-be-quieter-after-the-pandemic

[115] Stokstad, E. (2020, August 13). The pandemic stilled human activity. What did this "anthropause" mean for wildlife? *Science*. www.science.org/content/article/pandemic-stilled-human-activity-what-did-anthropause-mean-wildlife

[116] Schrimpf, M. B., Des Brisay, P. G., Johnston, A., et al. (2021). Reduced human activity during COVID-19 alters avian land use across North America. *Science Advances, 7*(39), eabf5073.

[117] Ezra Klein Show. (2022, May 24). *A conversation with Ada Limón, in six poems*. www.stitcher.com/show/the-ezra-klein-show-2

[118] McKean, T. (2021, May 12). "Sometimes I miss the lockdown." *The Nation*. www.thenation.com/article/society/covid-lockdown-nyc/

CHAPTER 9

[1] www.kreau.com/

[2] Interview with Knutson/Kreau (2021, September 10).

[3] Hipple, M. (2020, April 28). Seattle artists create murals on shuttered stores – in pictures. *The Guardian*. www.theguardian.com/us-news/gallery/2020/apr/28/seattle-artists-murals-stores-coronavirus

[4] Pauly, T., Chu, L., Zambrano, E., Gerstorf, D., & Hoppmann, C. A. (2022). COVID-19, time to oneself, and loneliness: Creativity as a resource. *Journals of Gerontology: Series B, 77*(4), e30–35.

[5] Sofo, A., Galluzzi, A., & Zito, F. (2021). A modest suggestion: Baking using sourdough – a sustainable, slow-paced, traditional and beneficial remedy against stress during the COVID-19 lockdown. *Human Ecology, 49*(1), 99–105.

[6] Kiernan, F., & Davidson, J. W. (2022). How can music engagement address loneliness? A qualitative study and thematic framework in the context of Australia's COVID-19 pandemic lockdowns. *International Journal of Environmental Research and Public Health, 20*(1), 25.

[7] Kapoor, H., & Kaufman, J. C. (2020). Meaning-making through creativity during COVID-19. *Frontiers in Psychology, 11*, 595990.

[8] Güzel, P., Yıldız, K., Esentaş, M., & Zerengök, D. (2020). "Know-how" to spend time in home isolation during COVID-19; restrictions and recreational activities. *International Journal of Psychology and Educational Studies, 7* (2), 122–31.

[9] Hill, A. (2020, November 7). "It's reawakened something": Creative ambitions blossom for lockdown 2. *The Guardian.* www.theguardian.com/world/ 2020/nov/07/its-reawakened-something-creative-ambitions-blossom-for-lockdown-2

[10] Pitstick, E. (2021). Baking during COVID-19: Coping, connecting, creating. *Denison Student Scholarship, 50.* https://digitalcommons.denison.edu/ studentscholarship/50

[11] Kletter, H. (2016, April 29). Defining resilience [Blog post]. *OUPblog.* https://blog.oup.com/2016/04/defining-resilience-ptsd-psychology/

[12] Werner, E. E. (2000). Protective factors and individual resilience. *Handbook of Early Childhood Intervention, 2*, 115–32.

[13] Luthar, S. S., Cicchetti, D., & Becker, B. (2000). The construct of resilience: A critical evaluation and guidelines for future work. *Child Development, 71* (3), 543–62.

[14] Cicchetti, D. (1993). Defining child maltreatment: The interface between policy and research. In *Child abuse, child development, and social policy.* Ablex.

[15] Warren, A. E., Schmid, K. L., Agans, J. P., et al. (2012). Resilience across the life span. *Annual Review of Gerontology and Geriatrics, 32*(1), 275–99.

[16] American Psychological Association. (n.d.). Resilience. In *APA dictionary of psychology.* https://dictionary.apa.org/resilience

[17] Maul, S., Giegling, I., Fabbri, C., et al. (2020). Genetics of resilience: Implications from genome-wide association studies and candidate genes of the stress response system in posttraumatic stress disorder and depression. *American Journal of Medical Genetics Part B: Neuropsychiatric Genetics, 183*(2), 77–94.

[18] Mao, W., & Agyapong, V. I. (2021). The role of social determinants in mental health and resilience after disasters: Implications for public health policy and practice. *Frontiers in Public Health, 9*, 658528.

[19] Ozbay, F., Johnson, D. C., Dimoulas, E., et al. (2007). Social support and resilience to stress: From neurobiology to clinical practice. *Psychiatry (Edgmont), 4*(5), 35–40.

[20] Ozbay, F., Fitterling, H., Charney, D., & Southwick, S. (2008). Social support and resilience to stress across the life span: A neurobiologic framework. *Current Psychiatry Reports, 10*(4), 304–10.

[21] Sippel, L. M., Pietrzak, R. H., Charney, D. S., Mayes, L. C., & Southwick, S. M. (2015). How does social support enhance resilience in the trauma-exposed individual? *Ecology and Society, 20*(4), 10. www.jstor.org/stable/26270277

[22] Li, F., Luo, S., Mu, W., et al. (2021). Effects of sources of social support and resilience on the mental health of different age groups during the COVID-19 pandemic. *BMC Psychiatry, 21*(1), 1–14.

[23] Weinstein, N., Hansen, H., & Nguyen, T.-V. (in press). Who feels good in solitude: A qualitative interview analysis of the personality and mindset drivers of well-being when alone. *European Journal of Social Psychology.*

[24] Thomas, V., & Azmitia, M. (2019). Motivation matters: Development and validation of the Motivation for Solitude Scale–Short Form (MSS-SF). *Journal of Adolescence, 70,* 33–42.

[25] Lian, S. L., Sun, X. J., Liu, Q. Q., et al. (2021). When the capacity to be alone is associated with psychological distress among Chinese adolescents: Individuals with low mindfulness or high rumination may suffer more by their capacity to be alone. *Current Psychology, 43,* 5110–22.

[26] Lay, J. C., Pauly, T., Graf, P., Biesanz, J. C., & Hoppmann, C. A. (2019). By myself and liking it? Predictors of distinct types of solitude experiences in daily life. *Journal of Personality, 87*(3), 633–47.

[27] Iyer, A., Tanushree, V. L., & Chakravarty, S. (2020). *Self-regulatory solitude: A qualitative exploration of solitude in Indian youth.* https://psyarxiv.com/uxm97/

[28] Pascal, B. (2006). *Pascal's pensées* (p. 139). www.gutenberg.org/files/18269/18269-h/18269-h.htm

[29] Ost Mor, S., Palgi, Y., & Segel-Karpas, D. (2021). Exploring gaps in positive solitude perceptions: Older adults vs. gerontology professionals. *International Psychogeriatrics, 33*(12), 1253–63.

[30] Smallwood, J., & Andrews-Hanna, J. (2013). Not all minds that wander are lost: The importance of a balanced perspective on the mind-wandering state. *Frontiers in Psychology, 4,* 441. https://doi.org/10.3389/fpsyg.2013.00441

[31] Killingsworth, M. A., & Gilbert, D. T. (2010). A wandering mind is an unhappy mind. *Science, 330*(6006), 932.

[32] Whitehead, N. (2014, July 3). People would rather be electrically shocked than left alone with their thoughts. *Science.* www.science.org/content/article/people-would-rather-be-electrically-shocked-left-alone-their-thoughts

[33] Wilson, T. D., Reinhard, D. A., Westgate, E. C., et al. (2014). Just think: The challenges of the disengaged mind. *Science, 345*(6192), 75–77.

[34] Cross, C. P., Cyrenne, D. L. M., & Brown, G. R. (2013). Sex differences in sensation-seeking: A meta-analysis. *Scientific Reports, 3*(1), 1–5.

[35] Webb, J. (2014, July 4). *Do people choose pain over boredom?* BBC. www.bbc.co .uk/news/science-environment-28130690

[36] Singer, J. L. (1955). Delayed gratification and ego development: Implications for clinical and experimental research. *Journal of Consulting Psychology, 19*(4), 259–66.

[37] Singer, J. L. (1961). Imagination and waiting ability in young children. *Journal of Personality, 29*, 396–413.

[38] Antrobus, J. S., & Singer, J. L. (1964). Visual signal detection as a function of sequential variability of simultaneous speech. *Journal of Experimental Psychology, 68*(6), 603–10.

[39] Singer, J. (1964). Exploring man's imaginative world. *Teaching College Record, 66*(2), 1–13.

[40] Singer, J. L. (1966). *Daydreaming: An introduction to the experimental study of inner experience.* Random House.

[41] Singer, J. L. (1974). Daydreaming and the stream of thought: Daydreams have usually been associated with idleness and inattentiveness. Now, however, through an empirical research program, their general function and adaptive possibilities are being elucidated. *American Scientist, 62*(4), 417–25.

[42] Singer, J. L. (1975). Navigating the stream of consciousness: Research in daydreaming and related inner experience. *American Psychologist, 30*(7), 727–38.

[43] McMillan, R. L., Kaufman, S. B., & Singer, J. L. (2013). Ode to positive constructive daydreaming. *Frontiers in Psychology, 4*, 626. https://doi.org/10 .3389/fpsyg.2013.00626

[44] https://violet-scarlet-dasj.squarespace.com

[45] Kaufman, J. C., & Beghetto, R. A. (2009). Beyond big and little: The four c model of creativity. *Review of General Psychology, 13*(1), 1–12.

[46] Beghetto, R. A., & Kaufman, J. C. (2007). Toward a broader conception of creativity: A case for "mini-c" creativity. *Psychology of Aesthetics, Creativity, and the Arts, 1*(2), 73.

[47] Kaufman, J. C., & Sternberg, R. J. (Eds.). (2006). *The international handbook of creativity.* Cambridge University Press.

[48] Interview with James Kaufman (2022, March 1).

[49] Franklin, M. S., Mrazek, M. D., Anderson, C. L., et al. (2013). The silver lining of a mind in the clouds: Interesting musings are associated with

positive mood while mind-wandering. *Frontiers in Psychology, 4,* 583. https:// doi.org/10.3389/fpsyg.2013.00583

[50] Royal Institution. (2022, June 30). *Mindwandering – with Moshe Bar* [Video]. YouTube. https://youtu.be/rz7MhCDRZlU

[51] Baird, B., Smallwood, J., Mrazek, M. D., et al. (2012). Inspired by distraction: Mind wandering facilitates creative incubation. *Psychological Science, 23* (10), 1117–22.

[52] Gable, S. L., Hopper, E. A., & Schooler, J. W. (2019). When the muses strike: Creative ideas of physicists and writers routinely occur during mind wandering. *Psychological Science, 30*(3), 396–404.

[53] Irving, Z. C., McGrath, C., Flynn, L., Glasser, A., & Mills, C. (2022). The shower effect: Mind wandering facilitates creative incubation during moderately engaging activities. *Psychology of Aesthetics, Creativity, and the Arts.* Advance online publication.

[54] Smallwood, J., Schooler, J. W., Turk, D. J., et al. (2011). Self-reflection and the temporal focus of the wandering mind. *Conscious Cognition, 20,* 1120–26.

[55] Immordino-Yang, M. H., Christodoulou, J. A., & Singh, V. (2012). Rest is not idleness: Implications of the brain's default mode for human development and education. *Perspectives on Psychological Science, 7*(4), 352–64.

[56] Franklin, M. S., Mrazek, M. D., Anderson, C. L., et al. (2013). The silver lining of a mind in the clouds: Interesting musings are associated with positive mood while mind-wandering. *Frontiers in Psychology, 4,* 583. https://doi.org/10.3389/fpsyg.2013.00583

[57] American Psychological Association. (n.d.). Introversion. In *APA dictionary of psychology.* https://dictionary.apa.org/introversion

[58] Nguyen, T. V. T., Weinstein, N., & Ryan, R. M. (2022). Who enjoys solitude? Autonomous functioning (but not introversion) predicts self-determined motivation (but not preference) for solitude. *PLoS One, 17*(5), e0267185.

[59] Mikulincer, M., Shaver, P. R., & Gal, I. (2021). An attachment perspective on solitude and loneliness. In R. J. Coplan & J. C. Bowker (Eds.), *The handbook of solitude: Psychological perspectives on social isolation, social withdrawal, and being alone* (pp. 31–41). Wiley.

[60] Huberman, A. (2022, January 24). *Dr. Alia Crum: Science of mindsets for health and performance. Huberman Lab Podcast #56* [Video]. YouTube. https://youtu .be/dFR_wFN23ZY

[61] Crum, A. J., & Langer, E. J. (2007). Mind-set matters: Exercise and the placebo effect. *Psychological Science, 18*(2), 165–71.

[62] www.merckmanuals.com/home/multimedia/table/placebo-i-shall-please

[63] Ostenfeld-Rosenthal, A. M. (2012). Energy healing and the placebo effect: An anthropological perspective on the placebo effect. *Anthropology and Medicine, 19*(3), 327–38.

[64] Legg, T. (2017, September 7). Is the placebo effect real? *Medical News Today.* www.medicalnewstoday.com/articles/306437

[65] Hurt, A. (2022, June 3). The placebo effect: A mystery in potential therapy. *Discover Magazine.* www.discovermagazine.com/health/the-placebo-effect-a-mystery-in-potential-therapy

[66] Crum, A. J., Corbin, W. R., Brownell, K. D., & Salovey, P. (2011). Mind over milkshakes: Mindsets, not just nutrients, determine ghrelin response. *Health Psychology, 30*(4), 424–29.

[67] Kojima, M., & Kangawa, K. (2005). Ghrelin: Structure and function. *Physiological Reviews, 85*(2), 495–522.

[68] Rodriguez, M., Bellet, B. W., & McNally, R. J. (2020). Reframing time spent alone: Reappraisal buffers the emotional effects of isolation. *Cognitive Therapy and Research, 44*(6), 1052–67.

[69] Thomas, V. (2021). Solitude skills and the private self. *Qualitative Psychology, 10*(1), 121–39.

[70] Lay, J. C., Pauly, T., Graf, P., Biesanz, J. C., & Hoppmann, C. A. (2019). By myself and liking it? Predictors of distinct types of solitude experiences in daily life. *Journal of Personality, 87*(3), 633–47.

[71] Degges-White, S., & Kepic, M. (2020). Friendships, subjective age, and life satisfaction of women in midlife. *Adultspan Journal, 19*(1), 39–53.

[72] Holt-Lunstad, J., Smith, T. B., & Layton, J. B. (2010). Social relationships and mortality risk: A meta-analytic review. *PLoS Medicine, 7* (7), e1000316.

[73] Han, S. (2021, May 20). You can only maintain so many close friendships. *The Atlantic.* www.theatlantic.com/family/archive/2021/05/robin-dunbar-explains-circles-friendship-dunbars-number/618931/

[74] Lees, N. (2022, June 10). How many friends do you really need? *New York Times.* www.nytimes.com/2022/05/07/well/live/adult-friendships-number.html

[75] Davies, M. G. (1996). Solitude and loneliness: An integrative model. *Journal of Psychology and Theology, 24*(1), 3–12.

[76] Jiang, D., Fung, H. H., Lay, J. C., et al. (2019). Everyday solitude, affective experiences, and well-being in old age: The role of culture versus immigration. *Aging and Mental Health, 23*(9), 1095–104.

[77] Coplan, R. J., Zelenski, J. M., & Bowker, J. C. (2017). Leave well enough alone? The costs and benefits of solitude. In *Subjective well-being and life satisfaction* (pp. 129–47). Routledge.

[78] Epley, N., & Schroeder, J. (2014). Mistakenly seeking solitude. *Journal of Experimental Psychology: General, 143*(5), 1980–99.

[79] Zessin, U., Dickhäuser, O., and Garbade, S. (2015). The relationship between self-compassion and well-being: A meta-analysis. *Applied Psychology: Health and Well-Being, 7*, 340–64.

[80] Neff, K. D. (2003). Self-compassion: An alternative conceptualization of a healthy attitude toward oneself. *Self and Identity, 2*(2), 85–102.

[81] Hobbes, T. (1894). *Leviathan; or, The matter, form, and power of a common-wealth ecclesiastical and civil* (Vol. 21, p. 34). Routledge.

[82] Calaprice, A. (2010). *The ultimate quotable Einstein* (p. 20). Princeton University Press.

[83] Gruber, M., & Valihi, A. (2019, September 13). Curiosity: We're studying the brain to help you harness it. *The Conversation.* https://theconversation.com/curiosity-were-studying-the-brain-to-help-you-harness-it-122351

[84] Gruber, M. J., Gelman, B. D., & Ranganath, C. (2014). States of curiosity modulate hippocampus-dependent learning via the dopaminergic circuit. *Neuron, 84*(2), 486–96.

[85] Litman, J. (2005). Curiosity and the pleasures of learning: Wanting and liking new information. *Cognition and Emotion, 19*(6), 793–814.

[86] Kashdan, T. B., & Steger, M. F. (2007). Curiosity and pathways to well-being and meaning in life: Traits, states, and everyday behaviors. *Motivation and Emotion, 31*(3), 159–73.

[87] Leavitt, C. E., Butzer, B., Clarke, R. W., & Dvorakova, K. (2021). Intentional solitude and mindfulness: The benefits of being alone. In R. J. Coplan & J. C. Bowker (Eds.), *The handbook of solitude: Psychological perspectives on social isolation, social withdrawal, and being alone* (pp. 340–50). Wiley.

[88] Santorelli, S. (Ed.). (2014). *Mindfulness-based stress reduction (MBSR): Standards of practice.* Center for Mindfulness in Medicine, Health Care, and Society, University of Massachusetts Medical School.

[89] Zenner, C., Herrnleben-Kurz, S., & Walach, H. (2014). Mindfulness-based interventions in schools – a systematic review and meta-analysis. *Frontiers in Psychology, 5*, 603. https://doi.org/10.3389/fpsyg.2014.00603

[90] Cavanagh, K., Strauss, C., Forder, L., & Jones, F. (2014). Can mindfulness and acceptance be learnt by self-help? A systematic review and meta-analysis of mindfulness and acceptance-based self-help interventions. *Clinical Psychology Review, 34*(2), 118–29.

[91] Strauss, C., Cavanagh, K., Oliver, A., & Pettman, D. (2014). Mindfulness-based interventions for people diagnosed with a current episode of an anxiety or depressive disorder: A meta-analysis of randomised controlled trials. *PLoS One, 9*(4), e96110.

[92] Regehr, C., Glancy, D., Pitts, A., & LeBlanc, V. R. (2014). Interventions to reduce the consequences of stress in physicians: A review and meta-analysis. *Journal of Nervous and Mental Disease, 202*(5), 353–59.

[93] Brewer, J. (2014). Mindfulness in the military. *American Journal of Psychiatry, 171*(8), 803–6.

[94] Lomas, T., Medina, J. C., Ivtzan, I., Rupprecht, S., & Eiroa-Orosa, F. J. (2019). A systematic review and meta-analysis of the impact of mindfulness-based interventions on the well-being of healthcare professionals. *Mindfulness, 10*(7), 1193–216.

[95] Antonova, E., Chadwick, P., & Kumari, V. (2015). More meditation, less habituation? The effect of mindfulness practice on the acoustic startle reflex. *PLoS One, 10*(5), e0123512.

[96] Taren, A. A., Gianaros, P. J., Greco, C. M., et al. (2015). Mindfulness meditation training alters stress-related amygdala resting state functional connectivity: A randomized controlled trial. *Social Cognitive and Affective Neuroscience, 10*(12), 1758–68.

[97] Brewer, J. A., Worhunsky, P. D., Gray, J. R., et al. (2011). Meditation experience is associated with differences in default mode network activity and connectivity. *Proceedings of the National Academy of Sciences, 108*(50), 20254–59.

[98] Goyal, M., Singh, S., Sibinga, E. M., et al. (2014). Meditation programs for psychological stress and well-being: A systematic review and meta-analysis. *JAMA Internal Medicine, 174*(3), 357–68.

[99] Mateer, T. J. (2022). Developing connectedness to nature in urban outdoor settings: A potential pathway through awe, solitude, and leisure. *Frontiers in Psychology, 13*, 940939.

[100] Keltner, D. (2023). *Awe: The new science of everyday wonder and how it can transform your life.* Penguin.

[101] Monroy, M., & Keltner, D. (2022). Awe as a pathway to mental and physical health. *Perspectives on Psychological Science, 18*(2), 17456916221094856.

[102] Resilience Symposium. (2021, October 1). *Using virtual reality to elicit awe* [Video]. YouTube. https://youtu.be/mMH3vmBB2cg

[103] Stellar, J. E., John-Henderson, N., Anderson, C. L., et al. (2015). Positive affect and markers of inflammation: Discrete positive emotions predict lower levels of inflammatory cytokines. *Emotion, 15*(2), 129–33.

[104] Shiota, M. N., Neufeld, S. L., Yeung, W. H., Moser, S. E., & Perea, E. F. (2011). Feeling good: Autonomic nervous system responding in five positive emotions. *Emotion, 11*(6), 1368–78.

[105] Greater Good Science Center. (2016, August 17). *Lani Shiota: How awe transforms the body and mind* [Video]. YouTube. www.youtube.com/watch?v=uW8h3JIMmVQ

[106] Bai, Y., Maruskin, L. A., Chen, S., et al. (2017). Awe, the diminished self, and collective engagement: Universals and cultural variations in the small self. *Journal of Personality and Social Psychology, 113*(2), 185–209.

[107] Monroy, M., & Keltner, D. (2022). Awe as a pathway to mental and physical health. *Perspectives on Psychological Science, 18*(2), 17456916221094856.

[108] Sturm, V. E., Datta, S., Roy, A. R., et al. (2022). Big smile, small self: Awe walks promote prosocial positive emotions in older adults. *Emotion, 22*(5), 1044–58.

[109] Perlin, J. D., & Li, L. (2020). Why does awe have prosocial effects? New perspectives on awe and the small self. *Perspectives on Psychological Science, 15* (2), 291–308.

[110] Piff, P. K., Dietze, P., Feinberg, M., Stancato, D. M., & Keltner, D. (2015). Awe, the small self, and prosocial behavior. *Journal of Personality and Social Psychology, 108*(6), 883–99.

[111] Rudd, M., Vohs, K. D., & Aaker, J. (2012). Awe expands people's perception of time, alters decision making, and enhances well-being. *Psychological Science, 23*(10), 1130–36.

CHAPTER 10

[1] Moskowitz, B. A. (2020, December 2). Widow walks into wall, finds hope. *New York Times*. www.nytimes.com/2020/04/10/style/modern-love-corona virus-widow-walks-into-wall-finds-hope.html

[2] Interview with Bette Ann Moskowitz (2020, July).

[3] Email correspondence with Bette Ann Moskowitz (2022, November).

[4] Ortiz-Ospina, E. (2020, December 11). *Who do we spend time with across our lifetime?* Our World in Data. https://ourworldindata.org/time-with-others-lifetime

[5] Snell, K. D. M. (2017). The rise of living alone and loneliness in history. *Social History, 42*(1), 2–28, quotes on 3, 7.

[6] Ausubel, J. (2020, March 10). *Older people are more likely to live alone in the US than elsewhere in the world*. Pew Research Center. www.pewresearch.org/fact-tank/2020/03/10/older-people-are-more-likely-to-live-alone-in-the-u-s-than-elsewhere-in-the-world/

[7] Ortiz-Ospina, E. (2019, December 10). *The rise of living alone: How one-person households are becoming increasingly common around the world*. Our World in Data. https://ourworldindata.org/living-alone

[8] Sharfman, A., & Cobb, P. (2022, March 9). *Families and households in the UK: 2021*. Office for National Statistics. www.ons.gov.uk/peoplepopulationand

community/birthsdeathsandmarriages/families/bulletins/familiesandhou
seholds/2021

[9] US Census Bureau. (2022, November 17). *Census Bureau releases new estimates on America's families and living arrangements.* www.census.gov/newsroom/press-releases/2022/americas-families-and-living-arrangements.html

[10] US Census Bureau. (2021, November 29). *Living arrangements over the decades.* www.census.gov/library/visualizations/2021/comm/living-arrangements-over-the-decades.html

[11] Ogunwole, S. U., Rabe, M. A., Roberts, A. W., & Caplan, Z. (2021, August 12). *US adult population grew faster than nation's total population from 2010 to 2020.* US Census Bureau. www.census.gov/library/stories/2021/08/united-states-adult-population-grew-faster-than-nations-total-population-from-2010-to-2020.html

[12] Pampel, F. C. (1983). Changes in the propensity to live alone: Evidence from consecutive cross-sectional surveys, 1960–1976. *Demography, 20*(4), 433–47.

[13] US Census Bureau. (2022, February 14). *The single life.* www.census.gov/library/visualizations/2022/comm/the-single-life.html

[14] Hill, D. (2021, December 16). *Population estimates by marital status and living arrangements, England and Wales: 2020.* Office for National Statistics. www.ons.gov.uk/peoplepopulationandcommunity/populationandmigration/populationestimates/bulletins/populationestimatesbymaritalstatusandlivingarrangements/latest

[15] Michael, R. T., Fuchs, V. R., & Scott, S. R. (1980). Changes in the propensity to live alone: 1950–1976. *Demography, 17*(1), 39–56.

[16] Khosravi, P., Rezvani, A., & Wiewiora, A. (2016). The impact of technology on older adults' social isolation. *Computers in Human Behavior, 63,* 594–603.

[17] Sironi, M., & Furstenberg, F. F. (2012). Trends in the economic independence of young adults in the United States: 1973–2007. *Population and Development Review, 38*(4), 609–30.

[18] Gibson, D. W. (2022, June 7). 10 years and counting: Her heart belongs to the Upper West Side. *New York Times.* www.nytimes.com/2022/06/07/realestate/renters-upper-west-side.html

[19] DePaulo, B. M. (2007). *Singled out: How singles are stereotyped, stigmatized, and ignored, and still live happily ever after.* St. Martin's.

[20] DePaulo, B. M. (2017). *Alone: The badass psychology of people who like being alone.* Independently published.

[21] DePaulo, B. (2014). *The best of single life.* Independently published.

[22] DePaulo, B. M. (2015). *How we live now: Redefining home and family in the 21st century.* Atria Books/Beyond Words.

[23] Gillespie, R. (2003). Childfree and feminine: Understanding the gender identity of voluntarily childless women. *Gender and Society, 17*(1), 122–36.

[24] Crowe, C. (Dir.). (1996). Jerry Maguire [Film]. TriStar Pictures.

[25] Agnihotri, A. (2022, November 10). Singles' Day 2022: Surprising benefits of being single. *Hindustan Times.* www.hindustantimes.com/lifestyle/festivals/singles-day-2022-surprising-benefits-of-being-single-101668067858377.html

[26] Nguyen, T. T., & Taylor-Bower, E. (n.d.). *Solitude in context: A systematic review of how social norms and physical environment shape perceptions of solitary experiences.* Preprint. https://doi.org/10.31234/osf.io/xb8gd

[27] Chadwick, K. A., & Collins, P. A. (2015). Examining the relationship between social support availability, urban center size, and self-perceived mental health of recent immigrants to Canada: A mixed-methods analysis. *Social Science and Medicine, 128*, 220–30.

[28] Richardson, C. (2008). Working alone. *New Labor Forum, 17*(3), 69–78.

[29] Kerns, A. (2010). *Wizards and witches* (p. 19). Lerner. (Original work published 1959)

[30] BBC News. (2005, September 14). *RIP bachelors and spinsters.* http://news.bbc.co.uk/1/hi/magazine/4141996.stm

[31] Coyle, C. E., & Dugan, E. (2012). Social isolation, loneliness and health among older adults. *Journal of Aging and Health, 24*(8), 1346–63.

[32] Community Life Survey. (2019–20). https://assets.publishing.service.gov.uk/government/uploads/system/uploads/attachment_data/file/940089/OFFICIAL-SENSITIVE_-_Community_Life_Survey_2019_20_Focus_On_Report.pdf

[33] Hawkley, L. C., Wroblewski, K., Kaiser, T., Luhmann, M., & Schumm, L. P. (2019). Are US older adults getting lonelier? Age, period, and cohort differences. *Psychology and Aging, 34*(8), 1144–57.

[34] Fokkema, T., De Jong Gierveld, J., & Dykstra, P. A. (2012). Cross-national differences in older adult loneliness. *Journal of Psychology, 146*(1–2), 201–28.

[35] Nguyen, T. T., Lee, E. E., Daly, R. E., et al. (2020). Predictors of loneliness by age decade: Study of psychological and environmental factors in 2,843 community-dwelling Americans aged 20–69 years. *Journal of Clinical Psychiatry, 84*(4), 22m14622.

[36] Qualter, P., Vanhalst, J., Harris, R., et al. (2015). Loneliness across the life span. *Perspectives on Psychological Science, 10*(2), 250–64.

[37] Galanaki, E. (2004). Are children able to distinguish among the concepts of aloneness, loneliness, and solitude? *International Journal of Behavioral Development, 28*(5), 435–43.

[38] Thomas, V., & Azmitia, M. (2019). Motivation matters: Development and validation of the Motivation for Solitude Scale–Short Form (MSS-SF). *Journal of Adolescence, 70*, 33–42.

[39] Pauly, T., Lay, J. C., Nater, U. M., Scott, S. B., & Hoppmann, C. A. (2017). How we experience being alone: Age differences in affective and biological correlates of momentary solitude. *Gerontology, 63*(1), 55–66.

[40] Ost Mor, S., Palgi, Y., & Segel-Karpas, D. (2021). Exploring gaps in positive solitude perceptions: Older adults vs. gerontology professionals. *International Psychogeriatrics, 33*(12), 1253–63.

[41] Ernest, J. M., and Cacioppo, J. T. (1999). Lonely hearts: Psychological perspectives on loneliness. *Applied and Preventive Psychology, 8*, 1–22.

[42] Ost Mor, S., Palgi, Y., & Segel-Karpas, D. (2020). The definition and categories of positive solitude: Older and younger adults' perspectives on spending time by themselves. *International Journal of Aging and Human Development, 93*(4), 943–62.

[43] Erikson, E. H. (1959). *Identity and the life cycle.* International Universities Press.

[44] Cumming, E., & Henry, W. E. (1961). *Growing old: The process of disengagement.* Basic Books.

[45] Kim, J. E., & Moen, P. (2001). Is retirement good or bad for subjective well-being? *Current Directions in Psychological Science, 10*(3), 83–86.

[46] Carstensen, L. L., Pasupathi, M., Mayr, U., & Nesselroade, J. R. (2000). Emotional experience in everyday life across the adult life span. *Journal of Personality and Social Psychology, 79*(4), 644–55.

[47] Freund, A. M. (2020). The bucket list effect: Why leisure goals are often deferred until retirement. *American Psychologist, 75*(4), 499–510.

[48] Wirth, M., & Kunzmann, U. (2018). Age differences in regulating negative emotions via attentional deployment. *Psychology and Aging, 33*(3), 384–98.

[49] Scheibe, S., English, T., Tsai, J. L., & Carstensen, L. L. (2013). Striving to feel good: Ideal affect, actual affect, and their correspondence across adulthood. *Psychology and Aging, 28*(1), 160–71.

[50] Jiang, D., Fung, H. H., Sims, T., Tsai, J. L., & Zhang, F. (2016). Limited time perspective increases the value of calm. *Emotion, 16*(1), 52–62.

[51] Chu, S. T. W., Fung, H. H., & Chu, L. (2020). Is positive affect related to meaning in life differently in younger and older adults? A time sampling study. *Journals of Gerontology: Series B, 75*(10), 2086–94.

[52] Sands, M., & Isaacowitz, D. M. (2017). Situation selection across adulthood: The role of arousal. *Cognition and Emotion, 31*(4), 791–98.

[53] Carstensen, L. L., Fung, H. H., & Charles, S. T. (2003). Socioemotional selectivity theory and the regulation of emotion in the second half of life. *Motivation and Emotion, 27*(2), 103–23.

[54] Yang, Y. C., Boen, C., Gerken, K., et al. (2016). Social relationships and physiological determinants of longevity across the human life span. *Proceedings of the National Academy of Sciences, 113*(3), 578–83.

[55] Nicolaisen, M., & Thorsen, K. (2017). What are friends for? Friendships and loneliness over the lifespan – from 18 to 79 years. *International Journal of Aging and Human Development, 84*(2), 126–58.

[56] Carmichael, C. L., Reis, H. T., & Duberstein, P. R. (2015). In your 20s it's quantity, in your 30s it's quality: The prognostic value of social activity across 30 years of adulthood. *Psychology and Aging, 30*(1), 95–105.

[57] Chen, Y., & Liu, X. (2022). How solitude relates to well-being in old age: A review of inter-individual differences. *Scandinavian Journal of Psychology, 64*(1), 30–39.

[58] Littman-Ovadia, H. (2019). Doing–being and relationship–solitude: A proposed model for a balanced life. *Journal of Happiness Studies, 20*(6), 1966–71.

[59] Rogers, C. (1980). *A way of being.* Houghton Mifflin.

[60] Raichle, M. E., & Snyder, A. Z. (2007). A default mode of brain function: A brief history of an evolving idea. *Neuroimage, 37*(4), 1083–90.

[61] Plass, J. L., Moreno, R., & Brünken, R. (2010). *Cognitive load theory.* Cambridge University Press.

[62] Weinstein, N., Nguyen, T. V., & Hansen, H. (2021). What time alone offers: Narratives of solitude from adolescence to older adulthood. *Frontiers in Psychology, 12*, 714518.

[63] Cross, S. E., Bacon, P. L., & Morris, M. L. (2000). The relational-interdependent self-construal and relationships. *Journal of Personality and Social Psychology, 78*(4), 791–808.

[64] Dwyer, C., & Schneider, C. M. (2021, December 22). *How solitude can help you regulate your mood.* NPR. www.npr.org/2020/07/15/891564595/how-solitude-can-help-you-regulate-your-mood

[65] Roth, G., Vansteenkiste, M., & Ryan, R. M. (2019). Integrative emotion regulation: Process and development from a self-determination theory perspective. *Development and Psychopathology, 31*(3), 945–56.

[66] Thomas, V. (2021). Solitude skills and the private self. *Qualitative Psychology, 10*(1), 121–39.

Index